Caring and Compassion

First Hospital.

First St Ann's Convent
1858-1864.

First Orphanage.

The first St. Ann's Convent in Victoria. This building is now installed at the Royal British Columbia Museum opposite Dr. John Sebastian Helmcken's home, which sits on its original site. SSAA P0031

*To the many Sisters of St. Ann
who demonstrated care and compassion
in their health care ministry*

Contents

Irrespective of creed or nationality, St. Joseph's Hospital will open its doors to such as are afflicted with sickness; it will afford relief and comfort to persons of every condition and standing in society; it will give shelter within its walls to the poor, the needy, the friendless, and the houseless.

—Bishop Charles John Seghers
(at the laying of the cornerstone
of St. Joseph's Hospital,
August 21, 1876)

The enjoyment of the highest attainable standard of health is one of the fundamental rights of every human being without distinction of race, religion, political belief, economic or social condition.

—Constitution of the World Health Organization
(signed on July 22, 1946)

Foreword

In 1858, when the Sisters of St. Ann accepted an invitation to leave Quebec to provide schooling for children in Victoria, they expected to be asked for nursing services. Little could they have imagined that their work in visiting the sick would evolve into St. Joseph's Hospital, a major general hospital and training school for nurses and for X-ray and laboratory technicians. Once St. Joseph's was well established, the Sisters accepted calls to open hospitals or extended-care homes in Campbell River, Smithers, Oliver, Victoria and Nelson.

It is these health care institutions that are the focus of this book, and many common threads run through their histories. The Sisters insisted on serving all who needed care, no matter their religious persuasion, race, or ability to pay their bills. Yet the Sisters regretted that for many years local antipathies and regulations of the federal Department of Indian Affairs meant that they had to establish racially segregated wards.

The hospitals varied according to the needs of their communities. In Campbell River, logging accidents provided many patients; in Smithers, gunshot wounds were common; in Oliver, miners and fruit pickers were prominent on patient rolls.

The Sisters were well versed in the current developments in medical care. The first Sisters took short courses in nursing before venturing west; antiseptic surgery and anaesthesia were introduced early at St. Joseph's. Later, through postgraduate studies and participation in health-related organizations, the Sisters extended their professional knowledge and ensured that their hospitals were accredited.

Financing the hospitals was always a problem. Although the Sisters

11

subsidized the institutions with their own labour and money, they also depended on the support of local communities: physicians, service clubs, women's auxiliaries and grateful patients. At times, the provincial and federal governments made grants, but religiously based institutions were not always eligible.

Shortly after the Second World War, the province introduced a hospital insurance scheme. This provided more secure funding, but also more bureaucracy and greater government control. Hospital insurance and population growth also created a need for larger hospitals. In some cases building new structures was beyond the financial resources of the Sisters. As a result of that and changes in the Roman Catholic Church that sharply reduced vocations to the religious life, the Sisters gradually withdrew from their hospitals and, in most cases, turned them over to local hospital boards. Today, only one of the institutions covered in this book remains as a legacy of the Sisters of St. Ann and the health care they provided to British Columbians.

Darlene Southwell is to be commended for her work in recounting this history and the Sisters of St. Ann are to be commended not only for their past work, but also for sharing their story, an important part of the social history of the province.

—PATRICIA E. ROY
Professor Emeritus of History
University of Victoria

Introduction

In approaching a history of the kind that follows, readers may find a little foreknowledge particularly useful.

The Congregation of the Sisters of St. Ann (often referred to as simply "the congregation" in this book) originated in Quebec in 1850 under their founder, who became known as Mother Mary Ann. In their home province, she was called Soeur Marie Anne and most of the Sisters' names were spelled in the French manner. When the Sisters pioneered in the west, the name Ann was spelled without the *e* and the name Marie generally became Mary. Some of the early Sisters in Victoria retained the French version of their names in religion, but many assumed the Anglicized translation. Some were known by both French and English names, which could be confusing. After a specific point in the first chapter of this book, the English spelling is used wherever possible, with a few historically necessary exceptions (some non-francophone Sisters brought the name Anne from Europe and continued to use the *e* in the west, for example).

It should be noted that, since Mother Mary Ann's beatification in Rome on April 29, 2001, she has become known as Blessed Marie Anne Blondin. Beatification is a step in the process to sainthood in the Catholic Church.

Various titles were attached to the Sisters. When they first arrived in Victoria, children called them "Auntie." In leadership they were known as Mother and retained that title during their lifetime. Following the Second Vatican Council and the emergence of a more current sensibility, the majority of Sisters resumed the use of their family names in the late 1960s, around the time they stopped wearing the religious habit. Each woman who entered the novitiate—a time of training and discernment of her vocation—was given her religious name and, as well, a number that reflected her place in the order of entering. It was possible that a deceased Sister's name could be used again.

Each area in which the Sisters expanded became known as a "province," hence British Columbia, the Yukon and Alaska became St. Joseph's province, with a provincial or province leader. Each of these provinces was attached to the motherhouse in Lachine, Quebec, which was the seat of authority for the congregation. Final decisions on large matters, financial or other, were made at the motherhouse by the mother general and the general council. Requests were initiated by the school, hospital, or orphanage through their local councils, progressing from this level to the provincial council for approval before being forwarded to Lachine.

Each "house" the Sisters occupied recorded its activities in chronicles. The provincial location gathered the information from these chronicles from all the houses, compiling a regular journal that relayed the activities of each. The chronicles contain a wealth of lore about the Sisters' daily lives and activities—both the mundane and the memorable. Researchers can often find details such as what type and colour of flowers were used in the chapel on special occasions or the colour of paint in the parlour or the type and colour of a new carpet or what it was like to experience an earthquake at a certain point in history. This kind of knowledge was invaluable while St. Ann's Academy, the seat of the provincial leadership and the official name of the Sisters' school in Victoria, was being restored in the 1990s. The Sisters of St. Ann maintain these records in their archives in Victoria (abbreviated to SSAA in endnotes in this book). Minutes of hospital boards of management, as well as annual reports and ledgers, minutes of medical advisory committees, official acts, yearbooks, pamphlets and monographs are available to fill in the history of the Sisters and often to provide a view of the outside community. In the case of the hospitals, these resources show vividly the circumstances and conditions that brought patients to be treated.

St. Joseph's Hospital and School of Nursing and, later, Mount St. Mary, were the largest institutions the Sisters established in British Columbia and take up more of the story than the smaller hospitals. Regardless of their size, these smaller hospitals were crucial to the life of the small towns and villages they inhabited. There are similarities in their individual development and demise, and the Bulkley Valley District Hospital in Smithers, also known as Sacred Heart Hospital, is given fuller treatment because it represents the struggles and accomplishments of them all.

This story records the history of caring and compassion of the Sisters of St. Ann as they participated in the development of health care and hospitals in British Columbia.

PART ONE

The First Hospital

St. Joseph's Hospital circa 1905, facing Humboldt Street. SSAA P0044

Chapter 1

In the Beginning

The deeper a tree sinks its roots into the soil, the greater its chances of growing and producing fruit.

—Mother Mary Ann

A new religious community, the Daughters of St. Anne, began in the mid-nineteenth century in the country parish of Vaudreuil, Quebec, a community just west of Montreal with a population of about three thousand.[1] This was the forerunner of the Sisters of St. Ann, and within a few years these first roots had spread and strengthened to embrace not only rural Quebec but the farthest western points of a developing country and a "little Canada" in the northeast corner of the United States.

Surely only deep humility had emboldened Marie Esther Blondin to propose to Bishop Ignace Bourget of Montreal that she initiate this new community of women religious.

Marie Esther was born on April 18, 1809, in Terrebonne, Quebec, the third child of Jean Baptiste Sureault-Blondin and Marie Rose Blondin (née Limoges); only four of the couple's twelve children survived infancy, and Marie Esther and her much-loved brother Jean Baptiste would be the only two to live to an old age.[2] They were raised in a pious and devoted family. Their father, tended by his loyal wife, exemplified patience and submission while enduring a disfiguring illness during the last five years of his life. Marie Rose Blondin also suffered physical frailty—once, following the birth of a child, she was left paralyzed for many months, and she also endured a long, debilitating illness before dying in 1862.[3] These examples

Born into a pious family and illiterate for most of her childhood, Marie Esther Blondin was led in 1848 to start a new congregation of women religious dedicated to teaching and to caring for the poor and the sick. The new congregation was formally established in 1850 when Mother Mary Ann and four other women professed their vows. SSAA P0050

of patient and uncomplaining acceptance supported Marie Esther in the trials she was to endure during the second half of her life.

From an early age, Marie Esther exhibited the virtue of charity to the sick and the poor. She was conscious of the needs of the neglected members of her society, feeling compelled to help them in any way a young girl could. She felt it imperative to educate the disadvantaged even though her own education was rudimentary for the first two decades of her life, until she attended the school operated by the Congregation of the Sisters of Notre Dame at Terrebonne and learned to read and write. Thus it seemed a natural progression when her parents accompanied her to Montreal in 1830 and she entered the novitiate of the Notre Dame Sisters. On completing her novice year she donned the holy habit and was given the name Sister Marie Christine. A short time later poor health forced her to return home, which she did in disappointment.[4]

Still she felt called to educate. When her health was restored she was recommended to Miss Suzanne Pineault, who needed an assistant in her girls' school in Vaudreuil. Their shared experience in the novitiate, their dedication to educating the poor and their aptitude for such work enabled them to work closely and in harmony for six years. When Pineault wished to leave the school in 1839, it logically fell to her former assistant to become the director of what was known as the Blondin Academy, an established school that enjoyed an enviable reputation in the area.[5]

Though she gave herself wholly to this enterprise, still the new director was drawn to another path. During Lent in 1848 she shared with

her pastor, Father Paul-Loup Archambeault, her aspiration to start a religious community devoted to teaching poor country children. Knowing
her stellar qualities he advised her to proceed and sent her off with an
introductory letter to Bishop Bourget in Montreal, who would decide
if her enterprise was indeed inspired by the Holy Spirit. Persuaded by
his interview with her, the bishop gave permission, encouraging her to
continue with prayer as she sought out the first candidates for the new
community.

Before speaking to Bishop Bourget she had informed her brother, now
head of the Blondin family, of her intentions:

> God helping, I will organize a congregation of young women, whose aim
> will be threefold: first, to work under a common rule; second, to teach
> girls in boarding-schools, and accept control of district schools; third, to
> care for the sick, the poor, and the orphaned.[6]

And so the fledgling group began on September 6, 1848, with a retreat conducted by Father Archambeault in the austere two-storey
school building consisting of six rooms on the main floor and four in
the attic. Seven women embarked on the venture. The founder, Marie
Esther Blondin, was thirty-nine years old. Others soon joined them,
notably Suzanne Pineault, who brought money that helped establish the
novitiate. This step into the unknown culminated in the canonical establishment of the Daughters of St. Ann with the religious profession of five
of the women in the presence of Bishop Bourget on September 8, 1850.
Henceforth, the bishop decreed, the community would be under the
protection of Saint Ann, the Mother of Mary, and Marie Esther would
be known as Sister Mary Ann.*

Vaudreuil remained the site of their administration until 1853, when
the motherhouse was moved to Saint-Jacques. In 1864 it moved to its
permanent home in Lachine, near Montreal.[7] In the words of one writer:

---

* Note that the francophone spelling is "Marie" and "Anne," but to avoid confu-
sion we are using the English spelling from this point on—with the inevitable
historical exceptions—since that is in fact what happened when the Sisters went
to the West Coast.

The Congregation grew and thrived. However, the price of this growth was heavy. The crushing debts that the Congregation assumed in order to build day schools and boarding schools led the sisters to deprive themselves even of necessities and to do extra handiwork to earn or to save money. On this regime, their health rapidly faltered; tuberculosis and typhoid fever wreaked havoc among them . . . The average age of those who died in the first half-century was 34 years.[8]

Undeterred, they continued to answer the call to ministry. They were ready when Bishop Modeste Demers requested their help on the West Coast. He had gone to Quebec, the site of his ordination in February 1836, to solicit the help of clergy and religious communities for his Diocese of Vancouver Island.[9] On October 19, 1857, with the blessing of Bishop Bourget, he had his first meeting with the Sisters of St. Ann, hoping to secure their commitment to the mission on Vancouver Island. They gladly accepted this call.[10]

While understanding that their first priority was the education of the young and the care of the poor and orphans, they fully appreciated that they would be called upon to care for the sick. Aware of their lack of knowledge for this duty, two of them went to Montreal to gain basic nursing experience—one to the Sisters of Providence Hospital and one to Hôtel Dieu.[11] When Bishop Demers returned to Saint-Jacques on February 12, 1858, preparations were under way to have four Sisters accompany him: Sister Mary of the Sacred Heart (Salome Valois), Sister Mary Angèle (Angèle Gauthier) and Sister Mary Lumena (Virginie Brasseur), all from Vaudreuil, and Sister Mary Conception (Mary Lane) from Rawdon, Quebec. At a time in history when people were born and raised in virtually the same area in which they would live and die, these women were embarking on a unique life journey.

Though truly faithful women, they were not a homogeneous group with unexamined motives. Rather, they sacrificed much and sublimated their personal desires to the needs of the community they served in God's name. It is difficult today to fully imagine the prospects these missionaries envisioned as they made their farewell rounds of students, families and their own Sisters. The Sisters, along with one laywoman companion, Marie Mainville, were leaving home with no expectation of ever returning.[12]

The first four Sisters arrived in Victoria after a long and arduous journey. Sister Mary Angèle's (Angèle Gauthier) journal provided an invaluable description of their journey to her family and to historians. Together with Sister Mary of the Sacred Heart (who also served as the first superior for a year), Sister Mary Angèle dedicated herself to serving the sick. Sister Mary Lumena (Virginie Brasseur) suffered severe seasickness on the journey, but went on to teach at St. Mary's School in Mission. Sister Mary Conception (Mary Lane) first dedicated herself to the mission in Cowichan, and then also went to serve at St. Mary's in Mission.

SSAA P0018, P0023, P0024 & P0025

Sister Mary Lumena wrote "I have gone from the home in which I was born, to go and live with strangers whom I am adopting as my own kindred"[13] as they departed to an unknown land of wilderness they believed to be inhabited only by aboriginal peoples and fur traders.

Travelling by road and water—including on boats that had to plow through ice on the St. Lawrence River—they arrived in Montreal, visited other convents where gifts were given to them, and attended an elaborate farewell party hosted by Bishop Bourget. They left Montreal by train on April 14, 1858, and after arriving in New York they boarded the ship *Philadelphia,* which was scheduled to depart three days later. Bishop Demers had not only secured the aid of the Sisters of St. Ann, but was able to take with him two priests, Fathers Pierre Rondeault and Charles Vary, and two Brothers of St. Viateur (a congregation founded in France), Joseph Michaud and Gédéon Thibodeau.[14] Not knowing who they would meet in the coming days, and not wishing to draw undue attention, the bishop and clergy dressed in secular garb and the Sisters hid their crosses and rosaries.

They sailed to Havana, Cuba, then changed to the *Grenada* and sailed on to the Isthmus of Panama, where they endured filthy hotel accommodation. They crossed the steamy fifty-one-mile length of the isthmus by train to board a very crowded steamship, the *J. Ellis Steeven*, proceeding on May 1 to San Francisco. Upon arrival they were grateful for the hospitality of the Sisters of St. Vincent de Paul and a modicum of the life they had left behind in Quebec. On May 28 they left on the *Sea Bird* for their final destination.

* * *

Very rough seas caused much discomfort. They also left Sister Mary Lumena, who had suffered seasickness throughout the two-month journey, practically skeletal; she had subsisted mainly on water. When they anchored briefly off Portland, Oregon, the local priest and Catholic community importuned them to jump ship and stay right there. However, they were resolved to stay on with Bishop Demers and proceeded out to sea.

What was it like to see their future home on the afternoon of Saturday, June 5, 1858? For Sister Mary Angèle it was "impossible to describe our joy on touching our Land of Promise."[15]

What unfolded before them was a shock even to Bishop Demers, who had been away from the West Coast for less than a year. On the bishop's departure from Fort Victoria in 1857, it was a place that politician and writer Alfred Waddington described as "a quiet village of about 800 inhabitants. No noise, no bustle, no gamblers, no speculators."[16] As Hudson's Bay Company chief factor, James Douglas had built Fort Victoria in 1843 (it was known at first as Fort Camosun or Camosack, after the First Nations name for the area). The fort extended from what is now bounded in the modern city of Victoria by Bastion to Courtney Streets and from Wharf to Government. Two large entry gates and two three-storey corner bastions joined with twenty-foot-high palisades, which enclosed accommodation for the chief factor, the doctor and a chaplain, as well as providing space for the daily business of the colony. There was a "sunset bell inside the great gates, which was rung every evening to warn the trading Indians that it was time to go out" to their settlements along the banks of the harbour.[17]

In 1849, Douglas established his full-time residence at Fort Victoria. Shortly thereafter, Britain designated Vancouver Island a colony. The British government appointed the tall, imposing Douglas governor in 1851, after Richard Blanshard resigned from the job, in part because he could not work with Douglas, whose employer, the Hudson's Bay Company (HBC), controlled most of the colony's activities. Douglas remained chief factor of the HBC for the years immediately after he became governor.[18] This "Scotch West Indian" had married Amelia Connolly, Métis daughter of Fort St. James's chief factor, in 1828, according to the "custom of the country."[19] Many of the fur traders and HBC men such as Douglas, lonely and isolated, had formed liaisons with aboriginal women. Certainly white women had not yet arrived in any numbers on the West Coast. These unions were often regularized later, and given religious sanction, as was the Douglas marriage in 1837 by the Church of England. While travelling about the Pacific missions, Fathers Demers and Blanchet (as they were known in those days) had "performed numerous marriage ceremonies for couples who had previously been wed a la facon du pays." These Roman Catholic priests "did acknowledge the existence of a marital bond" by considering that a cohabiting couple was living in a state of "natural marriage" and formally recognized "the legitimacy of their children."[20]

By the spring of 1858, the year in which Bishop Demers and his entourage arrived in the settlement, the fort and its surroundings housed "a fair seasoning of gamblers, swindlers, thieves, drunkards, and jail birds, let loose by the Governor of California for the benefit of mankind, besides the halt, lame, blind and mad," according to Waddington.[21] The Fraser Valley Gold Rush had changed the face of the young colony, and many gold seekers arrived in the area by way of Fort Victoria. Expecting to see twenty tent cabins surrounding the fort, the newcomers instead were facing two hundred houses and a sea of tents.[22] Sister Mary Angèle numbered this "City of Tents" at thirty thousand.

There were many other firsts in 1858. The arrival of the *Commodore* on April 25, 1858, with 450 men, the first of the gold seekers, presaged the advent of almost 25,000 more.[23] The British Royal Engineers, based at Esquimalt, began the process of civilizing Fort Victoria by surveying and laying out roads. The colonial secretary appointed Matthew Baillie Begbie, a Lowland Scot born in Africa and an 1841 graduate of Cambridge, as the first judge of the new mainland colony of British Columbia, to establish the British system of law.[24] Fort Victoria showed new signs of permanence and stability with the opening of the first bookstore, the purchase of two fire engines and the founding of a first library by W.F. Horre and a butcher shop by Thomas Harris, who was to become the first mayor when Victoria was incorporated as a city in 1862. The very Britishness of the colony was highlighted by the first cricket match, played by the Royal Navy.[25] Governor Douglas, at his own expense, commissioned the erection of five buildings by contractor Gideon Hallcrow to house the new colonial Legislative Assembly. Their design resulted in the affectionate nickname "the Birdcages."[26] Of more importance to the Church was the installation of the Oblates of Mary Immaculate in Esquimalt. These priests stayed only seven years in Victoria before leaving in 1865 for the newly formed Diocese of New Westminster, but the Oblates' connection to the Sisters of St. Ann throughout the province was to continue for a great while longer. Another religious group established itself in Fort Victoria in 1858, with the arrival of the first Jewish residents—also lured by the gold rush.[27]

Recording all these events for the population was Amor de Cosmos ("Lover of the Universe"), born William Alexander Smith, a colourful Nova Scotian and later the second premier of British Columbia, who founded the *British Colonist* in December 1858.

After disembarking at Victoria and leaving the rowboats that had carried them from the *Sea Bird* to shore,[28] the Sisters and the others in their group walked with Bishop Demers to his home, accompanied by clergy and members of the Catholic community. Here they prayed in the presence of the Blessed Sacrament and shared a meal of venison prepared by the Helmckens, a family with whom their lives would intertwine for the next two centuries.[29] Dr. John Sebastian Helmcken had come to the colony in 1850 as the Hudson's Bay Company's surgeon and in 1852 had married Governor Douglas's eldest daughter, Cecilia; he would serve as Speaker in the first Legislative Assembly of Vancouver Island from 1856 to 1871—though it was hardly a democratic institution.[30]

Bishop Demers and eight priests were among the group who led the spiritually and physically replenished Sisters to their log cabin in the early evening. The Sisters surely appreciated the bishop's blessing as they faced life in this thirty- by eighteen-foot log shell with no ceiling, no window coverings, a dirt floor and no well or outhouse.[31] Bishop Demers had purchased this building plus two lots in 1855 from Leon Morel, an HBC employee whose Stikine wife, Adelaide, had died of tuberculosis at the age of thirty in February.[32] The bishop had asked parishioners to prepare the

Built in the 1860s by Governor Douglas, the original legislative buildings were nicknamed "the Birdcages." This 1880s picture also shows the James Bay Bridge, built in 1859 across the bay to provide easier access to the government buildings.
SSAA P0052

house to receive the missionary Sisters, but unfortunately it had been left in total disrepair.

Undaunted, the Sisters draped their aprons over the bare windows, laid their mattresses on the floor and sank into exhausted sleep. But not for long. They rose at 4 a.m. to attend 5 a.m. Mass at the bishop's house, then proceeded to prepare their cabin for the reception of its first students the next day. It took them only one week to become self-sufficient enough that they no longer needed to depend on the bishop's hospitality for their meals. Yet getting to their humble abode was not easy. Outside the fort, passage was made difficult by muddy, potholed roads filled with obstacles. The Sisters' residence was on a hill that could be reached when the tide went out over the stinking mud flats twice a day. Not until 1859 did Governor Douglas have a bridge built to span this odorous section of James Bay. However, from the moment of their arrival Douglas took an interest in the Sisters of St. Ann; he immediately sent three of his daughters—Agnes, Alice and Martha—to the convent school as students.

Already the Sisters' role had expanded beyond teaching First Nations and Métis pupils to receiving all children who wanted an education. Their mission included, for example, the children of the Hudson's Bay employees and the sons and daughters of the black community, most of whom had come as well-educated Californians to escape the racial discrimination that was rampant before the American Civil War.[33] Needless to say, this outreach extended to the sick.

For want of space in their small convent, the Sisters visited the sick in their own homes. What this meant in practice was that recess and school breaks were filled with home visits to nurse the sick and that there were often all-night vigils at the bedside of the seriously ill. All of the Sisters engaged in these works of mercy, assisting the dying and helping in the laying out of the dead. Marie Mainville, their lay companion, frequently served as their messenger, which enabled them to enjoy a type of seclusion from the world, despite the fact that they left their convent for their ministrations to the sick. Sister Mary Conception and Sister Mary of the Sacred Heart answered the first call for assistance that came from the home of a Mrs. Forbes on Collinson Street, the future site of St. Joseph's Hospital. They tended to Mrs. Forbes, promising to bring a priest to administer the last sacraments against the initial opposition of her husband, but he welcomed their ministering to his wife, and gave them a donation after her death, when they had laid out her body. He subsequently built the pews for the new St. Andrew's Cathedral.[34]

The lack of space in their small log convent was soon alleviated with an addition designed and built by Brother Joseph Michaud that doubled its size. This was not the only Church building going on. Bishop Demers was constructing the first cathedral, also designed by Brother Michaud. On the day of his installation in Fort Victoria in 1852, Bishop Demers had whimsically stated: "The reason that my installation did not take place in the Cathedral is that the timber for its construction is still standing in the forest."[35] As Sister Mary Angèle wrote home in the fall of 1858, "We are building our wing, and His Lordship is building his cathedral."[36] A public subscription campaign for the new cathedral garnered $100 from Governor Douglas, who was recorded as the first donor. The Sisters contributed from gifts they had received from their families and other religious communities to ease their way in their new home after leaving Quebec.[37]

The cathedral witnessed the consecration of three bishops: Louis d'Herbomez, OMI (Oblates of Mary Immaculate); Charles John Seghers; and Jean Baptiste Brondel. Here, on March 25, 1860, Bishop Demers ordained Joseph Michaud in the church he had built,[38] which was dedicated to Saint Andrew on July 18, 1861. How fitting that, after serving the diocese for twenty-six years until it was outgrown, this original cathedral would be put on log rollers and pulled across Humboldt Street by horses in 1886 to become the permanent and much-loved chapel at St. Ann's Academy.

Contrary to the experience of some religious orders in North America with their local bishops, the Sisters of St. Ann enjoyed a mutually respectful relationship with Bishop Demers. Modeste Demers had proven his mettle from the time he was first sent west in 1837 on his and Father Francis Norbert Blanchet's mission to convert the First Nations peoples of the Pacific Coast. He was a gifted linguist who learned sufficient of "the Chinook dialect [the lingua franca of the West Coast] to preach, to translate prayers and to compose hymns in it" and he was also an "architect, surveyor, carpenter, mason, silversmith, printer and editor."[39] The recognition of his skills led to his appointment as bishop of Vancouver Island, including New Caledonia and the Queen Charlotte Islands. On November 30,

The first Catholic bishop of Vancouver Island, Bishop Modeste Demers invited, in 1858, the Sisters of St. Ann to help him build his diocese. A native of Quebec, Demers first travelled to the West Coast in 1837, and soon became fluent in the Chinook language.

SSAA P0056

1847, the feast of St. Andrew, he was consecrated bishop in Oregon City by his friend, now Archbishop Blanchet. Bishop Demers first set foot in his new diocese on August 29, 1852—landing at Cadboro Bay—following years of travelling throughout North America and Europe trying to recruit priests and find financial support for his See.

Bishop Demers followed the progress of the Sisters closely. It was he who printed the first prospectus for the school—dated December 2, 1858—on the first printing press in British Columbia.[40] In addition to outlining the school's courses, the prospectus, printed on blue paper with gold lettering, stated that "the Sisters are also prepared to attend to the sick at any time their services are needed."[41] (Eventually this very press, anglicized from its original French and used for many other purposes throughout the province, would be returned to the Sisters in 1912 for their Victoria museum at St. Ann's Academy.[42])

* * *

In their first months on the West Coast, the Sisters' relationship with the community was a little up and down. Most of the population were happy to have them there. Vancouver Island was a relatively tolerant place during the gold rush years, although there was some opposition and antipathy to the Catholic presence. The Sisters tried to lessen gossip and speculation by ensuring that open fences surrounded their houses and that any priest knocked loudly when arriving so that the students could see that he came from outside the building.[43] Sister Mary Conception reported to Sister Mary of the Purification in Lachine in 1859 that "the people . . . find our conduct strange, many criticize what we do, and others are afraid of us."[44] Anglican Bishop George Hills, who arrived in 1860, was also wary of the Roman Catholics, calling them "idolators."[45]

This caused some discouragement among the four Sisters and perhaps a feeling that they were not equal to the overwhelming task they faced. But help was on the way. In 1858, the motherhouse gained ten new novices.[46] Thus the congregation felt able to provide two more missionaries for the west in 1859. Despite misgivings about travel due to the American Civil War, eight more recruits from the Quebec motherhouse arrived safely in 1863.

Of the Sisters who arrived in 1858 and 1859, one, Sister Mary Providence (Mary Ellen McTucker), accomplished so much of merit within and without her religious community that it was said: "The consensus of the public is that this nun, who seldom left the convent grounds, exerted a far-reaching and beneficent influence which distinguished her as the greatest woman of the time in British Columbia."[47] She had entered the convent at fifteen years of age and made her profession in 1853. A chance mistake by the priest switched her religious name with that of another Sister who was to be called Providence. Since this seemed providential, she was left with the name. It was also not originally intended that she should be named to the west, but when Sister Mary Elizabeth contracted typhoid fever, Bishop Bourget agreed that Sister Mary Providence should go in her stead. She and Sister Mary Bonsecours embarked from Montreal in a kind of apostolic caravan, with Archbishop Blanchet, who had many years earlier made the prescient remark to the young novice: "God probably destines you, my little Sister, for the missions in the West."[48] Following the same arduous route of their predecessors, the two arrived on October 26, 1859, knocking on the door of the convent late in the evening. Their response to "Who goes there?" was a hearty "Canada, Canada—open to us."[49] A truly joyful and happy welcome greeted them.

Sister Mary Providence, twenty-two, was a well-educated Irish woman. She was appointed "Superior of the West," a position whose responsibilities she took to heart throughout the next forty-five years, expanding the Sisters' work in Victoria to include a large boarding school, a superb hospital, an orphanage, a day school and an aboriginal school, as well as seven other foundations throughout what became the province of British Columbia in 1871.[50] Despite these far-reaching activities, she lived out her life in a convent, fostering a cloister spirit. How could she escape the world, though, when it approached the convent? More than once a knock on the door heralded the arrival of a newborn, unwanted and abandoned, left with the hope that the kind Sisters would care for the baby. Sister Mary Providence soon opened a second school in town for children of the elite, but the first school remained to teach First Nations and Métis children and accepted little boys, orphans and a few homeless sick persons.[51]

Sister Mary Providence set about training the Sisters how to teach in English, and learned the Chinook language herself, as did Sister Mary Bonsecours. She wanted the students to study in English and used biographies as "a great aid in ennobling character (to have the young learn

the traits strongest in the world's best and greatest leaders)."[52] Her own biography could provide an example of a life well lived. She was not an impractical dreamer but a woman of wisdom and vision and superior intelligence who was calm, organized and faith-filled.

Bishop Demers, exhausted from his attempts to be pastor to his flock in the huge area that his diocese covered, was greatly relieved when Pope Pius IX erected the Vicariate Apostolic of New Westminster in 1865. That detached the mainland from the bishop's jurisdiction, even though he lost the service of the Oblates of Mary Immaculate in the process. He now also had a welcome assistant in Father Charles John Seghers, recruited from the American College

Arriving as a young Sister in Victoria in 1859, Mother Mary Providence (Mary Ellen McTucker) soon gained a reputation as one of the most influential women of her time in British Columbia, though rarely leaving the convent grounds. Mother Mary Providence served as Superior of the West for forty-five years, spearheading the Congregation's expansion in education, health care and caring for orphans. SSAA P0030

of Louvain in Belgium, which had been founded in 1857 to prepare young men for the missions of America. Three months after his ordination in 1863, Father Seghers arrived in Victoria eager to assume his missionary work. To him would pass the task of realizing the dream of Bishop Demers and the Sisters of St. Ann.

Bishop Demers took Father Seghers with him to attend the 1869–70 ecumenical council in Rome. While travelling through France, Bishop Demers was seriously injured in a train accident. His weakened condition led to a stroke and incapacitation, and he succumbed in the early morning of July 28, 1871, in Victoria. During his final illness his good friend Sir James Douglas, who had welcomed him and Father Blanchet to Fort Vancouver in 1838, was a frequent visitor. They were kindred spirits in their mutual love of cultured French, their mastery of several First Nations languages, their love and sympathy toward the aboriginal peoples and their support of the Sisters of St. Ann. Vancouver Island and the mainland had become one colony in November 1866, with Victoria named as its capital two years later. Both the bishop and the knight were sympathetic to the cause of Confederation over annexation to the United States and lived to see British Columbia become a Canadian province in 1871 (with Victoria now the provincial capital). James Douglas survived Bishop Demers by six years, until August 2, 1877. The young province lost another link to its pioneer beginnings.

Succeeding Modeste Demers in 1873 as bishop, Charles John Seghers was instrumental in assisting the Sisters build St. Joseph's Hospital in 1875. Originally from Belgium, Seghers was recruited in 1863 as a missionary for the West Coast. He served with zeal until his untimely death in Alaska in 1886, by a gunshot wound from a mentally unstable companion. SSAA P0059

Charles Seghers was destined to become the second bishop of Vancouver Island, the second archbishop of Portland, Oregon, and to return to his original See of Vancouver Island with the permission of Pope Leo XIII. Sadly, he was to die at the hands of his mentally ill companion Frank Fuller in Alaska in 1886. To the Sisters of St. Ann he was a kind chaplain who conducted retreats, encouraged them in the work in their schools and orphanages, and generally took their interests to heart. He has been described as "a man of surpassing wisdom, zealous and prudent, entirely devoted to his work."[53] His breadth of intellect was evident in the number of languages he spoke and the depth of his personal library.[54]

The five women from Saint-Jacques who had arrived in 1858 saw many changes in Victoria society as they expanded their own horizons. Sister Mary of the Sacred Heart, a woman of profound humility, was the first superior, albeit just for a year, and she soon turned from teaching to caring for the sick. Sister Mary Lumena spent most of her religious life at St. Mary's School in Mission, on the mainland. Sister Mary Conception was posted to Cowichan (also known as Duncan) after six years, a position where physical strength from her farming background stood her in good stead. Previous to this move she was charged with "teaching and visitation of the sick at domicile."[55] On one occasion she almost ran afoul of the Victoria medical community. She offered a gravely ill baby an old home remedy consisting of powdered pork bone mixed with milk and honey. In the mistaken notion that she had been practising medicine, Dr. John Davie, Jr. threatened to have her jailed until he found that she had only given the baby a cordial used by her own mother to cure dysentery.[56] Marie Mainville, a discreet, shrewd and trustworthy woman, remained their helpmate for twenty-nine years, until she returned to Quebec in 1887 to formally join the Congregation of the Sisters of St. Ann, making her religious profession in 1894 under the name Sister Marie des Sept Douleurs.

Sister Mary Angèle's journal provided her family, her religious community and posterity with a detailed account of the arduous pioneer journey to their new world. She arrived on the West Coast at the age of thirty-one and missed her native French—she struggled throughout her life with the difficult English language. In good spirit she took care of household duties, worked at the bishop's residence and, like the other Sisters, visited the sick wherever they might be lodged. One of her letters home told of visiting a leper who had suffered for many years and was shunned by everyone; she was able to console him and alleviate his sense of isolation. When the

wife and sister of Matlahaw, Chief of the Hesquiats in Barclay Sound, succumbed to smallpox, the chief took out his anger and pain by shooting
Father Auguste Brabant in the hand and the back.[57] Father Brabant, former
teacher at St. Louis College in Victoria, had come as a missionary to the
west coast of Vancouver Island. Sister Mary Angèle nursed him for three
months while he recovered from this near-fatal attempt on his life. Thus,
although the care of the sick initially had a secondary role in their mission
on Vancouver Island, almost immediately the Sisters found their nursing
services in great demand.

Chapter 2

St. Joseph's Hospital—A Dream Realized

Solidly rooted in charity, Christian health care institutions continue Jesus' own mission of caring for the weak and the sick.

— Message of Pope John Paul II
for World Day of the Sick 2002

When Bishop Modeste Demers in the 1850s purchased six lots between Humboldt and Collinson Streets in what was then Fort Victoria from the Hudson's Bay Company, through its chief factor, James Douglas, he did so with the desire that part of the property would be used at some future time for a hospital under the auspices of the Sisters of St. Ann. After interested citizens collected $1,054 toward this end in 1865, Bishop Demers headed to Central America in the hope of raising more funds. Unfortunately the poor economy there stopped all donations, postponing any immediate hope of fulfilling this goal.

However, Victorians were not completely without access to hospital care. The Sisters of St. Ann acted to fill this void with the support of Bishop Charles John Seghers, Bishop Demers' successor.

As early as 1855 during the Crimean War, the British Navy had asked Governor Douglas to provide temporary hospital accommodation because it feared that Russia might attack Vancouver Island. The governor constructed three buildings in Esquimalt—which is now a municipality next to Victoria—for $5,000 encompassing all the provisions needed for patients who did not materialize.[58] In 1858, however, the House of Assembly resolved that it did "not consider that such an institution [hospital] should be supported by the Colonial Government, but think that such benevolent objects should be left to the good feeling and charity of the Public."[59] Such charity did exist. In the year the Sisters of St. Ann arrived, then Anglican Rev. Edward (later Bishop) Cridge took in a homeless sick man, then rented a cottage at Yates and Broad as a temporary hospital. Later a more permanent hospital for male patients was built on the Songhees Indian Reserve. Accommodation for female patients was also opened on the reserve, but moved in 1864 to a new building on Pandora Street that became known as the Royal Female Infirmary. The male and female hospitals merged in 1869 as the Victoria Royal, the forerunner of the Royal Jubilee Hospital.[60] The small francophone community rented space for a hospital in 1860 on Herald Street, in 1865 building a new hospital between Collinson and Maclure Streets that closed in 1884. They had also formed a relief society to which anyone who was healthy at the time of joining could belong for the fee of one dollar a month; if illness struck, hospital admission, medication and doctors' fees would be free. The society continued after the French hospital closed and joined the Royal Jubilee Hospital in 1890.[61] And of course there were ad hoc hospitals during epidemics. For example, Dr. John Sebastian Helmcken attended children in the Sisters of St. Ann View Street Convent who contracted smallpox in 1868. He advised two Sisters to look after the sick at the small log convent. He himself took three little patients to this semi-isolation hospital to be under the Sisters' care. When one of the little ones died, Father Seghers presided at her nocturnal funeral, which was conducted secretly in order not to panic the local people.[62]

In March 1875, many interested citizens of Victoria joined with Bishop Seghers and Dr. Helmcken in importuning the Sisters of St. Ann to erect a hospital to supplement the government-supported Victoria Royal Hospital and the declining French hospital. Sister Mary Providence heeded their request to build an independent hospital to help serve the population, which according to the 1875 Census numbered eight thousand.

Her assets were both land and personnel. Bishop Seghers had given the Sisters the three lots on Collinson Street that Bishop Demers had purchased. In addition, when more missionary Sisters had arrived—five in 1866 on the steamship *Pacific*, three more in 1872 and eight in 1875—their increased numbers allowed the Sisters to expand their horizons. Moreover, in 1867 when Mother Mary Jeanne de Chantal, the superior general, returned to the motherhouse after her first official visit to the houses on the West Coast, she was accompanied by five young Victoria laywomen who wished to enter the Lachine novitiate.[63]

The Sisters had no actual money. Nevertheless, Sister Mary Providence agreed to open a hospital on faith and prayer. Dr. Helmcken, the Sisters' enthusiastic champion, once reached in his pocket, drew out a gold coin, placed it on the table and said: "Plant this and water it with your prayers and it will grow."[64] Architect James Syme was commissioned to draw up the plans.

How were they to furnish this new hospital? With no hospital supply company near at hand, the Sisters were responsible for even the tedious and dirty job of mattress making. Their chronicler of the day wrote:

> In preparation for the home manufacture of the hospital mattresses, all hands are at work picking the wool from off sheepskins. Thirty-six were plucked today. Seventy-five still remain to be done. The work is repugnant to touch and smell . . .
>
> Sixty-five among us, including Sisters, orphans, and even boarders, sat courageously before the task of picking two hundred and fifty pounds of wool, while two Sisters made up the mattresses. Our fun was spoiled by the excessive heat.[65]

Bishop Seghers donated beds and other needed equipment he had ordered from a hospital supply firm in Belgium. He invited the Sisters to furnish the hospital chapel from his private oratory. Some of the many local women advocating for the new hospital planned to hold a three-day bazaar in November 1875 to raise funds, but they feared it might go unnoticed when the sidewheeler *Pacific* sank on November 4 shortly after leaving Victoria, resulting in the loss of more than 250 lives.[66] Their fears were unfounded: the bazaar was a success, garnering a substantial donation of $2,000 to aid the cause.

On the morning of June 16, 1875—at 6 a.m., to be precise—Bishop Seghers, accompanied by the Sisters, the convent students and the orphans, blessed the site. The western Sisters would follow the role of their mother founder, Mother Mary Ann, who had also established herself in the early days as the first infirmarian during a typhoid epidemic in Quebec. The Sisters had been unstinting in their service to the sick in their homes, but often they would get sick themselves or carry an illness from house to house. Now they would have an efficient hospital in which to provide twenty-four-hour attention to those in need of it.

The congregation, determined to have well-prepared staff to operate their efficient new hospital, sent Sister Mary Bridget and Sister Mary Virginia to receive professional training at the Sisters of Providence's St. Vincent's Hospital in Portland, Oregon. In turn,

Serving for over sixty-five years, Sister Mary Bridget saw Victoria transform from a gold rush waypoint to a modern city. She became the first superior of St. Joseph's Hospital and died in 1933, aged 87. SSAA P0085

these two would instruct other nurses. They, along with Sisters Mary of the Sacred Heart, Mary of the Rosary and Mary Albert (Georgianna Morin), were to be co-labourers at the new hospital, with Sister Mary Providence adding the role of superintendent to her other duties. Sister Mary Bridget, a young nun who had come from Quebec with Sister Mary Jeanne de Chantal in 1866, assumed the reins as the first hospital superior. Throughout her nursing and teaching careers, she was known for her spirit of self-sacrifice, compassion and unselfishness. Her "kindness of heart," her "earnest and practical Christianity" and her "unselfish and devoted service" prompted then Mayor David Leeming of Victoria to write on her death in 1933 that she had the "respect and high regard of all those with whom she came in contact."[67] Clearly the Sisters and their work had become an appreciated facet of Victoria life.

*   *   *

Work on constructing the hospital began on July 28, 1875, and at the August 22 laying of the five-hundred-pound cornerstone, Bishop Seghers—in the presence of the clergy, the doctors and many prominent citizens—addressed Dr. Helmcken:

> Irrespective of creed or nationality, St. Joseph's Hospital will open its doors to such as are afflicted with sickness; it will afford relief and comfort to persons of every condition and standing in society; it will give shelter within its walls to the poor, the needy, the friendless, and the houseless.
>
> Let me express my hope and earnest conviction that the care, devotedness, and self-sacrifice of the Sisters will supply this want to the general satisfaction of the public at large.
>
> In selecting you, Honourable Sir, to lay the corner stone of this charitable institution, our object is to honour in you the friend of the poor and the humane reliever of human suffering and misery in its multiplied forms.

Dr. Helmcken reciprocated with thanks for the honour bestowed on him and other members of his profession, noting that they followed in the footsteps of Christ and the Apostle Luke. The *Daily British Colonist* noted on August 23, 1875:

> He contended that the main object of our sojourn on this world was to provide for those who come after us. The hospital was to be open to all without distinction or question, of creed or nationality, and on this ground all could meet and lend a helping hand. . . . He thought it a great point in favour of this particular institution, that it should be under the care of the Sisters of St. Ann, as that would guarantee good nursing which was of more importance than medicine, and it would be valuable if only as a school for nurses.

Prophetic words indeed.

With the moment upon them to place the cornerstone, Syme presented the inscribed silver trowel to Dr. Helmcken, who smoothed mortar over the stone that the contractor then lowered into place. Syme deposited items within, including an inscription that finished with the words "for the relief of suffering humanity and in the name of the virtue of Charity"; a copy of both the *British Colonist* (the name of the paper went through several variants over the years) and the *Standard* of August 21, 1875; a *Canadian Illustrated News* with a portrait of the Irish hero Daniel O'Connell (perhaps to recognize Sister Mary Providence's Irish roots); coins of that year; and religious articles.[68] The corroded copper box surfaced in 1949 when this original building was about to be demolished. By then "all but the [1875 US] silver dollar, which sparkled like new, had disintegrated beyond recognition."[69]

John Helmcken continued a close working association and friendship with the Sisters of St. Ann and St. Joseph's Hospital for the remainder of his life, as did his doctor son, James Douglas Helmcken. The elder Helmcken's first introduction to the Sisters came with a call to the early log convent in October 1859 to attend a sick nun. Totally unfamiliar with religious women, he was none-theless completely taken with the young Sister Mary Providence, who answered the door. At her death in 1904, when he asked for time to sit alone in reflection by her bier, he was to describe her as a beautiful young woman of grace and dignity with intelligent, serious eyes. Many years later, John Helmcken's daughter Edith (Dolly) summed up their connection: "Dad and Sister Mary Providence always argued when they met and always parted the best of friends."[70]

Hon. J. S. Helmcken, friend and medical adviser of Sisters of St. Ann, Victoria, B.C. 1851–1908

A leading figure in the young colony and province, Dr. John Sebastian Helmcken also became a close friend and supporter of the Sisters. In addition to his medical practice and raising his family after being widowed, Dr. Helmcken helped to negotiate the joining of British Columbia to Canada, and was the first president of the British Columbia Medical Society.
SSAA P0228

Because of his close connection with the hospital, John Helmcken deserves more attention here. He had been a member of the first Legislative Assembly and was appointed along with Joseph Trutch and Robert Carrall as a delegate to Ottawa during negotiations in 1870 over British Columbia joining Canada. He ended his political life after Confederation, citing personal and financial reasons and writing to Prime Minister Sir John A. Macdonald that "political life is not conducive either to domestic comfort or pecuniary gain."[71] Moreover, the death of his wife, Cecilia, in 1865 had left him with a family to raise and once again the Sisters of St. Ann played an important role since the doctor was able to send Dolly, his youngest child, as a boarder to the convent, just as he had sent her older sister Amy as a day student, confident that they would receive loving care. All the while, as well as maintaining a busy private practice, he was surgeon to the Hudson's Bay Company (until 1885), coroner for a time, and the surgeon at the jail. In 1885 he was elected the first president of the new British Columbia Medical Society, which was formed to set adequate standards for medical doctors.[72] He filled these roles for almost sixty years, until he retired with a pension from the provincial government in 1910.[73]

*   *   *

Construction of the hospital continued until April 1876, barely slowed by a heavy snowfall at Easter on March 28. The brick building included a basement and two floors for patient care and administration. Surmounting the front facade was a large marble cross. A modern hot-air system heated the rooms, doing away with the need for a messy, labour-intensive coal furnace. The rooms had gaslight fixtures similar to those recently installed in the 1871 three-storey convent across the street. Pipes that were connected to the city water system, which had been installed in 1873, pumped water throughout the building. To the right on the first floor was the chapel; to the left, rooms for amputations and major surgeries, as well as patient wards. All had been built and decorated "for the comfort and well being of those who may hereafter become inmates of the building," according to the *Daily British Colonist* on April 12, 1876. A few days later, on April 17, the hospital was open for public viewing, with musical entertainment, lunch and a bazaar making it a festive day.

Assisted by Father John J. Jonckau, Bishop Seghers celebrated the first Mass in the chapel on June 7. On June 25 he presided over the official

The newly opened St. Joseph's Hospital facing Collinson Street, in 1876. It had all of the modern conveniences, including hot air heating, running water and gas lights. SSAA P0086

opening and solemn dedication of the new hospital to Saint Joseph. Sister Mary Providence had chosen Saint Joseph because he was the guardian of the Holy Family; he was known as the patron of a happy death, which made him an appropriate protector of all who entered the hospital and particularly those who might succumb there. A statue of Saint Joseph donated by a Mr. Jones of Victoria was carried at the front of a procession of the bishop, clergy and congregation from the cathedral to the new hospital, where the statue was reverently placed on its permanent pedestal. James Syme presented the keys of the hospital to Bishop Seghers, commending "the intelligence of the builders and the skill of the workmen who have carried out the plans laid before them with personal interest and care."[74] The bishop ceremoniously placed the keys on a silver salver held by two young convent students, then turned and solemnly presented them to Sister Mary Providence. This two-storey, thirty-five-bed red brick hospital, built for the cost of $13,900, was now wholly in the hands of the Sisters of St. Ann.[75] "This action officially added nursing to the works of the Sisters of Saint Ann on Vancouver Island."[76] (That fall, Mother Mary Eulalia, the superior general from the motherhouse in Quebec, would visit along with her assistant. Unlike the earlier Sisters who had had to follow a long and torturous route via the Isthmus of Panama, these two travelled by train via Chicago and San Francisco. Mother Mary Eulalia endorsed the establishment of the hospital and would help the pioneer Sisters to endure the loss of Sister Marie des Sept Douleurs, the first Sister to die in St. Joseph's Hospital.[77])

Hospital work began in earnest. A Mr. Bowden, an indigent man, was admitted and would remain in hospital until his death in early 1877.[78] Later in 1876 Victoria experienced another smallpox epidemic, which followed outbreaks in 1862, 1868, and 1875, all of which taxed health care resources and threatened to decimate the population. Unfortunately city authorities thought to alleviate the threat by expelling First Nations peoples who lived in the vicinity rather than by quarantining and vaccinating, thus spreading the disease farther afield.[79]

Working under conditions that would be considered the most primitive today, the Sisters and hospital staff nevertheless achieved amazing results. There was no operating room, but that did not mean patients went unaided. Describing the removal of a pelvic tumour, Sister Mary Bridget wrote:

> That first operation was performed on a table in the nurses' commons room. Clean newspapers were spread on the floor. Instruments and white cotton gloves were made sterile in a wash boiler. The doctors wore those gloves wet and frequently rinsed their hands in bichloride of mercury solution. Sponges were cleaned, squeezed, washed and disinfected for 48 hours then kept in jars filled with carbolic acid until needed. The patient was anaesthetized with chloroform. The operation was performed under the anxious eyes of all the nursing sisters. None of the staff went to bed afterward. They stayed up to sit, in turn, with the patient. Mary Bridget finally took a few hours rest but soon returned to stay for the night.[80]

There were no apparent complications and the patient recovered.

The Sisters ran a hospital as current in medicine as any in the country. It was only in 1846 that the first operations under ether anaesthetic had been performed anywhere in the world, and only in 1847 that chloroform had first been used for an operation. (Queen Victoria is widely reported to have allowed chloroform to be used for her own deliveries in the 1850s.) Anaesthetics were gradually introduced in Canada after 1848 and by the time St. Joseph's opened the medical staff were ready to use these modern methods.

The Sisters immediately set up a system to help potential patients assure themselves admission and care at St. Joseph's and to provide a source of income for the hospital. Neither the City of Victoria nor the provincial government provided a social safety net for constituents or subsidies for the hospital. St. Joseph's Hospital Society was born with clearly set out rules and the stated objective to provide "mutual relief and gratuitous charity."[81] The rules stated that anyone in good health, whatever their age, gender, colour or beliefs, could become members of the society. Members were entitled to free admission to the hospital, including a consult with the visiting doctor, plus free medicine. For a premium of $1 a month and an initial fee of $5, if applying after September 1876, those eligible could join, or even opt for a one-time payment of $100 to ensure care for a lifetime. On December 14, 1883, a Mr. David Berry availed himself of the lifetime payment opportunity, promptly became ill, was admitted to hospital and "was a constant inmate of the institution [for thirty-eight years] and died there 1921."[82] Thankfully this was not the norm, but it was not unusual for patients to be in care for months and months, perhaps years. A Mrs. Feland, ailing with an "ingrowing toenail," stayed from October 20 to 27, 1904. Her toe must have been infected to elicit such a lengthy stay. A sprained ankle kept a Mr. McDowell in for a five-day stay in the same year. Non-members were not excluded but could pay $2.50 per day, and any surplus funds of the society were directed to the care of those unable to pay. An entry in the beautifully handwritten hospital ledger of July 1903 informs us of the month's expenses entailed in the hospital operation: wages, $125.50; provisions, $384.15; drugs, $70.75, and an income of $1,629.00.[83]

Early "Patient Registers" reflect the social history of Victoria. Many names familiar to historians appear on the pages, though there are also entries listed only as "Indian" or "Chinaman." Lack of facilities in remote areas caused aboriginal people from Hesquiat, Nootka, Clayoquot, Cape Mudge and even the Queen Charlotte Islands (known today as Haida Gwaii) to arrive at St. Joseph's for treatment. The admitting diagnosis, physician's name, date of admission and discharge, country of origin and current residence, and religious persuasion are mentioned. Few listed themselves as Canadians. Many single men listed their home as one of the local hotels. Admissions for appendicitis, "summer complaint" and rheumatism were common, though gunshot wounds and even an injury caused by a bite from a monkey are in evidence. Blood poisoning as a diagnosis appeared to mean certain death. Many women entered hospital accompanied by their young children, but not until the early 1900s were maternity cases entered in any number.[84] Home births were the norm until this time.

*　*　*

The new hospital signified one of several major steps in the growth and civilizing of Victoria in the 1870s. In anticipation of the transcontinental railway that had been promised around the time British Columbia became a Canadian province in 1871, for example, the city looked forward to growth in its population and economy. The foundation of modern city waterworks in 1873 promised better health and ease of access to water and contributed to the efficient operation of the new hospital when it opened three years later. Since the original fort had been demolished in 1864, Victoria had extended its boundaries. One farm in particular—Beckley Farm—had been divided and sold in lots that now boasted big houses, outbuildings for chickens, cows and horses, and homeowners who depended on underpaid Chinese labour to tend to them.[85] Welcome new neighbours who surrounded the convent and the hospital included the Church of Our Lord on the corner of what are now Humboldt and Blanshard Streets. The church was built for Dean Edward Cridge, the last of the Hudson's Bay chaplains, who had broken away from the Anglican Church because of a conflict over ritualism.[86]

The hospital was of course open by the time Sir James Douglas died in August 1877, and the Sisters, who deeply felt the loss of this good friend and benefactor, marked the sombre occasion by draping the facade of both the hospital and the convent in black and white until after his funeral. Then, on February 7, 1878, Pope Pius IX—who had blessed the inauguration of their congregation—died. Shortly beforehand, the Sisters in Victoria had sent him a tablecloth adorned with their own needlework to honour the fiftieth anniversary of his consecration. Locally, Bishop Seghers, who had nurtured and encouraged them through the construction and opening of their new hospital, was moved to Oregon in 1878 and succeeded by another graduate of the American College at Louvain in Belgium, Jean Baptiste Brondel.

The *Daily Colonist* reported on October 12, 1877, that St. Joseph's Hospital was "a model of cleanliness, cheerfulness and comfort." Victoria citizens patronized the hospital as soon as it was built. Sister Mary Bridget was superior during the first year of operation; then that position was held by Sister Mary Winifred, who was the first pharmacist as well as a nurse noted for her self-denial and complete dedication to her patients. Her unexpected death on April 21, 1885, at the age of forty was attributed to her having exhausted herself in her zeal to tend her patients and thus picking up a fatal illness from one of them. She had not been able to hide her light under a bushel, however. Her reputation drew many Victoria residents to her funeral, which was conducted by Bishop Seghers at the cathedral. From there she was laid to rest in the convent cemetery across the street, alongside other deceased members of her congregation.

★   ★   ★

The reputation that St. Joseph's Hospital quickly gained ensured a steady flow of patients, most of whom were men, although women began to feel more comfortable with a hospital stay once the Sisters and other women were on hand to care for them. By the end of 1876 the hospital had treated six paying patients in-house and ten who received treatment free of charge. The *Daily Colonist* noted on March 16, 1881, that St. Joseph's had treated 286 patients since its 1876 opening, 161 of them Catholics and 125 of them of other persuasions. All this accomplished in a thirty-five-bed hospital! But already the flat gravelled roof had deteriorated badly—rain soaking through the pebbles had perforated it.[87] This damage and "greater public patronage" caused Bishop Brondel to appeal to the citizens of Victoria for help in 1881. "This is a charity not confined to creed or nationality, but open to all regardless of church, country or color," he was quoted as saying, in the *Daily British Colonist* of March 22, 1881, and the Sisters "have nothing to give but their untiring zeal and unremitting attention day and night to God's poor." The hospital statistics give credence to his statements.

But nothing concrete happened until 1888, when the Sisters considered it absolutely necessary to improve and enlarge the hospital. John

Teague, a local self-taught architect who was best known for his design of the City Hall in 1878 (a building he would occupy as mayor from 1894 to 1895), was commissioned to draw up plans. He had also designed the Church of Our Lord (1875), and the addition to St. Ann's Academy (1886) across Humboldt Street. Teague is credited with "bringing architectural beauty and charm to the city" and being responsible for the "initial groundwork that had set the foundation and would establish the pattern for the new twentieth century appearance of the city."[88]

The new addition incorporated many modern conveniences, such as chutes to take soiled linen directly from the wards to the laundry, where a new washer and extractor washed, dried and ironed everything so rapidly that the linen could be turned around and sent right back to the wards, according to the *Daily British Colonist* of October 23, 1888. This was a distinct improvement over the small, poorly lit room in the basement that staff had to use in the original building. Sanitation standards were of the highest, a condition that contributed to the safety and comfort of the patients. St. Joseph's Hospital now had its first operating room, a third storey and thirteen private rooms—which increased the bed capacity to forty-eight.

Naturally there was a high price to pay for these improvements. Adjacent land had been purchased for the laundry at a cost of $2,000 and the laundry itself cost $6,380. The addition to the hospital cost $31,000. Borrowing money from local supporters such as a member of the Bossi family was not sufficient, so a loan of $31,500 was procured from the Credit Foncier of Montreal at 5-percent interest. Not until 1898 did a $20,000 loan from friend James McNamee enable the hospital to reduce this debt to $11,500.[89] The result seemed worth the expense and the Sisters were not unaccustomed to incurring debt in order to fulfill their mission.

Constant work was the lot of the Sisters, but the visit of the governor general, the Marquis of Lorne (whom Queen Victoria, his mother-in-law, had appointed), and his wife, Princess Louise, occasioned a festive break in routine in October 1882. The dignitaries' task was to "investigate and encourage industry in the province,"[90] but the princess and her husband deviated from the schedule to attend a reception at St. Ann's Academy, then crossed the street to tour St. Joseph's Hospital. So favourably impressed were they that the princess wrote to the provincial superior (Mother Mary Anne of Jesus had been appointed by then):

> I shall tell my mother, the Queen, of your great work here. You are caring for humanity from the cradle to the grave. I shall relate what I have seen, also tell of your white-curtained wards, filled with suffering humanity, your bright class-rooms, and above all the self-sacrifice and service your sisterhood contributes at this distant post of the Empire.[91]

In this loyal outpost of the British Empire, this was strong praise. Despite the variety of ethnic origins represented in the local population and the fact that most of the Sisters of St. Ann were French-speaking, individuals had to be British loyalists to feel accepted. The Sisters, who had always been loyalists, chose the tune of "God Save the Queen" as the tune of their own community song, "Two Houses by the Sea."[92]

During the reconstruction of St. Joseph's Hospital, Mother Mary Providence was the administrator; it was a position she had occupied once in the past and was to assume for a third time in 1900 until her death in 1904. Since her arrival in Victoria in 1859 she had been the mother vicar,[93] but in 1881 it was necessary to name her replacement; she had held the title for twenty-two years, a circumstance that could not repeat itself following a recent revision in canon law by Pius X restricting tenure to triennial appointments, with a nine-year total limit.[94] Enter a young Irish Sister from Rawdon, Quebec—Sister Mary Anne of Jesus, who, despite her courage and enthusiasm, was overwhelmed at the prospect of becoming superior at the age of twenty-six. How was she to succeed someone as capable, compassionate and competent as Mother Mary Providence? Fortunately she had the trust and support of her predecessor. A great friendship developed between the two women as they alternated positions of provincial and local superior and hospital administrator. "On the one side, there was the reverence, the confidence of youth for age, and on the other, deep-rooted admiration of age for competent youth."[95] This confidence and admiration were not misplaced. Once installed as mother superior, Sister Mary Anne of Jesus proved her mettle. She was an excellent teacher and excelled at nursing. Her special affection for the sick and elderly led her to anonymously perform small favours to distract and amuse them. This same

Overwhelmed in 1881 at being appointed mother superior at the age of twenty-six, Mother Mary Anne of Jesus soon proved her worth, showing equal care and concern for the sick and for her fellow Sisters. Unfortunately, this led her to ignore her own health problems, and she died prematurely at age forty-six. SSAA P0019

consideration was shown the Sisters under her care. She was well aware of her charges' need to balance work and play and she made sure those she supervised took time for recreation. Exhausted retreatants from the hospital were relieved of any manual labour, which guaranteed them rest and rejuvenation. In an unheard-of benefit, she sent two ailing young Sisters to Harrison Hot Springs in the hope of restoring them to health.[96]

A deep sense of charity led Mother Mary Anne of Jesus in 1899 to invite an ailing Father Pierre Rondeault to stay at St. Joseph's Hospital, where she spent many hours tending and comforting him toward the end of his life (1900). Her care exhibited the gratitude the Sisters felt to this priest who had accompanied the original four pioneer Sisters to Victoria in 1858. She herself suffered from excruciating migraines and a painful facial nerve complaint, tic douloureux, but she tried to mask her suffering in order to continue her work. Her inability to stave off these debilitating disorders no doubt led to the fluid tumour on her brain that caused her premature death on April 23, 1901, at the age of forty-six.[97]

*   *   *

Back in 1890, the Sisters in Victoria had mourned the death too of their founder, Mother Mary Ann. But they could take comfort in the growth of their congregation in the west.

The Victoria novitiate had been officially inaugurated on December 8, 1889. A few young women came from Lachine to serve their probationary period of study and formation, but local aspirants also entered.[98] These women were the future nurses and teachers for ministries in British Columbia, the Yukon and Alaska. More institutions, including a small hospital that had opened in Juneau, Alaska, in 1886, had to be staffed.

The Sisters continued their life of twenty-four-hour commitment. Sister Marie Jean Berchmans, who had been appointed to serve the Catholics of the Songhees Nation for eighteen years (1893–1911), taught on the reserve in the daytime and after hours tended the sick in their homes and prepared them for death.[99] As was true for most of the population in these years, people were still nursed mainly at home.

Though the promise of the Canadian Pacific Railway terminus in Victoria had not been realized, Victoria was blossoming. Prime Minister Sir John A. Macdonald visited in the summer of 1886 with his wife, Lady Susan Agnes Macdonald, to drive the last spike on the Esquimalt and Nanaimo Railway at Shawnigan Lake.[100] Victoria and Esquimalt Telephone Company began operating in 1880, a scant four years after Alexander Graham Bell had made his first telephone call.[101] John Blair, a Scot with an excellent background in landscape architecture, was hired to design and build the gardens at Beacon Hill Park in 1889.[102] Along with the successes there was a darker side to the city's life. The many saloons and the influx of labourers and gold seekers from all over the world were a volatile combination. No wonder the jail was fully occupied.

In 1887 the other lay general hospital in Victoria was named the Royal Jubilee to commemorate the Jubilee of Queen Victoria, and it opened in its present location in 1890.[103] With foresight, the Sisters in that year purchased additional property adjacent to St. Joseph's Hospital from Bishop Nicholas Lemmens for $13,000. Their vision allowed for needed development over the coming years. In 1897 the second expansion was undertaken at a cost of $38,000. This meant twenty-four additional patient beds, bringing the number to seventy-two, with three operating rooms, a modern X-ray facility and a passenger elevator. Everything was done that could be done to make the hospital up to date both in its physical plant and in the nursing skills it offered. Money was hard to come by, but the Sisters were excellent stewards who could make every penny count—and this was at a time in Victoria history when the Francis Rattenbury-designed Parliament Buildings, meant to replace the old "Birdcages," were being built for an ultimate cost of $923,000 (by their completion in 1898), for a provincial population of only 175,000.[104] While the hospital was completing its addition in 1897, British Columbia spent more money to celebrate the sixtieth anniversary of Queen Victoria's reign by illuminating the front of the not-yet completed legislative buildings with 3,333 light bulbs.[105] The provincial government, however, still did not contribute to the care of hospital patients, a position harking back to the first days of the House of Assembly.

The Klondike gold rush signalled the end of the pioneer years. The streets of Victoria are said to have "bustled with strange men—Scots, Irish, French, German, Australian, American—garbed in outlandish costumes and dragging oxen and horses through roadways piled high with sacks of provisions, knockdown boats, fur robes, and Klondike knickknackery."[106] Many of these gold seekers instead became local merchants and developers, settling down and raising families. Many of them sent their children to St. Ann's Academy and many of them had cause to use St. Joseph's Hospital.

The Sisters who had arrived in 1858 and in the following years had filled a multitude of roles—teacher, nurse, substitute mother, gardener, labourer, builder. They had made and sold needlework and handcrafts to support themselves. Their lives had been full of poverty and penance, which they happily accepted. Those who spoke only French on arrival had the added burden of learning English. Juggling spiritual and temporal matters, they managed to find a balance while contributing a great deal to the development of British Columbia and Alaska. The remaining Sisters bid a sad goodbye to Sister Mary Angèle, one of the first four, when she died in 1898 after forty years of service in the west. But they had all made a lasting impression on those they served. In his dying days Bishop Demers played down the importance of his ministry but mused "I have done one good thing. I have brought the Sisters of St. Ann into my diocese."[107]

Chapter 3

A New Century

A woman's influence is not limited; life will be mostly what women truly wish it to be.

— Mother Mary Providence

You will declare this fiftieth year sacred . . .
This fiftieth year is to be a jubilee year for you . . .
The jubilee is to be a holy thing to you.

— Leviticus 25

As the Congregation of the Sisters of St. Ann was about to celebrate the golden jubilee of its foundation in 1900, Archbishop Paul Bruchesi of Montreal thought the occasion of such import that he offered to pay the way back to Quebec for the Sister who had served longest on the West Coast without returning to the motherhouse. Forty-two years of living away from Quebec entitled Sister Mary Bonsecours, who had arrived in Victoria with Sister Mary Providence in 1859, to this honour. She did not travel alone. Eastern relatives of other Sisters had sent money enough to defray the cost of twenty other women attending the celebrations in Quebec.[108]

Moving into modern times, fifty years after its founding, the congregation was established and secure, even though continually trying to recruit new members to serve the many ministries it was asked to assume. Only 10 percent of the religious community resided in British Columbia, but the Sisters could point with pride to the presence in Victoria of both a boarding and a day school, a kindergarten, an aboriginal school, an orphanage and the efficient St. Joseph's Hospital. In addition, they had established eight other foundations throughout the province.[109] Though fast disappearing, a few of the first pioneers still survived. Sister Mary Bonsecours and Sister Mary of the Sacred Heart celebrated their golden jubilees in 1901 and 1902 respectively.

In 1908, when the congregation celebrated the fiftieth anniversary of its arrival in the Victoria area, the whole city celebrated with the Sisters. Sailors from HMS *Shearwater* decorated the convent and its grounds with flags of all nations.

> [A] canopy of them [were] arranged row after row extending from the gateway down the long avenue to the porch. The B.C. Electric Company illuminated the convent and its grounds with hundreds of bulbs. The electric firm also sent a corps of workers to prepare an illumination on the Convent façade and the grounds. Hundreds of bulbs gleaming among the flags produced the effect of a fairyland.[110]

The guests of honour were Mother Mary Anastasia, who had come from Lachine for the occasion, Sister Mary Conception and Sister Mary Lumena. These latter two women gave witness to the early development of their congregation in the west, and the growth of the city of Victoria and the province of British Columbia.

With the death of Queen Victoria on January 22, 1901, this distant part of the British Empire went into official mourning. The day afterwards, the *Daily Colonist* carried the headline "Victoria the Good Has Passed Away," and reported that flags had been "floated at half mast and the bells tolled for several hours" in Vancouver; the same happened in Victoria. The Sisters experienced a more intimate sorrow at the death on April 23 of Mother Mary Anne of Jesus, their current provincial superior and the former superior at the hospital. This loss was tempered by the happy celebrations of Sister Mary Bonsecours' golden jubilee that summer. The following year Sister Mary of the Sacred Heart—one of the first four pioneers, the first superior at the log convent and a woman devoted to caring for the sick—marked this same milestone.

Mother Mary Providence, recovering from a stroke, again accepted the role as superior of St. Joseph's Hospital in 1900.[111] Though she conducted all her business transactions in the parlour of St. Ann's Academy, she nevertheless became known to the business people of the city for her penetrating mind and accurate judgment. Her golden jubilee festivities in 1903 gave an opportunity for the larger community to demonstrate appreciation for her contribution to the city.[112] Some of her former students, including Mrs. J.D. Helmcken, planned the festivities, which were attended by the humble and the elite, including Sir Henri-Gustave Joly de Lotbinière, lieutenant-governor of British Columbia; Mayor Alexander McCandless; Admiral Andrew Bickford; almost all of the city's physicians; and the elderly Bishop Edward Cridge of the Reformed Episcopal Church. Seven months later Mother Mary Providence suffered a massive stroke and collapsed at her desk. She died four days later, on May 29, 1904, at the age of sixty-seven.

*   *   *

Throughout the years, even with nursing care available at the hospital, people relied on the Sisters to visit the poor and the sick in their homes, making them the forerunners to the modern public health nurse and social worker. Some visits were follow-ups to hospital stays. Many were not. They visited regardless of whether the individual or family was Catholic, and were particularly solicitous in situations where young children were involved. Their sensitivity was known and appreciated, leading to unexpected requests such as conveying the news to a Victoria woman that her son had been arrested in Quesnel, British Columbia, for theft. "The poor mother," the register recorded in April 1924 "was greatly afflicted."[113] Special feast days called for special attention to those sick in their homes. At Easter of 1924 the Sisters delivered gift boxes that each contained Easter eggs, a roast of pork, some doughnuts, apples and a tin of lard.

The Sisters who worked in the hospital worked very hard indeed. Unlike the teaching Sisters, they could not take a lengthy, restorative holiday at Christmas or in the summer. Moreover, they often had more than one job and frequently went weeks without a day off. Because the Sister in charge of the operating room was overworked, sometimes working all day and then getting up in the night four or five times a week, the staff was increased. Sister Mary Flore's responsibilities were "washing that is done at the hospital, sewing, garden, accounts, night nurse—sleep from 1 p.m. to 9 p.m., go on duty at 10 p.m. until Mass," which would have been six o'clock in the morning. Sister Mary St. Sauveur was the druggist and tended to the sacristy, the operating and dressing rooms.[114] Working conditions deteriorated as the admission of more patients resulted in overcrowding.

The nature of hospital work sometimes made it difficult for the nursing Sisters to observe the Rule of the Sisters of St. Ann, the Vatican approved standard by which they lived their daily lives, "the expression of the Will of God."[115] One could not leave a patient in the middle of treatment or counselling, nor could one routinely observe silence when always in contact with patients, doctors and staff. In times of short staffing, a Sister might be unable to make her monthly day-long retreat. However, the spirit of the rule was always held. "The Customary" was written to help in the observance of the rule. It outlined the community practices on a daily, weekly, monthly and yearly schedule and the duties of each individual occupation[116] and for the nursing Sisters included such regulations as being careful not to begin laying out the dead "till three hours after duly certified death."[117] Science had progressed a long way since the days when a feather

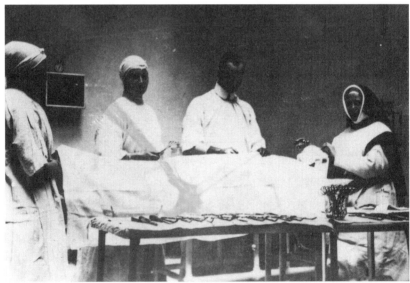

The doctor and nurses at the ready in the operating room in 1903. Note the large mask over the patient's face on which either chloroform or ether anaesthetic will be dripped. SSAA P0250

or a mirror had been placed under a patient's nostrils to determine if life was present.[118]

Until the new wing was opened in 1908, the nurses at St. Joseph's laboured under the handicap of small quarters, a too-small chapel, no dormitory for the nurses and an unsuitable men's ward.[119] In September 1906, Sister Mary Bridget, the superior of St. Joseph's, appealed to her provincial council for permission to build an annex to the hospital, 100 by 110 feet, with a front-facing main entrance on Humboldt Street and a new wing for private patients. After examining the plans for the proposed new wing, this council submitted them to the general council in Lachine, which approved them. St. Joseph's called for bids and signed a contract for $114,800 with Messrs. Gribble & Skene, who were also the contractors for the new Empress Hotel, where the first major fundraising event—a costume ball sponsored by the Knights of Columbus—realized $915.50 as a contribution to St. Joseph's Hospital.[120] The construction of the Empress Hotel was particularly welcome, since the filling in of the mud flats that the original four Sisters had had to traverse—and on which the city dumped its garbage—eliminated the stink and the plague of rats that had been endured for many years.

The general council in Lachine also authorized St. Joseph's to borrow $30,000 from Canada Life Assurance for this addition. In anticipation of further expansion, in June 1911 the hospital purchased Peter Carr's adjacent small house for $4,000, with half down and the balance to be paid when the hospital was able.[121] Among the dignitaries present at the opening of the new wing on October 3, 1908, were Mother Mary Anastasia, superior general; Mother Marie des Cinq Plaies (she kept her French name to be true to her roots), provincial superior; and Dr. John Sebastian Helmcken, who reiterated that "it does not matter in the least what the creed, or the nationality of a patient may be, he or she is equally acceptable" and informed the crowd that the Sisters "are independent of all outside aid."[122] In formally opening the new wing, Premier Richard McBride spoke of the immense debt owed the Sisters for the "attention and skill" they brought to their patients.[123] While Dr. Helmcken spoke of the Sisters' independence from outside aid, and the premier of the peoples' debt to them, the Sisters still owed a considerable amount on the new addition. Some of the burden was eased by donations of furnished rooms by Father Auguste Brabant, the apostolic administrator of the diocese; architect Thomas Hooper; and other supporters.

The new five-storey unit designed by Hooper cost $135,000. With sixteen rooms on each floor—the third floor for men, the fourth for women, nurses' dormitories on the fifth and sunrooms on either end for convalescing—the hospital now had 150 beds. A roof garden gave patients access to the fresh air, with a beautiful view as a bonus. Fireproof walls and doors and two fire escapes ensured the safest building possible. Sister Mary Bridget remained as superior, a position she held until 1917, with sixteen Sisters and fourteen nurses under her jurisdiction.

Among the staff was Mary Macnamara, a nurse who lived in the hospital until her death in 1935. She had been the first night supervisor when St. Joseph's occupied the old building on Collinson Street, but she had later moved to San Francisco. After escaping the 1906 earthquake, she returned to Victoria to organize the first maternity unit in St. Joseph's Hospital. In retirement she gave invaluable advice to the Sisters, the nurses and volunteer organizations. Her interests included landscaping the grounds of the hospital and Vernon Villa across the street.[124] No doubt she earned her keep.

As Victoria grew, the city decided that farm animals could no longer be kept in the city. In 1912 the hospital purchased a farm on the Saanich

Patients enjoying the air from the rooftop of St. Joseph's Hospital. Beacon Hill Park is in the distance. SSAA P0089

Peninsula to supply food and provisions for the patients, staff and Sisters, which meant that in addition to administering the hospital, St. Joseph's Council had to decide when to buy and sell cows, pigs and sheep, and what and when to plant. The farm, however, lessened their dependence on local suppliers and reduced the high costs of dairy products, meat and produce.

The registers indicate that patients of many nationalities and origins were cared for, including Japanese, Chinese, aboriginal, Jewish, Buddhist and pagan persons, as per the promise made at the opening of the hospital in 1876. In the 1890s, when there were 3,167 patients, 2,260 of them—or 71 percent—were not Catholics.[125] Given the demography of the province, that is not surprising. In 1901 there were 33,000 Catholics in a total population of 179,000 and one-third of them were aboriginal people.[126] Despite this, the Sisters' congregation had grown.

Although white BC residents had long complained that Chinese people were taking jobs from white men, the hospital employed Chinese men in the kitchen and on the grounds. The Sisters resisted pressure to fire their Chinese help and continued to employ them, particularly as cooks, because they appreciated the men's contribution to the operation of the hospital. The Sisters provided their Chinese staff with sleeping rooms in the basement of the hospital. They felt this pressure again when the public

Ignorant of the changes they represent, these cows stand on the farm on the Saanich Peninsula that the hospital purchased in 1912 when Victoria decided that farm animals could no longer be kept in the city. Though an additional—and different—responsibility, the farm did serve to reduce food costs and lessen dependence on local suppliers. SSAA P0242

agitated for what became the exclusionary *Chinese Immigration Act* of 1923.

These exclusionary sentiments also meant separating "Oriental" and other foreign patients from the Caucasian patients. Among the Chinese patients was a Mr. Bong, "houseboy" to the Carr family, whose famous artist daughter Emily remembered that "we were all as fond of him as anyone could be of anything holding itself so completely aloof."[127] Sister Catherine Moroney, laboratory director and medical records librarian at St. Joseph's for many years, recalled how Ward 4B was used to segregate "Oriental," aboriginal, Japanese and Sikh patients from the hospital's white patients. The Sisters were greatly distressed at the need for this, but the mood of the population was such that the hospital would not have been sustainable before the Second World War if it had tried to mingle ethnic groups. As the excesses of the war drew people's attention to the evils of racism, British Columbians became more tolerant of other races. Soon after the war, the hospital quietly integrated its wards.[128]

Another relationship was also of great importance to the Sisters. Though occasionally difficulties surfaced between the diocesan bishop and the congregation in the first half of the twentieth century, most encounters were mutually cordial and respectful. In the period between Bishop Bertram Orth's resignation in 1908 because of failing health and the arrival of Bishop Alexander MacDonald in May 1909, Very Reverend Auguste Brabant, a priest originally from Flanders, acted as apostolic administrator. A genuine friend to the Sisters, in their golden jubilee year he honoured the four pioneer Sisters by paying the travel expenses of four young women who came from Ireland to enter the Victoria novitiate.[129] More notably, he purchased a large plot in the Catholic section of Ross Bay Cemetery for the burial of the Sisters. He wrote that the least the church could do to show appreciation "for all the sacrifices and the good works of the Sisters of St. Ann, is to supply a spot where their holy remains may rest till the day of their glorious resurrection."[130] He entrusted his "mortal remains" and his "worldly goods" to their care upon his death, which came on July 4, 1912.

The physicians who served at the hospital were among its benefactors, giving generously of their skills, without charge to the Sisters—Dr. O.M.

Jones, twenty-four major operations, 1895 to 1918; Dr. J.C. Davie, major operations and services, 1878 to 1915; Dr. R.L. Fraser, professional services given willingly and gladly; Drs. Gibson and Keys, specialists in eye, ear, nose and throat trouble "freely and agreeably respond to the Sisters' many demands on their skilled services, 1912 to 1918."[131] And the Sisters never forgot the charity of their great friends Drs. John Sebastian and J.D. Helmcken, father and son, "who for sixty years have been father and brother in their care of the health of Sisters and Orphans."[132] The many kindnesses made it an easy decision for the hospital to have John Avery build a concrete shed for the doctors' horses and buggies in 1909.[133]

* * *

Nursing Sisters seemed to be an invisible presence in health care. When we realize that the 1911 Canadian Census omitted religious nursing sisterhoods from the list of 5,476 female professional nurses, it is clear that their contribution was not being recognized.[134] Fortunately, recognition was not their goal, as the Sisters of St. Ann, like many other religious congregations, continued their work, always looking for new recruits. In 1912, several Sisters went on a recruiting mission to the Maritimes. They carried a letter from Bishop Alexander MacDonald, a native of Nova Scotia, describing St. Joseph's Hospital as "easily the finest and best equipped institution of its kind in the whole province." He explained that the congregation was unable to find candidates locally due to "the newness of the country, [and] the comparative smallness of the Catholic element in the population."[135] Despite this dearth of Catholics, other religious groups were coming to Vancouver Island. Three members of the

Son of Dr. John Sebastian Helmcken, Dr. James Douglas Helmcken continued his father's friendship and devotion to the Sisters. SSAA P0227

contemplative order of Franciscan Poor Clares arrived in 1911 and the Sisters of St. Joseph of Toronto opened a hospital in Comox in 1913.[136]

When England declared war on Germany in August 1914, Canada—as a member of the British Empire—was at war too. By the time of the signing of the armistice that ended the war on November 11, 1918, more than ten million had died, six million of them civilians.[137] The sinking of the *Lusitania* by a German submarine in May 1915 had consequences locally. The twenty-one-year-old son of James Dunsmuir, a former premier and lieutenant-governor, was among the thirteen Victoria victims. With local anti-German sentiment running high, many citizens participated in attacks on the Kaiserhof Hotel, the German Club and German Consulate, but there were no serious casualties.[138]

Although the European battlefields were far away, many wounded veterans were brought to Victoria for treatment. St. Joseph's rearranged the wards to accommodate casualties. The Sisters gave up their dormitory for a women's ward that in turn became a soldiers' ward. Throughout the war, and in the years immediately following, many visitors came to

Dressed in her military uniform, Myrtle Starrett was the only nurse graduate (1917) of St. Joseph's Hospital to see active service in both World War I and World War II. SSAA P0307

the hospital to pay tribute to these soldiers, including Colonel Issaly, aide-de-camp and physician of the commander-in-chief of Allied armies in the Far East; the Prince of Wales; and the former "Baron Byng of Vimy" (in his capacity as governor general of Canada), who visited each soldier.[139] The military authorities in Ottawa, in appreciation for the care the hospital gave the soldiers, in 1920 donated one hundred beds and mattresses with a value of $3,000.[140]

Women, particularly nurses, had joined the army, essentially a male domain at the advent of the First World War, and proven themselves indispensable caregivers, earning a respect and prestige they had not previously enjoyed. Canada supplied more than two thousand women to war service, fifty-three of whom died in the line of duty.[141] St. Joseph's sent twenty-eight of its graduates overseas with the expeditionary forces, four of whom were honoured with the Royal Red Cross, 1st Class, for their service—Thora Bloomquist, Ethel Saunders, Martha McBride and Myrtle Starrett, the last seeing active service in both wars.[142]

*   *   *

Through the war years the hospital continually improved its facilities. The laundry was enlarged, new operating room equipment was purchased, more land was cleared on the farm, and a motor truck procured to bring in milk, eggs, chicken and pork from the farm. Ironically, the motherhouse in Lachine did not give permission to replace the dangerous 1896 passenger elevator at St. Joseph's until 1914, a year after Mother Mary Anastasia, who was then mother general, died as the result of an accidental fall down an elevator shaft in Lachine. St. Joseph's purchased radiography equipment in 1915—only twenty years after Wilhelm Roentgen's 1895 discovery of X-rays, for which he received the 1901 Nobel Prize in Physics. Dr. Geoffrey Jefferson, who had urged the purchase of a proper Roentgen table and equipment so patients would not need to be sent to the Royal Jubilee Hospital, became the first head of the department, with a Dr. Flumerfelt as assistant radiographer. The X-ray department staff took ongoing training, and their equipment was continually upgraded to keep step with improvements to the technology. The School of Radiography was established in 1920.

In 1915 the Medical Association of Victoria, through its doctor delegates, suggested that St. Joseph's establish an advisory board of physicians who would confer with hospital authorities once a month, as a medium of communication between the association and the hospital. This suggestion was adopted, but not that of appointing a medical superintendent. Since the hospital ran without regular financial grants from the province or the municipality and had a very low death rate (19 per 1,000), indicating satisfactory patient treatment, it did not deem such a position necessary at this time. Sister Mary Modeste and Sister Mary Josephine were sent to the Mercy Hospital in Chicago, the first to take a course in anaesthesia and the second a course in surgical technique, with other Sisters to follow. The medical association encouraged and advised them in these plans for professional development at the same time that they made the previous suggestions.[143]

War was not the only vehicle of death. Working in the hospital had its own perils, as evidenced by an entry that Nurse Amos had "poisoned herself in mistake," causing her death on August 11, 1901,[144] but this was an isolated example. From time to time, however, epidemics caused severe illness and sometimes death. In 1916, thirteen Sisters at St. Ann's Academy and the Chinese gardener contracted typhoid fever. Two died, including Sister Mary Ruth, a young postulant who was permitted to take her vows on her deathbed. The doctors devoted themselves to their care, particularly Dr. Jim Helmcken. Twenty women from St. Joseph's— fifteen lay nurses and five Sister nurses—tended them. Health officers examined every aspect of St. Ann's building and premises, but found no flaw in the sewage system or water pipes to explain the outbreak. The provincial council decided that "as a slight remuneration for the un-tiring and invaluable services rendered by the nursing staff of St. Joseph's Hospital to the thirteen Academy Sisters suffering from typhoid fever, the semi-annual interest—three hundred sixty dollars on amount loaned to said Hospital—would be remitted."[145]

The Spanish influenza pandemic appeared postwar, transported most likely on returning troop ships. The death toll worldwide is estimated to have been between fifty million and one hundred million.[146] The impact of this pandemic might be most clearly illustrated by the fact that in-fluenza accounted for 32.6 percent of all insurance death claims against life-insurance companies in Canada in 1918.[147] Unlike other diseases, the flu struck people in the prime of life and was undeterred by face masks, drugs and therapies. No vaccine existed against it. "The most effective pro-cedure turned out to be the care provided by the nurses, who kept patients hydrated, rested, and warm"[148], which the Sisters did, in the hospital, in private homes, even sending help to their houses in New Westminster and Kamloops. The Sisters themselves were not immune to the scourge: Sister Mary Josephine and Sister Mary Alodie succumbed, while many others fell ill, were weakened and recovered only after a lengthy convalescence. Many were debilitated enough to require a later rising hour in order to properly fill their spiritual duties. Permission was given for arising at 5:30 a.m. instead of 4:50 a.m.

St. Joseph's also cared for many of the Sisters of St. Ann from throughout the province who required medical treatment. Recognizing that the previous sum of $200 per year for their care was insufficient, in 1921, the provincial council decided that "a uniform rate of one ($1.00) dollar a day be paid for each Sister" and to cover all material costs of the X-rays. [149]

Shortly after the end of the war a Jesuit priest, Father Charles Moulinier, founder and president of the Catholic Hospital Association of America (1915), and Dr. John Bowman, director of the American College of Surgeons, toured Canada in order to encourage the movement to standardize hospital care and organization in Canada, a movement initiated by the college to develop minimum standards for hospital practice, the principal ones being:

> 1. the restriction of operating privileges to surgical staff who had been trained and approved
> 2. the holding of regular staff meetings
> 3. the keeping of an efficient record system
> 4. the presence of laboratory and X-ray facilities and staff [150]

Following the visit of the two men to St. Joseph's in April 1919, the Sisters asked Drs. R.L. Fraser, W.T. Barrett and F.M. Bryant to serve as members of an advisory board, inviting one or two representatives from each medical specialty to join the consulting staff. The group met on April 29, elected officers and drew up and adopted a constitution and bylaws. On October 10, 1920, Dr. Malcolm T. MacEachern, president of the British Columbia Hospital Association, sent a telegram to the hospital announcing the good news that St. Joseph's had been ranked in Class "A" by the American College of Surgeons. [151]

The Sisters' concern for maintaining high professional standards had also been evident when three of them were among the 139 delegates who attended the founding convention of the British Columbia Hospital Association (BCHA) at the Vancouver General Hospital on June 26, 1918. St. Joseph's fulfilled the functions of a modern hospital set out by the first chair, Dr. MacEachern: (1) the care of the sick, (2) the training of doctors

Reflecting their concern for high professional standards, the Sisters participated in the first British Columbia Hospital Association (BCHA) convention in 1918. In this photograph of the delegates to the 1924 convention, held in Vancouver, the four Sisters of St. Ann (middle) are Sister Mary Noemi, Sister Mary Bertholde, Mother Mary Gabriel and Sister Mary Perpetual Help. PHOTO BY F.G. GOODENOUGH, SSAA P0230

and nurses, (3) the extension of medical knowledge and (4) the prevention of disease.[152] Through the long life of the BCHA, Sisters of St. Ann were attendees at all its conventions and sat on many of its committees.

*   *   *

Until 1921, St. Joseph's was proud of its independence from government. The hospital was busy, but by that year financial depression made it difficult to collect arrears and donations had declined sharply. The hospital might have managed, but it still owed $18,000 to the provincial administration. Thus, St. Joseph's Hospital Local Council considered petitioning the provincial government for recognition under the *Hospital Act*, in order that it might receive the grants accorded to so-called public hospitals. The provincial council wished to explore this matter further, asking permission to meet with the government's provincial secretary, then perhaps the premier, but felt "great prudence is necessary so that the rights and the independence of St. Joseph's Hospital may be safeguarded."[153]

St. Joseph's was not the only hospital suffering financial problems in

1921. That year the BCHA called on the government "to bring in a measure at the earliest opportunity to provide by a universal basis of taxation for the adequate financing of hospitals receiving aid under the Hospital Act."[154] The unexpected response to this request was an amendment to the *Liquor Control Act* to direct some of the profits to hospitals while giving these monies to the municipalities to administer—a change that was to prove untenable. Sister Mary Mark, superior, Sister Mary Bertholde and C.H. O'Halloran, the hospital's lawyer, attended the BCHA convention in New Westminster in 1922, believing it necessary for all Catholic hospitals to be represented, thus emphasizing their request that Catholic hospitals share in the public money appropriated to hospitals. The BCHA passed a resolution that liquor profits should be distributed through the provincial secretary and that all hospitals should share equally on a per diem rate provided they were open to government inspection and were willing to have

a government representative on the hospital board. In October 1922, St. Joseph's Hospital Council considered how to obtain recognition under the *Hospital Act*. The council consulted BC Finance Minister John Hart concerning the formation of a board of directors, and consulted the Sisters of St. Joseph at their hospital in Comox as to how they had managed this process.

Meanwhile the City of Victoria in November of 1922 grudgingly gave St. Joseph's Hospital a token $2,000 as part of the public hospital fund, but the hospital had to reapply regularly for these funds to help cover the cost of caring for its poorer patients, none of whom were ever turned away because they could not pay, a fact attested to by the doctors practising at St.

C.H. O'Halloran, the brother of Sister Mary Cornelius, served as legal counsel for the Sisters. One pressing issue he helped to address was getting legal recognition from the government, thereby making the hospital eligible for government funding. SSAA P0266

Joseph's. Father William O'Boyle, OMI (Oblates of Mary Immaculate), president of the BC arm of the Catholic Hospital Association of America, strenuously championed the right of the Catholic hospitals to a pro rata distribution of government monies marked for hospitals. He made it clear that, in St. Joseph's case, substantial public service had been given, as proven by the Sister superior's compilation of statistics for the previous eleven years, which demonstrated that $177,000 had been given in charity care.[155] Delegations from St. Joseph's and a BCHA memo to BC Provincial Secretary John MacLean suggested it would be discrimination if Catholic hospitals, which had officially signified their willingness to submit to government inspection, were not included in the funding proposal. In April 1923 MacLean announced that St. Joseph's Hospital would be recognized under the *Hospital Act* from April 1, 1923, thus assuring it would receive a per capita grant because it complied with government requirements. The only disadvantage was that, henceforth, the books would be subject to government inspection.[156] Sister superior now found herself with the onerous task, on top of her other duties, of preparing a monthly account report for the government, but was happy to receive the hospital's grant, of which the council earmarked $1,500 a year as salaries for the nursing Sisters.

As of January 1, 1926, however, an amendment to the *Hospital Act* took away this grant. Under this amendment each hospital would receive 70 cents a day from each municipality for patients—paying and non-paying—who had been resident for three months in that municipality before entering the hospital. But this per diem payment could be made only on behalf of "indigents" in one hospital per municipality.[157] In Victoria this was the Royal Jubilee. Indigent patients at St. Joseph's were not to be recognized. Since St. Joseph's always had a large number of patients who could not pay for their treatment, this was a financial blow. A few years later, in 1929, when it became evident that the system of having municipalities control funding for hospitals was not working, the government returned the responsibility for hospital grants to the provincial secretary.

Through all these deliberations the hospital carried on its daily life. The government and municipality may have struggled with their responsibilities, but the interest of Victoria citizens manifested itself in a variety of ways. Since 1909 the annual "linen shower" had been an important event that had elicited support from the community. Each year on March

19, the Feast of St. Joseph, supporters would bring a donation of a specific linen item to a tea. Organized by Miss Frances Meyer, a long-time resident of the hospital, and taken over in the 1920s by Mrs. Alex McDermott, another faithful friend of the hospital, the shower garnered much in the way of needed linen supplies—1,200 towels in 1921 alone. That year, on June 11, the energetic women who supported the hospital held the inaugural meeting of a women's auxiliary. The members took on the task of sewing, mending linen and making layettes, thus freeing the Sisters to devote more time to patient care. They convened bazaars, teas and other fundraisers. The BCHA recognized the invaluable service and the link that such auxiliaries formed between the community and the hospital, going so far as to alter its bylaws in 1923 to admit the auxiliaries of member hospitals as corporate members.[158]

Another way of promoting community involvement was participation in National Hospital Day. Beginning in 1921, St. Joseph's became one of the hundreds of hospitals throughout North America that adopted May 12, the birthday of Florence Nightingale, as an occasion to throw

Happily working at their booth, Ada McKenzie, Head Nurse on Maternity, and Sister Leanne Marie, Sister Mary Margaret of the Sacred Heart, Sister Mary Malachy and Sister Mary Grace (l–r) take part in an annual bazaar held by the Women's Auxiliary in the 1960s. SSAA P0253

open their doors to the public, to acquaint visitors with both the work of the hospital and the physical plant that supported it. St. Joseph's added a happy note by inviting as many as 150 new mothers and their babies born in the preceding year to visit and gather for a group photograph. And the public did come—500 people the first year, inspecting every part of the building, staying for tea and meeting the Sisters and men and women who staffed the hospital. Often the lieutenant-governor of British Columbia and the mayor of Victoria and his wife and other dignitaries would attend, giving added weight to the occasion.

Smiling for the camera, these mothers and babies are back at St. Joseph's for an annual tea. Sometimes this included a "best baby," who was given a trophy. This picture looks to be from the 1950s. PHOTO BY ALFRED TOONE, SSAA P0293

Chapter 4

The War-to-War Crunch

St. Joseph's never refuses assistance to any person who asks
for it and no matter from whence a person may come, no
matter what their creed may be, the doors of St. Joseph's are
ever open to receive them.
　　　　　　　　—Mayor Herbert Anscomb, May 23, 1929,
　　　　　　　　　　　　at the opening of the new wing

By 1919, eight thousand Victoria men and women had returned from serving overseas, to a city that had doubled in size to a population of sixty thousand.[159] St. Joseph's was feeling the crunch for space.

A pressing need to enlarge the facilities was evident in the early 1920s. An isolation ward was required in order to comply with the *Hospital Act*, which led to clearing rooms over the laundry for this purpose. The space was immediately filled with five patients, student nurses who had contracted measles. This plan was abandoned within two months because the laundry noise was detrimental to the patients' recovery, but the need to find extra space did not evaporate.

At a special meeting of St. Joseph's Hospital Local Council on October 26, 1923, Mother Mary Gabriel, provincial superior, was asked to present a request to the general council in Lachine for "permission to borrow two hundred thousand ($200,000) dollars, with which to enlarge and remodel the present hospital."[160] The council expected to meet the interest charges and pay off some of the capital by applying the $1,500 accruing annually from Sisters' salaries. Through the 1920s the hospital also attempted to accumulate surrounding property for the hoped-for expansion, a proposed nurses' residence and a separate tuberculosis centre. In November 1923 Lachine approved the request to borrow and build. St. Joseph's engaged a local architect, C. Elwood Watkins, junior partner of Thomas Hooper, to draw up plans for a new wing. However, building costs were rising, and under canon law in the Catholic Church, Rome must approve borrowing and expenditures over a set amount. By 1925 the amount requested to borrow had increased to $300,000. In January 1926, however, Mother Mary Leopoldine, superior general, secured the permission of Pope Pius XI to proceed.[161] When tenders were opened in the presence of Mother Mary Gabriel, St. Joseph's Council and the architect, the lowest bid was $524,000, which was $200,000 higher than they could finance. Changes were made to the plans and again they were put out to tender. In October 1927, they came within the budget.[162]

The contract was let to the local firm of Luney Brothers, who promised to complete the work by March 1929. An extraordinary visitor at the time, Most Reverend Andrew Cassulo, apostolic delegate to Canada and Newfoundland, was admitted for treatment. When he was discharged, Sister Mary Mildred—who had been hospital superior since June 1925—showed him exactly where the expansion was to be, whereupon he blessed the land and the undertaking. On November 23, 1927, Bishop Thomas O'Donnell and Mayor Carl Pendray turned the first sod, with the Sisters, medical and nursing staff and friends looking on. Mrs. Charles Lombard, who had been present at the original sod-turning in 1875, and Mary Macnamara, St. Joseph's first trained nurse, also took a turn with the shovel.[163]

Another special guest was Sister Mary Bridget, the hospital's first superior. In her first years in Victoria she had looked after the broke and the broken (as they were sometimes called) gold-rush miners, many of whom she continued to nurse as they became permanent residents of the hospital along with other homeless and elderly of the city. Her death on January 11, 1933, at the age of eighty-seven—well after celebrating her diamond jubilee—came after sixty-five years of fidelity, kindness and unselfishness as an accomplished nurse and in service to others.[164]

* * *

Apart from the funding given by the Sisters of St. Ann and 17 percent from a provincial government grant, St. Joseph's raised money through its first public appeal. The hospital's fiftieth anniversary in 1925 seemed an auspicious time to make such a solicitation. The Sisters still owed $75,000 from the 1908 addition. They appealed to the people on their record of treating anyone regardless of creed, noting that 90 percent of the patients were not Catholic. In a special brochure, they stressed that there was no intention to detract from "the noble work and services rendered by other hospitals. There is room and work for all. This is proved by the fact that at times both hospitals are taxed to capacity."[165] In fact, Victoria could be proud of "its two splendid hospitals."

With the turning of the first sod, the next step was the laying of the cornerstone for the new surgical and maternity unit. Bishop O'Donnell blessed the stone and, according to custom, passed the historic trowel to BC Lieutenant-Governor Robert Randolph Bruce to lay the stone on Sunday, March 18, 1928.[166] On the stone was the inscription:

A.M.D.G.

PRO DEO ET HUMANITATE

St. Joseph's Hospital

1928[167]

Within the stone was a small box containing a blessed medallion of St. Joseph, a hospital yearbook, coins of the year 1927, the most recent editions of the *Victoria Daily Times* and the *Daily Colonist*, and a book listing those who had been involved in building the addition; the present staff of Sisters; the graduating nurses of 1928 and those in training; the employees; and the names of prominent figures in the Catholic Church of the time. The program for the ceremony gave statistics relevant to the service the hospital provided. St. Joseph's had treated 56,751 patients in the previous fifty-three years. Its current annual payroll was $53,648, with the free hospitalization and care averaging $18,500 per year. Up to this date, 4,021 babies had been born at St. Joseph's.[168]

On May 23, 1929, Lieutenant-Governor Bruce declared the new wing officially open, the Firemen's Band playing for the hundreds, including George McGregor, president of the board of the Royal Jubilee Hospital, who gathered to hear the official speeches and tour the addition. Sister Mary Mildred and Bishop O'Donnell welcomed all; they were proud to say that only local people had worked on the construction. Dr. Gordon Kenning, president of the consulting staff, applauded the Sisters' courage and foresight. Victoria Mayor Herbert Anscomb added that "St. Joseph's never refuses assistance to any person who asks for it and no matter from whence a person may come, no matter what their creed may be, the doors of St. Joseph's are ever open to receive them."[169] Premier Simon Fraser Tolmie's announcement that St. Joseph's was giving free treatment to Victoria's needy to the tune of $18,500 a year should justifiably have embarrassed the mayor, knowing as he did that the city constantly dragged its heels about assuming its responsibility to offset this expense.

The new wing allowed greater efficiency and greater comfort for the Sisters. One central water-heating plant replaced three inefficient furnaces. The Sisters now had comfortable apartments that were separate from the rest of the first floor, which contained the X-ray department and a cheerful children's ward, with a separate tonsillitis ward. Two major and five smaller operating rooms occupied the fifth floor, the theory of the time being that the farther away from the road an operating room was, the less dirt would intrude. At the south end of each ward were bright solariums opening to

The new C wing of St. Joseph's Hospital, opened in 1929, contained, among other needed additions, new accommodation for the Sisters and a new children's ward.
SSAA P0064

Beacon Hill Park. The many donors of room furnishings, window treatments and other appointments included the Butchart family; architect C. Elwood Watkins and his wife; the builder; the students at St. Ann's Academy; and the Kiwanis Club.

St. Joseph's also hoped to construct a tuberculosis sanitarium. In 1924 it purchased four lots on Rupert Street for $4,300. In 1925 it submitted plans for a new building to the general council in Lachine, but late in the year decided instead to purchase the Vernon property across the street and more adjacent lots. With some alterations, the house would be well suited to long-term care for the chronically ill—it had glass-enclosed verandas and a spacious and well-established garden surrounded by a high stone wall. On May 1, 1926, Bishop O'Donnell blessed the house, and the first patients were installed three days later. The home was equipped for fifteen patients on two floors, and was always staffed with two Sisters and two lay nurses.[170]

In 1926, too, the Sisters assumed responsibility for Our Lady of Lourdes Hospital in Campbell River, and in 1929 built a new nurses' residence on the corner east of St. Joseph's Hospital.

The Sisters also concerned themselves with the running of St. Joseph's during the 1920s. To conform to the *Hospital Act*, they created an advisory

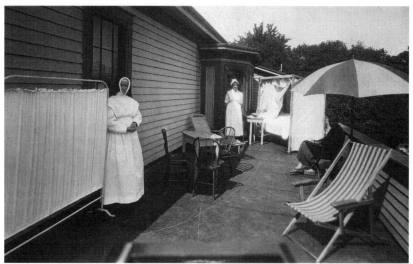

The Vernon Villa TB Sanitarium, shown in the late 1920s with Sister Mary Priscilla (left), treated those chronically ill with tuberculosis. It featured a glassed-in veranda and a large, secluded garden. SSAA P0107

board composed of members of the Victoria community. They had always availed themselves of the expertise of interested businessmen and physicians, but now they prepared to formalize this arrangement.

A preliminary meeting was held on October 22, 1923. The constitution and bylaws adopted on March 31, 1924, were signed by Sister Mary Gabriel, president; Sister Mary Mildred, vice-president and acting secretary for the Sisters of St. Ann; Sister Mary Anna, acting superior of St. Joseph's Hospital; and Sister Mary Good Shepherd, secretary for the hospital. They mandated a board consisting of nine members: six appointed by the Sisters of St. Ann, one by the lieutenant-governor in council as a representative of the BC government, one by the corporation of the City of Victoria, and one by the lieutenant-governor in council as a representative of the municipalities of Oak Bay, Saanich and Esquimalt.[171]

The first official meeting convened on April 29, 1924. The Sisters appointed Sister Mary Mark (superior and chair), Sister Mary Anna (superintendent of nurses), Sister Mary Catherine of Sienna and three men—Alex McDermott, Charles E. Wilson and C.H. O'Halloran. The government appointed two men—W.S. Fraser and E.D. Johnston, who was deputy minister of finance. The bylaws set for carrying out the business of the hospital stated that the board would meet once a month. The board formalized the hospital's practice of taking care of the needy by declaring that the hospital would admit—after inspection and the approval of the hospital's medical officer—any indigent person not suffering from smallpox who had a certificate from any resident medical practitioner of the province stating that he or she required hospital treatment. Anyone involved in an urgent situation or accident was to be admitted promptly without any formality.[172] McDermott would make evident his ongoing interest in St. Joseph's by sitting on the board for more than two decades, until his death in 1949. The board looked for means to finance building and programs in various ways, even passing a resolution in 1927 that stated

> The Federal Government [shall] be requested to amend the Income War Tax Act, 1917 . . . so that every person or corporation shall be entitled to deduct from his or its income all sums donated to charitable or educational foundations or institutions.[173]

The hospital's shortage of funds arose partly from the continued failure of the city to honour its obligation to pay for poor patients. That the city was so removed from considering the hospital's needs was evident when city council in 1937 refused to help St. Joseph's financially because the council was not represented on the board—which was curious given that on July 5, 1929, the city had appointed James Adam as its representative and he had been attending board meetings ever since. The hospital also had free provincial patients because the provincial inspector of hospitals had informed them in 1928 that since each hospital was obliged to care for a certain number of old people unable to care for themselves, it could not discharge these patients when they no longer needed acute care. In 1932 the city health officer sent a circular to members of the Victoria Medical Society requesting all doctors to send patients who were unable to meet their bills to the Royal Jubilee Hospital as a means of saving money, but the board explained that St. Joseph's would not refuse patients as that would defeat the end for which it was founded.[174]

* * *

Of all the individuals who supported the Sisters, Nellie Cashman, an Irish-born woman of extraordinary energy, was the most colourful. Known for her care and compassion, she nevertheless was tough enough to brave the harshest conditions to pursue her quest for gold in the North, travelling by dogsled and snowshoe and sleeping in the wild. She first learned of the Sisters' proposed hospital in the early 1870s, when she passed through Victoria on her initial excursion to Alaska. She took their cause to the Cassiar, BC, miners whom she had rescued from an early death from scurvy by bringing fresh limes to supply their vitamin C. She passed the hat among them, collecting $543.50 to send to the Sisters. During her years in the North she continued to be a benefactor, and "sometimes a cart laden with pillows and comforters would be delivered at the hospital in her name."[175] Her unconventional dress and lifestyle made her a target of gossip, but the Sisters appreciated her generous heart and realized the necessity for her to dress to suit her environment.

Back and forth Nellie went, to Arizona and California, to Alaska and

In August 1964, Sister Elizabeth Marie (Betty Janelle) walks among the graves of deceased Sisters in their section of Ross Bay Cemetery in Victoria. The section was purchased for them by their good friend and benefactor, Father Auguste Brabant, in 1909. SSAA P0067

the Yukon, raising her deceased sister's children, nursing and mothering children and miners alike, running a restaurant or a hotel, all the while prospecting or mining the properties on which she had staked a claim. Her wanderings put her in contact with two other well-known lovers of the North, Jack London and Robert Service. When she fell seriously ill she wished to spend her last days with the Sisters on whom she had bestowed her charity. She entered St. Joseph's Hospital in October 1924 and died of pneumonia on January 4, 1925. She was eulogized in many North American papers. She is buried in Victoria's Ross Bay Cemetery adjacent to the plot of the Sisters of St. Ann. They paid for her grave and for a monument that calls her "a friend of the sick and the hungry and to all men" and praises her "heroic apostolate of service among the western and northern frontier miners." Truly "the miners' angel."[176]

* * *

Of primary importance to the congregation was the ongoing education and pursuit of professionalism in education and nursing. In this respect the nursing Sisters were like lay nurses, though some of the women involved in the movement believed that a "vocation" and "profession" were mutually exclusive.[177] There was no contradiction in the Sisters' minds. They belonged to the Canadian National Association of Trained Nurses after it formed in 1908 (in 1924 it became the Canadian Nurses Association)[178] and the Graduate Nurses Association of British Columbia, formed in 1912 (whose name changed to the Registered Nurses Association of British Columbia, or RNABC, after the passage of Bill 67 on March 23, 1935, and changed again to the College of Registered Nurses of British Columbia on August 19, 2005).[179]

Representatives of the nursing Sisters of St. Ann regularly attended the meetings of these two associations, as well as the BCHA and the Catholic hospital associations of the province, Canada and North America. They travelled to take courses in current medical advances. Sister Mary Patrick and Sister Mary Bertholde took a two-week course at Vancouver General Hospital in 1923 to study diets prescribed under the new treatment regime for diabetics; Sister Mary Mildred and Sister Mary Gregory went to Milwaukee, Wisconsin, in 1926 for a mammoth hospital congress, and stayed on to take a three-week course in hospital management and administration at Marquette University. From there they visited hospitals in several major cities, finding the Mayo Clinic in Rochester, New York, of great interest. The mother general had sent them "in view of the very pressing need for fully trained and equipped hospital Sisters."[180] Sister Mary Beatrice advanced her knowledge of the X-ray at courses in Vancouver, qualifying in 1931 as a registered technician with marks of 86 percent in practical work and 93 percent for X-ray physics and theory. In the same year two Sisters and two student nurses were sent to "Tranquille," a sanitarium in Kamloops, to follow a two-month course in the "Care of the Tubercular Patient."[181] Hospital Sisters studied and took pedagogy exams that were intended mainly for teachers but useful for anyone in nursing education who was continuing their education and development efforts.

⋆　⋆　⋆

The stock-market crash in 1929 presaged the Depression of the 1930s. Victoria was of course not immune. Dr. Kenning admitted a Victoria businessman diagnosed as a "physical and mental wreck" due to the crash. World economies slumped and with them the fortunes of individuals and institutions such as St. Joseph's that may not have invested in stocks but felt the impact of others' losses. In February 1926 Rome had authorized the borrowing of $300,000 for the new addition, money loaned by the Bank of Montreal bearing an interest rate of 5.5 percent, and first drawn on in August 1928. A further loan of $50,000 was taken in November 1929 at 6 percent interest, both loans subject to retirement in May 1932. The hospital managed to keep up with interest payments, but by October 1930 the debt was crippling daily operations. The board deemed it prudent

Sister Mary Bertholde (nursing graduate, 1921, and medical technology graduate, 1923) hard at work in the modern laboratory at St. Joseph's Hospital. Throughout the Sisters' history in health care, they have insisted on maintaining the highest medical and professional standards to serve their patients. SSAA P0112

to ask the general administration in Lachine to try to refinance their loans and add more to it at a lower interest rate. The motherhouse came to their rescue staving off a more damaging financial situation.[182]

Belt-tightening occurred at every level. Due to the heavy cost of milk from local dairies, the hospital farm purchased three cows as an initial investment in milk self-sufficiency. A new elevator became necessary for staff and patient safety (Sister Mary Henrietta of Jesus and the elevator operator had a near-fatal accident) as well as liability concerns; its purchase was realized only due to a $6,000 bequest in 1930 from Mrs. Ann McTiernan, a patient since 1925.[183]

As the Depression deepened, the *Daily Colonist* on March 19, 1933, noted that "never before, perhaps, were our local hospitals more appealed to for long-term credit, by patients stricken by illness in a season of unemployment, and many are the cases unable to defray in any way the cost of treatment." The Sisters received property, a cow and even a piano in lieu of payment. They closed Ward 2A and Vernon Villa for a time as an economic measure. In 1934, Bishop John MacDonald—wishing he could send more—sent $1,000 from the sale of property to Sister Mary Mark, the provincial, to use where it was most needed. This perhaps was in response to her request for financial assistance, particularly for St. Ann's Academy, since the diocese was assisting the boys at St. Louis College, but not the girls at the academy where ninety-eight students paid no tuition largely due to their parents' situation during the Depression.[184]

In 1933 the government reduced its grants to hospitals, causing the board to look at other methods to survive. Already they had considered reducing employees' wages. In October 1932 any employee receiving more than $60 a month suffered a salary cut of 10 percent; Dr. Gerry Aylward, the anaesthetist, and other staff doctors also had their income reduced by 10 percent, while Father Sobry, the hospital chaplain, accepted a 50-percent drop in his stipend. They made do with one less male nurse and gave an engineer a cottage on hospital property to live in as part payment on his salary. In 1934 the hospital installed a sawdust burner in one of the boilers, hoping to reduce fuel costs by 30 or 40 percent, and adopted a one-piece uniform for nurses, a move aimed at reducing the work and cost in the laundry. The board considered and discarded the idea of running sweepstakes. More drastically, it did not renew its liability insurance in

1933 due to the extremely high premium, a practice it did not continue for long. The BC Hospital Association urged its members to besiege their members of the legislative assembly with pleas to reinstate the government grant to its former level, a pressure that resulted in a return to those previous amounts on April 1, 1934.[185]

Even in their straitened circumstances the Sisters managed to practise charity. Knowing a staff member had responsibility for an aging parent or a large family, they would add something to her monthly pay. The local clergy suffering deprivation during the Depression were offered free hospital care, and a 50-percent discount was given to any priest from outside the diocese. During 1938 they allowed graduate nurses, dietitians and other professionals a month of sick leave with pay and free hospital care for one month, excepting expensive medications. Other employees were given a 25-percent discount.[186]

Despite privation, many occasions—large and small—were celebrated with gusto. Milestones for the congregation included the opening of the

Mother Mary Leopoldine, after a number of leadership roles in BC, led the short-lived mission to Japan in 1934. After returning to Canada she eventually became the superior general of the congregation. SSAA P0310

Bulkley Valley District Hospital (a.k.a. Sacred Heart Hospital) in Smithers, BC, in 1933, and the departure of four Sisters on the *Empress of Russia* on October 6, 1934, to open a new mission in Japan, where Mother Mary Leopoldine, the current superior of St. Joseph's province and the former general superior, was to be the founding superior in Kagoshima. She and Sister Mary Ignatia would be sent from Victoria along with two Sisters from Eastern Canada— Sister Marie-Louise Agnes and Sister Marie-de-Bethlehem. The diamond jubilee of the Sisters' 1858 arrival on the West Coast deserved three days of celebration that drew the dignitaries of the day.

St. Joseph's could proudly point to the fact it now had 260 beds and eight operating rooms. Sixteen fully graduated staff nurses were Sisters of St. Ann.[187]

There were other milestones. On May 6, 1935, Sister Mary Ludovic as "matron" of the hospital received King George V's Silver Jubilee Medal, which was presented by Lieutenant-Governor John Fordham Johnson on the grounds of the legislature. A page in the Sisters' history was turned when Bishop John MacDonald gave them permission to vote in the federal election for the first time on October 14, 1935, at a polling booth set up in the hospital.[188] And small things gave pleasure to these Depression days of hard work and

Father Bernard Hubbard, SJ, earned his nickname, the "Glacier Priest," while climbing in the Austrian Alps. He became a world-renowned authority on arctic phenomena, leading thirty-one scientific expeditions into Alaska and the Arctic between 1927 and 1962. With thousands of photos and reels of film, he was a popular lecturer. SSAA P0231

penury: their first radio, bazaars and linen showers, dynamic visitors like writer G.K. Chesterton and Father Bernard Hubbard, SJ (Society of Jesus), the "Glacier Priest," to entertain them.

An ongoing benefactor appeared on the scene during the Depression. Mayo Singh, a successful lumberman who was grateful for the care given his wife at the birth of their third child, a son, in December 1933, immediately gave $100 to pay for the food required for hospital staff and patients for one day, as well as table linens and hankies to nurses on the maternity floor. Upon finding out from Sister Mary Ludovic, the superior, what might still be lacking after the annual linen shower in March 1934, he presented her with 264 white bedspreads.[189] From this time on, throughout the 1930s, 1940s, and 1950s, he assisted in any way he could, producing a litany of linens and in 1936 building a covered walkway from the nurses' home to the hospital. He is mentioned in the Sisters' chronicles in November 1950 for undertaking to pay the hospital's entire fruit

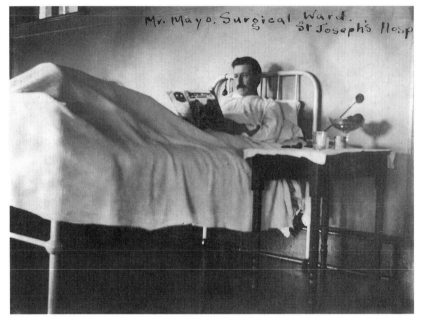

Lying in bed as a patient in the hospital he loved, Mayo Singh, a successful lumberman, was a constant benefactor over three decades following the birth of his third child in St. Joseph's in 1933. SSAA P0233

and vegetable bill for December as well as providing the Christmas turkey dinner for all patients, staff and Sisters. His final act of generosity was a substantial bequest in his will upon his death in 1956.

*   *   *

Partly to improve service to patients and partly to comply with future requirements of the American College of Surgeons, a professional body they wished their hospital physicians to belong to, St. Joseph's Hospital revised its bylaws and constitution and enlarged the medical staff in May 1935. After this date the staff included thirty-three "active" members and sixteen "visiting"; the active staff were divided into eleven departments, with a chief of service at the head of each, responsible to the chief of staff for the functioning of the service involved. These advancements would make St. Joseph's eligible to accept interns. Mother provincial and six of the nursing Sisters took courses in hospital administration at Providence Hospital in Seattle, under the auspices of Seattle College for academic credit, studying topics from hospital history to the organization and function of the hospital, X-rays, diagnostics, physical therapy, pharmacy, hospital economics, health insurance and social service.[190] The demands of running a modern hospital had become more complicated.

At the beginning of 1936 the hospital noted with satisfaction some improvement in its financial position. In February there were 186 patients, the highest number since before the Depression; presumably more of them were able to pay the cost of their treatment. There were wide swings in the number of in-patients, however—in September 1937 there were only 114 patients, so paying patients did not constitute a reliable monthly income. There were also many long-term patients unable to contribute to the cost of their care.[191]

In November 1936, the provincial legislature amended the *Hospital Act* to authorize "cities to remunerate hospitals other than City Hospitals for treatment given to indigent cases"[192], a step that should have removed one of the constant drains on the hospital, but in May 1937 the city was still balking at paying St. Joseph's. All the "houses" in St. Joseph's province were in debt to the provincial administration, unable to pay even interest during the Depression. With the desire to eliminate compound interest and hoping they could reduce their capital debt and accumulated interest, the general council in Lachine granted each institution a lowered rate of interest (dropping from 4 percent to 2 percent) for ten years beginning January 1938 on loans to the provincial administration. This enabled the hospital to engage a chartered accountant in 1938 to set up the books, do the auditing and complete the special report forms for monthly accounts required by the government, thus removing a time-consuming task from Sister superior.

Bishop Cody blessed and turned the first sod on February 29, 1940, for a new St. Joseph's Villa to replace Vernon Villa, which had become inadequate within ten years of its purchase in 1926. Tuberculosis patients were overflowing into Ward 4B across the street. The lot adjacent to Vernon Villa was purchased and in 1938 Henry Whittaker was retained to draw up plans for a new sanitarium, with Archie Sullivan as contractor. The provincial government guaranteed occupancy of twenty-five to thirty beds, provided the Sisters erected a new building for that purpose. The board voted in January 1940 to accept the proposal of the government's

Strong supporters of the Sisters' work, Henry Whittaker (left), the provincial architect, and Archibald (Archie) Sullivan (right), contractor, frequently worked together to build the Sisters' hospitals. SSAA P0079 & P0080

TB division to make an annual grant of $18,000 toward the maintenance of twenty TB patients. Lieutenant-Governor Eric and Mrs. Hamber, the board chairman and other friends came out to view the one-storey structure at its official opening on October 3, the Feast of Saint Teresa of Lisieux, who died of tuberculosis and is considered the patroness of TB patients. The new structure included thirty-eight beds for patients and staff, a small laundry and a chapel. The Kiwanis Club rented the old Vernon Villa for $30 a month to use as a workshop for the convalescent TB patients.[193]

Mother Mary Mark's term of office as provincial superior was extended by one year by special papal indult to 1941, in order to provide continuity through the current building programs—Mount St. Mary, St. Joseph's Villa, a new wing for the school of nursing and a new $38,000 X-ray unit. The financial squeeze had been alleviated, but the declaration of war in September 1939 brought many other restrictions, more belt-tightening and galvanized the population in support of Britain and the war effort. Employment increased, largely because of positions left vacant by those joining the armed forces, as well as Victoria's development as a major shipbuilding centre. With the movement of nurses and other medical personnel to serve overseas, local health care facilities suffered acute staff shortages, and called upon married and retired nurses to offer their skills to local hospitals. In 1941 there were 26,473 graduate nurses in Canada, and 4,000 were needed for military purposes.[194] Seventy-five graduates of St. Joseph's School of Nursing were on the active service roll, serving in various forces, with two—Norah Leahy and Eileen Robinson—receiving the Royal Red Cross and honourable mention in dispatches.[195] In the words of one author, "Women's contributions to the work force increased immensely. Industries traditionally closed to women welcomed their labour."[196]

Union membership in British Columbia increased from 14 percent in 1939 to 30 percent in 1943, a movement that was to affect the future operation of St. Joseph's.[197]

It was now impossible for staff of St. Joseph's to obtain gas for their personal cars, even for use on hospital business. In rural areas where there was no other transportation, gas may have been available but drivers were not. For the first time, Sisters at Bulkley Valley District Hospital were given permission to obtain driving licences and to operate vehicles, as no men were available.

Food was rationed and expensive and other supplies were difficult to obtain. The annual linen shower was a great boon to the hospital during these restrictions. The government demanded costly "black-out" procedures, while giving St. Joseph's 100 beds, mattresses, blankets and pillows so it could handle at least 100 emergency patients in case of disaster. Soon after the declaration of war, the hospital became very crowded due to the number of soldiers being admitted. In January 1940 the hospital had 54 soldiers as in-patients and by September their patient count was 288, rising in February 1941 to 301. This came on top of a record month for maternity patients, with the birth of 59 babies. The influx of soldiers continued, causing the hospital to convert the central linen room into a six-bed ward for them, paid for by the Junior Auxiliary.[198] The city requested that the dining room be converted, "not to say perverted"[199], into a storage area for gas masks. Adding to the Sisters' consternation, they heard on December 8, 1941, that war had been declared between the United States and Japan. Their hearts were with their Sisters in Japan as they prayed earnestly for God's protection and their safe return to Canada.

Because of the need for fuel oil in the war effort, "by order of the Department of Munitions and Supply," the hospital was forced to convert to coal for heating. It installed two Iron Fireman stokers at a cost of $8,000 and spent $4,000 to set up coal bins and automatic conveyors. The provincial government gave a $5,000 grant toward these installation costs.[200] The need to remodel the hospital to meet wartime needs and higher costs for food and other supplies imposed a heavy financial burden on the hospital. Recognizing this, both the general council in Lachine and the provincial council of the Sisters of St. Ann agreed not to demand interest payments from July 1, 1943, until July 1, 1945.

Given the increased patient load, however, the hospital was able to reduce its debt from $520,000 in 1934 to $123,000 in July 1945. Indeed, in 1945 the hospital paid off these debts and still had a surplus of more than $200,000. When salaries almost doubled over the war years, the hospital was able to pay them. The Sisters believed "God has shown that he is pleased that we should pay the living wage to our employees, because He has blessed us with the means to do so."[201]

Advances in medicine accelerated during the Second World War, just as they had in the First World War. St. Joseph's was gifted with an iron lung in August 1940, and it was used for the first time the following February for a patient with botulism poisoning and in future years mainly during polio epidemics. "Operation Blood Bank" began in mid-1943. The Junior Auxiliary donated $2,000 to set up the refrigeration and testing equipment. Sisters and lay nurses went to the armed forces bases, where donors gave blood to be tested in the hospital lab for purity and typing before being made available for use in emergency cases.[202]

In 1945 St. Joseph's became the first hospital in Canada to accept the Red Cross blood transfusion service.[203] The *Daily Colonist* of February 6, 1947, announced that St. Joseph's would receive its first shipment of blood through the Red Cross project, and two days later ran a picture of Sister Mary Loretto and a lay nurse giving the first transfusion to a patient.[204] What the world remembers more is the advent of penicillin. Margaret Doris, later Sister Mary Doris, recalled her five-year pharmacy apprenticeship at Royal Columbian Hospital in New Westminster in the 1940s, years when women were able to fill spots normally reserved for men. The day the first batch of penicillin arrived in the lab, "the head burst in the door with this little bottle of stinky fluid," this marvel of antibiotics they knew "was doing so much for the boys on the battlefield."[205] St. Joseph's witnessed its first use of penicillin in February 1944 on a young soldier with staph cellulitis in his neck. The drug could be obtained only through permission of a joint committee of the Armed Forces, which alone was empowered to release it.[206] The soldier's recovery seemed almost miraculous in an era when infections caused by such events as a ruptured appendix could be a death warrant.

St. Joseph's had been training lab technologists since the 1920s, but not until October 1944 did the Canadian Medical Association approve the courses taught, with the first students passing the exams given by the Canadian Society of Laboratory Technologists in January 1945. Four Sisters took a refresher course in 1943 in Vancouver on hospital adminis-tration, presented by Percy Ward, the provincial inspector of hospitals. In November 1944 the Vancouver Island branch of the Canadian Association of Social Workers held three days of meetings at St. Joseph's attended by Mother Mary Mildred and several Sisters. The next month the hospital organized a social service department, hiring an experienced social worker and a stenographer to assist her. Sister nurses continued to expand their education. Also in 1944, the congregation accepted another call to mission by establishing a "house" in poverty-stricken Haiti.[207] The Sisters in British Columbia demonstrated their solidarity with this expansion by sending $1,000 for this mission to the superior general, Mother Mary Leopoldine, to honour her golden jubilee.

The Sisters of St. Ann had been members of the British Columbia Hospital Association (BCHA) since its inception in 1918. They joined the Catholic Hospital Association of the United States and Canada in its early days and remained members when the Catholic Hospital Council of Canada (CHCC) was formed in 1942 to deal exclusively with matters pertaining to Canadian Catholic hospitals, particularly with respect to its francophone community and its regional composition.[208] The provincial voice, the Catholic Hospital Association of British Columbia (CHABC), held its inaugural meeting on April 12, 1940, in Vancouver led by Mother Mary Mark as its first president. She served for one year, followed by Sister Mary Kathleen (1943–44), Sister Mary Loretto (1952–54), Sister Mary Angelus (1957–59), and Sister Mary Lucita (1965), who was the last of the Sisters of St. Ann to preside over the CHABC, though they remain members to this day.[209] Each of the hospitals the Sisters operated in British Columbia was represented at the meetings of the BCHA, the CHABC and other professional associations in the province.

Chapter 5

Keeping Up with the Patient Load

The story of St. Joseph's Hospital is one of constant progress, of sacrifice, work, generosity, and constant devotion so the suffering of man could be alleviated.
—Jacob Villiers Fisher, deputy finance minister and hospital board member, March 19, 1952, the Feast of St. Joseph and the opening of the new Collinson Street addition

By mid-1943 the federal government was planning for postwar hospital construction. The Rowell-Sirois Commission contemplated adding rehabilitation annexes to St. Joseph's Hospital or the Royal Jubilee Hospital to avoid the duplication of staff and equipment that a separate military hospital in the Victoria area would entail. St. Joseph's submitted plans for consideration, without result. Nevertheless, it was evident that the hospital needed updating and more space.[210]

As early as June 1943 the board advised tearing down the original Collinson Street wing and replacing it with a modern new wing. Premier John Hart gave the Sisters permission in October 1944 to seek a grant and have government architect Henry Whittaker draw up plans. During a November 1944 meeting, Provincial Secretary George Pearson told Mother Mary Mildred and Sister Mary Kathleen that the BC government would contribute one third of the cost for erecting a modern two-hundred-bed, eight-storey addition and would finance a psychiatric department provided the plans were approved by Dr. A. Crease, the superintendent of Essondale, the provincial mental hospital in rural Coquitlam, BC.[211]

The federal government announced in January 1946 that it was prepared to make a grant of 15 to 20 percent towards hospital building and in 1948 it approved $65 million to be spent over the next five years toward hospital construction.[212] With these incentives, Sister superior purchased the Royal Canadian Air Force barracks located on Foul Bay Road for $3,010 and installed them on the grounds in May 1946 under the supervision of Archie Sullivan. They would provide temporary accommodation for sixty to seventy patients during the demolition. The barracks were opened for patients in late 1947, while the board awaited new figures for the proposed wing.

Unfortunately the need to raise funds for a new hospital wing collided with the Diocesan Development Drive for its 1946 centenary celebrations. Bishop John Cody wrote to Mother Mary Mildred early in 1945 that he expected the Sisters to donate $10,000 (10 percent of the $100,000 target) as their "fair share"—$5,000 in cash and $5,000 from one half-interest they had in property on Rockland Avenue. Lachine approved the first $5,000 donation immediately, but it was much later before the motherhouse felt

As part of the government's postwar hospital expansion plan, RCAF barracks (foreground) were purchased and installed on hospital grounds in 1948 to house up to seventy patients while part of St. Joseph's Hospital was demolished and rebuilt. SSAA P0054

that St. Joseph's province could pay the rest. In fact, the provincial council in Victoria felt this demand exceedingly heavy on top of their other financial burdens and asked Bishop Cody to accept payments at their convenience and in amounts they felt they could spare.[213] The bishop expected the Sisters to delay the hospital drive until the diocesan drive for centenary expenses was complete, at which time he would pledge the support of the diocese.[214]

Another source of revenue was again pursued. In view of the considerable number of poor city patients being treated, St. Joseph's approached the city in June 1946 for remuneration, asking the city to bear in mind that the Jubilee could not accommodate all these city patients. It would be cheaper to pay St. Joseph's than to build sufficient space to provide for them elsewhere. To aid in its appeals to city and government, St. Joseph's inaugurated a bookkeeping system early in 1946 that was already in use at Vancouver General Hospital and the Royal Jubilee and that made it possible to ascertain an exact statement of per capita cost, thus justifying the fee charged. However, the plea fell on deaf ears.

Even with the promised grants the Sisters would need to find about $500,000. With the support of Bishop Cody, the general council petitioned Rome to allow it to borrow this sum; permission was granted in February 1946. Bishop Cody blessed the grounds for the new wing on March 19, the Feast of Saint Joseph, always considered an auspicious date for events involving the hospital and also the month in which Bishop Cody had determined the hospital could begin its fundraising campaign following the diocesan drive. James Cardinal McGuigan, visiting for the diocesan centenary, turned the first sod on August 2, 1946, amid great publicity. Catholic Premier Hart led a delegation welcoming the cardinal not only to the diocesan celebrations, but also the seventieth anniversary of St. Joseph's Hospital. Hart, Mayor Percy George, the board chair, many of the medical staff and their wives and many other dignitaries graced the platform when Whittaker handed the ceremonial shovel to Cardinal McGuigan, who told the crowd "this first sod is turned by the same hands that have power to cast a vote for the choice of the Vicar of Christ on earth."[215] On Sunday the Sisters, nurses, island Catholics as well as Chinese and First Nations men in colourful costumes preceded the even more colourful hierarchy in their clerical garb on a two-mile Corpus Christi procession to Athletic

Proud local and church leaders gather on stage in 1946 for the turning of the sod ceremony to mark the beginning of the new building campaign. Eventually the original 1876 structure was demolished and a modern wing built. L to r — Dr. George Hall; Justice C.H. O'Halloran of the BC Court of Appeals; James Cardinal McGuigan of Toronto; the Honourable John Hart, premier of British Columbia; Victoria Mayor Percy George; John C. Cody, Bishop of Victoria. SSAA P0267

Park that culminated in a Benediction service of prayer and song. Prior to this Sister Mary Dorothea had written and produced a "magnificent entertainment" pageant presented at the Royal Theatre.[216] These events were the last presided at by Bishop Cody, who left on August 5 for his new posting in London, Ontario. Archbishop Joseph Charbonneau of Montreal made his first appearance on the West Coast for these celebrations with a surprise visit to Mother Mary Leopoldine, the superior general who was also present from Lachine for the occasion, little knowing that his association with the Sisters of St. Ann would soon take a historic turn.

★   ★   ★

Bishop James Michael Hill—described as a "stately and dignified, but kindly" man—arrived in his new diocese on September 5, 1946.[217] He celebrated his first Mass in the academy chapel the following day and watched as the steam shovel arrived at St. Joseph's for the initial excavation which would take place a week after his own arrival. By December 14, 1946, the first pillars for the new wing were ready for the pouring of cement. There were 332 patients in the hospital, a hospital trying to carry on its normal routines providing care and attention to this full house despite the chaos of demolition and construction work. As usual around Christmas time, choirs came to entertain the patients, employees held parties and constant friend and benefactor Joe North brought candy and fruit to every patient. New Year's Day always brought an influx of visiting dignitaries and the Sisters celebrated with their traditional singing of French hymns.

The Sisters always intended the hospital be open to people of every race and creed, a policy that extended to staff as well as patients. As noted earlier, they were sometimes challenged by the mores of the day to adhere to this policy. Early in the century they had retained Chinese employees even though pressured to release them; now, in 1947, a member of the medical staff asked the board to curtail the number of Jewish interns. The board, however, believed "that each applicant should be judged according to his personal merits and qualifications."[218] In that same year, the medical staff presented an application for internship from a man "of the negro race." Jacob Villiers Fisher, who was British Columbia's deputy finance minister and a board member, spoke for the Sisters on the injustice of racial discrimination. The board did state "it would not be to Dr. Thomas' advantage in the least if he were accepted as an intern, but given no cooperation or assistance by any appreciable number of the local physicians and surgeons" and "it was clearly their duty [medical advisory board] to decide the matter among themselves." Which they did in accepting him.[219] Legal and ethical issues consumed time too as they grappled with the rights of insurance companies' access to patient files in considering claims and with the issue of whether the armed forces could take responsibility for decisions about the treatment of incapacitated veterans.

The Sisters carried on the normal work of a hospital throughout all these challenges. Between March 12 and May 15, 1947, the maternity department was closed due to an unidentified epidemic among the newborns, who were transferred to an isolation ward with Sister Mary Beatrice in charge.

Sister Mary Beatrice (Beatrice Wambeke, 1929 graduate) as a young nurse at Our Lady of Lourdes Hospital in Campbell River. SSAA P0122

All the nurses who were available helped in the strenuous work of saving these infants. Sister Mary Alena came from Campbell River to help. The hospital was also in the public eye when it successfully treated Police Chief John A. McLellan, after a heavy ladder had fallen on him during a fire drill, causing a cracked pelvis, crushed vertebrae and internal injuries. He repaid his treatment by joining the hospital board of management in 1950.

The expenses of the hospital had risen unexpectedly due to increased salaries and the necessity of employing unskilled aides and maids to relieve a temporary shortage of student nurses when the entry age to nursing schools in British Columbia was raised to nineteen. And rising salaries continued to contribute to the high operating costs: in 1949 there was a drastic average increase of 48 percent, the bulk being for nurses whose salaries rose by 73 percent.[220] The hospital realized additional income by raising the nursing Sisters' salaries to the level of the lay registered nurses. For the previous thirteen years (July 1, 1936–July 1, 1949) the Sisters had taken only their living expenses from operating costs in order to pay down the hospital debt.[221] In 1947 the financial situation was eased only slightly by the receipt of just over $92,000 from the Spratt estate[222] and over $12,000 in 1948 from the provincial government, a grant given to the principal hospitals in British Columbia to "help maintain the hospitals in these times of financial difficulties."[223]

Sister Mary Kathleen said farewell in July 1947 to take up her post as superior at Lourdes Hospital in Campbell River. Her successor, Sister Rose Mary, was to shepherd the new construction through to its completion in 1953.

*   *   *

Construction continued, although halting briefly in July 1947 when the foreman, a Mr. Turnquist, became ill and gave his workers the week off. This was not the only frustration. The real worry was a dramatic rise in construction costs. By November 1947, Archie Sullivan's latest estimate for the new wing had risen to an astronomical $2,225,000. Though Bishop Hill had earlier been consulted concerning the building plans, he was consulted again in June 1948—should the Sisters abandon plans to build? The estimated cost had risen by then to $2,250,000. They would need approval from the Vatican to borrow $1.5-million on top of the $500,000 allowed in 1945, and the bishop could not support asking for such a loan. Thus, the initial plan had to be changed. On February 20, 1949, the general council approved (1) a central section linking the kitchen wing with existing Rupert and Humboldt Street blocks, (2) a westerly extension to the Humboldt Street "A" wing and (3) complete demolition of the original Collinson Street section, demolition being the best option since it was a fire menace and the demolition firm agreed to do this for the salvage.

The hospital expected that an extension to the Humboldt Street A wing would lead to a concentration of services and economy in nursing personnel.[224] This new wing would be a reinforced concrete addition with four floors, at a cost of $247,000. The federal government would pay $1,000 per bed (with 128 beds planned) and the provincial government would pick up one-third of the gross cost, thus the budget would remain within the limits of the 1945 permissions. Henry Whittaker, who had been instrumental in much of the Sisters of St. Ann's hospital building in British Columbia, had now moved from government service to private practice, but the Sisters were able to arrange with him and the government to retain his services until the new additions were complete.

Excavation for the new and demolition of the old commenced in April 1949 with new plans that would not interfere with future construction on the Collinson site. Work came to a standstill on August 6, 1949, over a disagreement with the newly minted British Columbia Hospital Insurance Service (BCHIS). All BC hospitals had been required to join effective January 1, 1949. Sister Rose Mary informed the provincial council "building operations on the new wing have been temporarily halted in protest to the action on the part of the government."[225] The authorities had arbitrarily changed the policy regarding the right of

Demolished in 1949, the original 1876 portion of St. Joseph's Hospital had aged to the point of being considered a fire hazard. In its place a new wing of the hospital was built. SSAA P0235

privately owned hospitals to control the room differential accruing between established ward rates and private room charges.[226] Since private hospitals (though St. Joseph's was a public hospital in practice) were not entitled to every grant afforded public hospitals, the amount received from "room differentials" was crucial in their budgets. Father J.A. Leahy, SJ (Society of Jesus), of the BC Catholic Hospital Association, along with Bishop Hill of Victoria, Archbishop William Duke of Vancouver, the Sisters of St. Ann and other representatives of Catholic hospitals, prepared a brief to bring to the provincial government. Behind-the-scene activity resulted in some adjustment that was acceptable to all parties, and it was satisfactory enough that Sullivan called the workmen back on the job on September 28.

Once resumed, construction continued apace. Dr. F. Bryant became the proud first patient in the new A wing on August 31, 1950—before its official opening. The T. Eaton Company, which had been contracted to furnish the new wing for about $28,000, generously provided flowers in every room of the new wing and huge baskets of flowers in the hallways for the September 8 opening. Generous doctors donated furnishings for one of the new wards; Mrs. David Spencer and Mrs. D'Arcy McGee led a long list of local patrons.

On the occasion of the formal opening and rededication of the 1875 foundation stone to be reset over the main entrance, Dr. L.W. Bassett, president of the medical staff, brought greetings, Bishop Hill blessed the addition and Mayor George and the Health and Welfare Minister A. Douglas Turnbull gave speeches. Not until February 1, 1951, did the ward fully open, admitting twenty-two old men. Eight days later the hospital set a new record, with four hundred patients.

*   *   *

The long road to universal health care insurance in British Columbia would be fraught with detours, but owes much to the BC Hospital Association, whose members proposed it as early as 1919. More than a decade later the BC government appointed a Royal Commission on State Health Insurance and Maternity Benefits (the second of its kind, in fact) to consider the concept, and the result was an explicit recommendation in its completed report in 1932 "that the public interest requires the introduction of a compulsory health insurance and maternity benefit plan in British Columbia."[227]

During the Depression the scheme was unworkable due to the meagre number of wage earners. St. Joseph's Hospital had community benefit groups for certain organizations. The local Rugby Union (1933), BC Telephone (1936) and the Canadian Pacific Railway (1937) contracted to pay coverage for their employees, until 1943 when the hospital cancelled all contracts but that of Blue Cross. However large this group, many patients were still without any coverage. The passage of the "Act to Provide for the Establishment of Hospital Insurance and Financial Aid to Hospitals" (known as the *Hospital Insurance Act*) in 1948 and the introduction of compulsory participation on January 1, 1949, promised better financing for the future. The growing pains of the BC Hospital Insurance Services presented other problems for hospitals as both sides tried to agree on budgets and financing arrangements. BCHIS representatives frequently came to survey the business office and other departments at St. Joseph's, as they presumably did at other hospitals. Premiums from July 1, 1951, increased to $30 a year for a single person and to $42 a year for a family. Co-insurance was introduced on April 1, 1951.

When a policy of "firm budgets" was introduced on January 1, 1951, each hospital was expected to submit "a budget of its proposed annual expenditures," in the words of A. Douglas Turnbull. "This budget would be examined by BCHIS and, if approved, the hospital was expected to keep its expenditure within it."[228] The administration at St. Joseph's met with BCHIS officials, endured many surveys, bore the brunt of public dissatisfaction with the new organization and tried to manage within a budget that was not set until six months after the start of the hospital's fiscal year. In 1960 the hospital Sisters had to ask their provincial administration to advance them regular funds on a temporary basis because the BCHIS advance cheque came after the date when payroll cheques must be issued, thus leading to a bank overdraft every month with a resultant interest charge of $300. If the congregation's provincial administration loaned the hospital $125,000 to $150,000 each month, to be repaid as soon as the BCHIS money came in, the interest paid at the rate of 5.75 percent went to the congregation rather than to the bank.[229]

The transition to hospital insurance was definitely not a smooth one, although the administration at St. Joseph's co-operated fully, believing that the plan must succeed. The hospital insurance scheme was a major item in the 1952 provincial election, which led to the installation of a new Social Credit government under Premier W.A.C. Bennett, who cancelled arrears in premiums and made participation in the insurance plan voluntary, retaining co-insurance at a dollar a day in an effort to balance accounts. Bennett introduced an additional 2-percent sales tax in 1954, yielding more than the amount lost in premiums, thus reducing constant stress on the hospital. Not until July 1, 1958, did British Columbia join a federal/ provincial health insurance plan under which the federal government took over about 50 percent of the cost of acute hospital care, leaving the province room to consider chronic and convalescent care needs.[230]

* * *

Building activities didn't overshadow the landmark anniversaries of 1950. On the one hundredth anniversary of the congregation in 1950, St. Joseph's province in British Columbia had eleven establishments: five boarding schools for girls, one boarding school for boys and five hospitals with seventy-one Sisters working in them.[231] The Sisters and their friends and supporters gave triple thanks—not only for the congregation's centennial, but also for the seventy-fifth year of St. Joseph's Hospital and the fiftieth year of the nursing school. Father Joseph Birch, OMI (Oblates of Mary Immaculate), the provincial of the Oblates, sent $500 for the centenary of the community because of "the immense work and the incalculable good accomplished" by these women.[232] The hospital received the prestigious 1950 "Honor Award" from the *American Institution Magazine* for achieving the highest standard of sanitation in food handling in an annual food service contest conducted nationally among mass-feeding institutions. Who could blame them for standing back, taking a breath and contemplating the fruits of their labour for a short time.

The celebrations and accolades were a reminder that underlying the mechanics of building and operating a hospital were the values of charity that had motivated the Sisters to pursue this ministry from the beginning. In charity they welcomed into their hearts and home a figure of significant importance in the history of Quebec and the Catholic Church in Canada. Archbishop Joseph Charbonneau lived out his exile on the West Coast as chaplain to the Sisters of St. Ann, living mainly at St. Joseph's Hospital where he had first stayed during the 1946 centennial of the diocese of Victoria. His first connection with the Sisters of St. Ann had been in 1943 when, as archbishop of Montreal, he had presided at the general council elections in which Mother Mary Leopoldine was elected general superior for a second term. He had later endorsed a request to the Pope to extend her term in office by one year so she might remain at the helm during the 1950 centennial of the congregation. On giving permission in 1945 to exhume the remains of Mother Mary Ann he said: "She deserves a place of honor in the Motherhouse of the Institute."[233] In Victoria his humble demeanour, hearty contagious laugh and dignified bearing made him a favourite of all.

When Rome announced Archbishop Charbonneau's "retirement" to Victoria in February 1950 for health reasons, there was much skepticism. The archbishop took the Church's views on social justice seriously, living out these beliefs as chair of the Canadian Bishops Committee on Political-Social Justice questions. The infamous "Asbestos Strike," which crippled major mines in Quebec for four months in 1949, led him to declare "the working class is the victim of a conspiracy and the Church has a duty to intervene."[234] When he ordered collections taken up in the parishes of his archdiocese to support the striking miners and their families, he was in direct conflict with Quebec Premier Maurice Duplessis. It appears that Duplessis's influence led to Archbishop Charbonneau's banishment to Victoria as a "martyr of conscience and of social justice." Pierre Trudeau described these events as "a turning point in the entire religious, political, social, and economic history of the province of Quebec"[235], the beginning of the so-called quiet revolution.

In Victoria the archbishop lived a quiet and modest life, teaching ethics in St. Ann's novitiate, teaching catechism in the classrooms at St. Ann's Academy, and ministering to the sick in hospital. He never mentioned the circumstances that had brought him west, but that didn't mean that others were unaware of his past. In 1958 Martin Johnson, then co-adjutor (or assistant) archbishop of Vancouver and the former bishop of Nelson, was taking part in the Sisters' centennial celebrations and asked Archbishop Charbonneau how tall he was. The response of six feet two inches prompted Johnson's reply: "Yes—in height—but sixty feet of man with humility that is a lesson to all ranks of the clergy and hierarchy."[236]

Archbishop Charbonneau died at St. Joseph's Hospital at 2:15 p.m. on November 19, 1959—two months after his nemesis, Duplessis. The archbishop's body lay in state at St. Ann's Academy, then at St. Andrew's Cathedral, until his funeral Mass was celebrated on November 24 by Archbishop Duke of Vancouver. From the funeral, his remains were taken by boat to Vancouver and then flown to Montreal, accompanied by Bishop Hill and two Sisters of St. Ann—Sister Rose Mary and Sister Mary Dositheus, his devoted nurse. Following the funeral at Our Lady Queen of the World Cathedral in Montreal on November 27, he was laid to rest in the bishops' crypt, which for many years carried a plaque attesting to the gratitude felt by the people of the Montreal archdiocese for the care given to their former archbishop by the Sisters of St. Ann.[237]

* * *

Before the new St. Joseph's A wing was up and running, plans were already under way for the deconstruction of the original Collinson site and for the new building to rise there to house administration, an emergency department, a new pediatric unit, central supply, a new operating theatre and rooms for the Sisters on the sixth floor. The hospital Sisters had vacated their accommodation in the old building and the Sisters in the nurses' home had given up their lower floor to house the interns.

Following approval of the final construction plans, the Sisters asked for and received permission in September 1951 to spend $850,000 above the original 1945 request in order to complete a new Collinson Street section. When Bishop Hill was convalescing from a coronary thrombosis in Santa Barbara, California, Sister Mary Angelus and Sister Mary Ann Celesta— who were there taking a course in hospital administration—visited him. Though debilitated, he assured them that he would be in Victoria for the official opening of the administration wing. And so he was, giving the blessing beneath the huge white cross on the face of the building on March 19, 1952, the Feast of Saint Joseph. Jacob Villiers Fisher, the deputy finance minister and board member, said: "The story of St. Joseph's Hospital is one of constant progress, of sacrifice, work, generosity, and constant devotion

Completed in 1951, the new section of St. Joseph's Hospital, facing Collinson Street, which replaced the original hospital building, was soon running at full capacity. SSAA P0236

so the suffering of man could be alleviated."[238] Dr. Douglas Roxburgh, the Sisters' chosen spokesperson, expressed thanks to the architect, contractor and every tradesperson whose skills contributed to the building on their behalf. The expansion that had started with the turning of the sod in 1946 was now near completion.

On the heels of this ceremony, the PAR (post-anaesthetic recovery) rooms opened on June 1, 1952, "providing the very latest mode of efficient and concentrated nursing care for post-operative patients."[239] On October 29 the new operating room built for surgical demonstrations was used for the first time, its two-way speaking device and observation tower allowing doctor and student observers to interact. A year later a new physiotherapy unit opened, with the executive of the Canadian Arthritis and Rheumatism Society (CARS) and BC Health Minister Dr. G.F. Amyot on hand. CARS had staffed an office in the hospital since 1950. The *Daily Colonist* of November 29, 1950, congratulated St. Joseph's for performing the first cerebral angiogram on Vancouver Island. In December, W.Q. Stirling, the BC representative on the Canadian Board of X-Ray Technicians, wrote that a survey by his organization showed St. Joseph's to be the only school in Canada where a full curriculum for X-ray technicians was being taught.[240] At this time St. Joseph's Villa operated as a thirty-four-bed tuberculosis unit under the direction of the BC Health Ministry's division of tuberculosis control, treating patients with "the latest advances in therapy and technique" and giving students "a thorough theoretical and practical education in the nursing of isolation patients."[241]

In 1951 the daily cost of operating the hospital had risen to $4,785—$3,376 of this going to salaries and $436 to food. The average daily fuel oil consumption was 1,100 gallons, and patients and staff consumed 350 pounds of meat, 5 sacks of potatoes, 100 gallons of milk, and 160 loaves of bread.[242]

Sister Rose Mary's six-year term as administrator ended in July 1953. St. Joseph's Hospital council spoke of its gratitude to her for the successful conclusion of the major expansion project, during which she had overseen

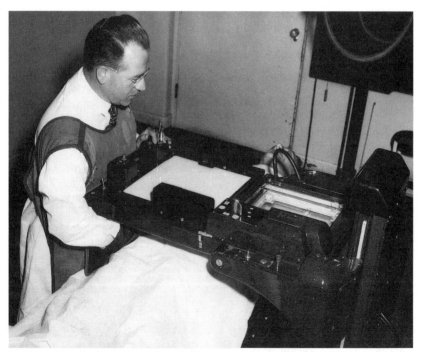

Dr. Frank Stuart, chief of radiology, is fluoroscoping a patient in this 1950s picture. Fluoroscopy is an imaging technique allowing the doctor to see the real-time movement of internal organs and structures. SSAA P0261

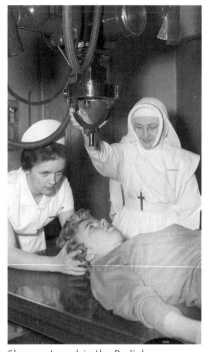

Shown at work in the Radiology Department, Sister Celine Marie (Marie Baines) graduated from the School of Nursing in 1934 and from the School of Radiography in 1945. SSAA P0315

the construction of three separate units, and controlled their cost and financing while maintaining service to a full capacity of patients. The council deemed it very gratifying to have "come out of a project of $2,184,986 with an outstanding debt of $403,000 of which $75,000 was an old debt carried over from the 1929 building project (the C wing) making $324,000 the true balance on loan."[243]

The Sisters, of course, also had to look after themselves. In 1951 various of their other houses in the province donated funds to erect a separate infirmary as an annex to St. Ann's Academy, which could no longer provide enough space for the Sisters needing care. They envisioned a four-storey reinforced concrete building of forty-five beds to cost $200,000 and to be built by Archie Sullivan, builder of other facilities for the Sisters of St. Ann. The general council in Lachine gave permission for Mother Mary Dorothea, the provincial, to take steps to obtain the federal old-age pension for the twenty-eight Sisters who were over seventy years of age, anticipating these funds would help finance the new infirmary. Though the new infirmary did not materialize, it was yet another example of the Sisters' willingness to cover expenses from their own resources.

They continued to care for their own sick and incapacitated at Mount St. Mary until it became an extended-care hospital (see Chapter 8) and was no longer permitted to take such patients. In 1959 they purchased Mount St. Angela, which had been built in 1865 as an Anglican girls' school in Victoria. It was officially opened and blessed by Bishop Hill on June 8, 1960, as a home for retired Sisters. One floor was set aside for nursing service when the need arose, with a full schedule of trained nurses. This remained their infirmary until 1983, when St. Ann's Residence was constructed in Saanich as a combined long-term-care hospital and home for retired Sisters.

* * *

The board first discussed the prospect of hiring a medical superintendent in September 1944. Sister Mary Kathleen solicited the opinion of the Catholic Hospital Association of British Columbia on the advisability of such an experiment.[244] A year later Dr. Roxburgh agreed to assume the joint positions of superintendent and pathologist, but he resigned on December 28, 1949, to give full attention to his increased duties in the pathology department and was not immediately replaced.

When Sister Rose Mary requested British Columbia Hospital Insurance Service (BCHIS) funding in January 1952 for a medical superintendent, BCHIS asked her to show how this appointment would prove an economy, despite the fact that other large hospitals in the province had already demonstrated the value of such a position. The secretary of the medical staff informed the board on September 30, 1952, of the unanimous agreement of the Sisters, the Medical Advisory Board and the executive of the medical staff that, "for the coordination of the various services of the hospital, the teaching program of the internes [sic], and the supervision of the surgical work," an early appointment of a medical superintendent must be made; the board recommended the immediate appointment of such. A full year passed before St. Joseph's welcomed Dr. Armand Brunet—formerly a hospital inspector for the Joint Commission of the American and Canadian College of Physicians and Surgeons—as Superintendent. He had inspected St. Joseph's in February 1953 and was well aware of any shortcomings, though St. Joseph's had received full accreditation in May. The forty-five-year-old, who had suffered a severe leg injury during the war, immediately restructured the X-ray department, organized staff, amended bylaws to include credentials and surgical tissue committees, and enforced the rules under which the hospital doctors were to operate, including addressing their perennial resistance to keeping records up to date. Sister Mary Angelus, now the administrator, told the board in February 1954 that Dr. Brunet was proving to be outstanding.[245]

Sadly, Dr. Brunet tendered his resignation less than three years later, in April 1956, to take a position in Edmonton where he would be paid more than BCHIS allowed in BC hospitals. He was succeeded by Dr. Ernest Boettcher of Toronto, who had a degree in hospital administration, that September. The new medical superintendent gave a detailed report to the board in January 1957, telling members of the excellent co-operation from the medical staff. His statistics showed increased bed occupancy, increased service, a decrease in the average stay per patient, an improved standard of care and a minimum number of unnecessary surgeries. He strongly recommended better facilities for the maternity department.[246] The next month Sister Mary Angelus and the board approved a press release highlighting the need to replace the current inadequate space.[247]

British Columbia was enjoying twenty years of almost uninterrupted growth, with workers enjoying "the highest per capita incomes in Canada."[248] Also in the 1950s, British Columbia saw the rise of powerful unions with province-wide jurisdictions. As early as 1946 nurses at Vancouver General Hospital had joined a union under the American Federation of Labor. St. Joseph's Hospital had been amicably bargaining with its engineers since 1948. Regular employees formed an association in July 1949, hoping to forestall unionization. Sister Mary Gregory, director of the nursing school, brought the board literature on the organization of a bargaining agency within the Registered Nurses Association of British Columbia who wished to offset the desire to unionize that was prevalent among some sections of nurses.[249] The Sisters based their bargaining on investigating comparable positions in government and agreeing to reasonable demands, also appreciating the long service and loyalty of many of their staff.

The Sisters also met with management from the Royal Jubilee Hospital in mutual agreement that wages should be on a par at both Victoria hospitals. The board met with members of the various bargaining committees in an atmosphere of mutual respect. When BCHIS was first formed, it brought the salaries of St. Joseph's employees in line with those paid by other large hospitals. From 1949 on, BCHIS sometimes was an obstacle to bargaining. Hospitals could set budgets based on agreements reached with their employees, but BCHIS "reduced, deleted or otherwise changed with no reference to the hospitals concerned" and presented fixed budgets to hospitals as long as six months after the beginning of the operational year.[250]

Not surprisingly, disagreements occurred. In 1952, hospital engineers were granted a union shop under the International Union of Operating Engineers and in the early 1960s the Hospital Employees Union came into effect at St. Joseph's. The BCHA appointed a "bargaining" person in 1951, forerunner to the appointment of Duncan Bradford in 1960 as a labour specialist charged with developing labour relations services for the member hospitals. The BCHA also held education workshops on labour relations, one of which was attended in 1959 by Mother Mary Luca, provincial superior; Sister Mary Angelus, superior of St. Joseph's; Sister Damian Marie; and Dr. Boettcher. Since there was no escaping the BCHIS dictums, Sister Mary Angelus innovatively decided in 1957 that since she couldn't give the employees the 10-percent raise agreed to, she would advance all employees by two increments on the pay scale.[251] Both sides accepted this solution. The Sisters also noted that age was not their criteria for retirement; rather, employees stayed on based on merit and ability.

Chapter 6

Parting of the Ways

The gift that the Sisters donate to the people of this area is more than land, buildings or equipment. It is a living institution with a long tradition of service to the sick and injured.

—Sister Eileen Kelly

As British Columbia thrived and its resource-based industry expanded, medical technology advanced. New treatments for tuberculosis meant that the number of patients throughout the province decreased. Consequently St. Joseph's Villa was fully closed in December 1955 and all patients sent to larger sanitariums. The old Vernon Villa was demolished. In February 1956 the minister of health approved the use of St. Joseph's Villa for general patient care and it reopened as "the Annex." This had financial benefits, as the hospital consistently had received only half the per diem cost for tuberculosis patients' care. After October 1956, the thirty-five-bed Annex was devoted to diabetic and longer-term patients.

To keep abreast of these advances in treatment and technology, the Sisters were constantly upgrading their skills and education. As members of the many professional bodies associated with their ministry, they attended workshops or presented them, on all aspects of health and hospital care, keeping their credentials current. Members attended regional hospital conferences, conferred with other institutions regularly and attended many summer education programs. For example, Sisters Mary Agnes Claire and Miriam Claire—also sisters by birth—were in Seattle in May 1951 for the former's graduation from Seattle University with a bachelor of science in nursing, while her sister took a course at the Virginia Mason Hospital on the care of diabetic patients. Also, Sisters Mary Angelus and Mary Lucita, along with Mrs. Ardena Simpson, associate director of nursing, attended a Nursing Service Institute of the American Hospital Association in September 1954. There, Sister Mary Angelus received a certificate of membership in the American College of Hospital Administrators. Sister Mary Angelus was again in Chicago in September 1956, along with Mother Mary Luca, provincial superior, to formally receive her membership in the hospital administrators' association at a university convocation, after she had passed gruelling oral and written exams. British Columbia had only one other member of this association.[252]

As well, Sister Mary Catherine of Sienna wrote exams in November 1955 in order to qualify for registration as a medical record librarian (MRL), an increasingly complex field. She later explored the idea of developing a school for MRLs in Canada, meanwhile lending her expertise to other hospitals in the country by giving workshops, and she was instrumental in forming the Vancouver Island chapter of the BC Association of Medical Record Librarians in 1958. She was president of the provincial body for several years. The British Columbia Hospital Insurance Service (BCHIS) sent some of its staff to St. Joseph's to be coached in hospital organization and management. In-house, Sister Mary Gregory established a bright and spacious medical reference library and reading room in 1955 on the fifth floor of St. Joseph's and furnished it with as many first-class books as the budget could afford, as well as suitable texts and

Sister Mary Catherine of Sienna conducting a pregnancy test in 1957 by injecting a Flemish Giant rabbit with urine. This method, called the rabbit test, was introduced in 1926 and lasted into the 1960s. If the woman was pregnant, the hormone hCG, found in the urine, would cause changes to the rabbit's ovaries. SSAA P0248

journals for the doctors. She was in charge of cataloguing and ran a very efficient operation.[253]

"Sister formation" was not neglected. Sister Mary Angelus stressed the necessity of preparing the Sisters for their work, "the intrinsic nature of the preparation being a spiritualizing of their motives, so that each one's work will be done with the right motive, and seen in proper perspective, according to God's plan."[254] One of Sister Marguerite Lalonde's cherished memories of the hospital was carrying a lantern and preceding the priest through the hospital wards in the early mornings, ringing a bell to announce the coming of Holy Communion.[255] Sharing the grief of a bereaved parent or dying patient was her introduction to pastoral care. The Sisters' holistic approach to nursing saw the patient as more than a "disease" to be treated. Part of this approach was being attentive and listening, often visiting to sit with the person and hear what was in the patient's heart. Their care extended over the entire twenty-four-hour day.

Compelling visitors and patients enlivened their days. After Bishop Cuthbert O'Gara, CP (Congregation of the Passion), had been their patient, recovering from the results of imprisonment in Communist China, Francis Joseph Cardinal Spellman invited the Sisters to St. Patrick's Cathedral in New York in September 1953 for a Mass of Thanksgiving for Bishop O'Gara's safe return, the speaker being Bishop Fulton Sheen. Former premier John Hart suffered a heart attack while visiting his dying brother at St. Joseph's, and so became a patient himself. Another premier, W.A.C. Bennett, was admitted in January 1960 suffering with kidney stones and thus missed the opening day of the provincial parliament. After an excellent recovery, this "cheerful and cooperative patient" was discharged home. A special phone had been installed to handle the inquiries about his condition and special measures had been taken to ensure his privacy. The Sisters had learned how to deal with the news media earlier, when triplets were born in 1954 and "the hospital . . . [was] besieged with photographers who were waiting for the birth with all the impatient interest of typical newsmen."[256] This experience also helped them deal with the invasion of police inspectors and news reporters when the hospital safe was robbed in February 1960.

The challenge of keeping the hospital staffed with Sister supervisors became more acute in the 1950s. At various times the minutes of the St.

Joseph's Council discussed this "alarming" shortage. The problem was compounded when severe "pneumonitis" felled several Sisters in 1953 and the "Asiatic flu" epidemic swept through the congregation in 1957. Even when fully deployed, they could not find the means to give a Sister supervisor a day off in October that year.[257] Occasionally a Sister would graduate from the school of nursing and quickly be made supervisor despite her feelings of unpreparedness.

Notwithstanding the continuing struggle to supply Sisters for their existing ministries, they received frequent requests to take charge of hospitals in other dioceses—for example, from Bishop H. O'Leary in Alberta (1935); Archbishop William Duke in West Vancouver, Surrey and Langley, BC (1944); Bishop Coudert in Atlin, BC (1952); Bishop Martin Johnson in Castlegar, BC (1967); and Zeballos Hospital Board in BC (1947). Chetwynd and District Hospital asked them to administer and open a pioneer hospital in the Peace River area in BC (1967); they were also asked to take over a hospital and nursery in St. Vincent in the West Indies (1968); and Victoria's Bishop Remi De Roo asked them to operate St. Mary's Priory (1968).[258] These were some of the needs they were unable to fill.

Great celebrations were held in 1958, marking the hundredth anniversary of the Sisters' arrival on the West Coast. The Sisters' "Pioneer Day" celebrated their arrival in Victoria on June 5; Bishop James Hill also blessed the centennial addition to the Heywood Annex to St. Ann's Academy, expressing the gratitude and thanksgiving of all those who had been the beneficiaries of the Sisters' uninterrupted love and service. The Sisters in turn thanked the doctors and hospital administrators, the nurses and the men and women who gave selflessly on boards and auxiliaries, as well as their many benefactors, private and public. On each of the following four days a Mass was celebrated: for Children's Day; for Alumnae Day (outdoors at St. Ann's Academy); for Visitors' Day; and finally a Requiem Mass was held on June 9 for their deceased Sisters, relatives and friends. Much enjoyment was had at a special pageant held in the Royal Theatre, a short walk up the hill from the hospital and scene of so many nursing graduations. Sister Mary Beatrice, with the co-operation of hospital photographer Les Spencer, mounted an exhibit for the Registered Nurses Association of British Columbia (RNABC) convention in Victoria showing the history of St. Joseph's Hospital from its inception. Sister Mary Geraldine, who had come from Lachine in 1888 as a young novice, observed her diamond jubilee, representing the senior Sisters among the three hundred Sisters now in St. Joseph's province. It was a year of reflection on the past and a time to look forward.

* * *

The record demand on maternity facilities in 1956, as well as the report of the national accreditation commission, pointed to the need for new, modernized accommodation. The 1,687 births in this year—compared with 828 in 1951—emphatically highlighted the lack of resources.[259]

The 1958 Centennial of the Sisters of St. Ann in BC brought together leaders of the Congregation from far and near to celebrate. Centre front—Mother Mary Liliane, superior general; Mother Mary Luca, BC provincial superior. Back row, l–r—Sister Mary Gladys, superior of St. Ann's Academy, Victoria; Sister Mary Angelus, superior, St. Joseph's Hospital; Sister Mary Stella, prefect of studies; Sister Mary Paul, annalist, Lachine; Mother Mary Thérèse de St. Anne, general councillor; Sister Mary Annunciata (hidden), provincial bursar; Sister Marie Anne Eva, general prefect of English, Lachine; Mother Mary Ludovic, former general councillor, superior of St. Joseph's Province 1947–1950; Mother Mary Velma, general councillor; Mother Mary Jean Cassien, general councillor, Lachine. Picture taken at the blessing of St. Ann's Annex, Victoria. SSAA P0068

The provincial council gave permission in 1957 for the hospital to pursue sketches of a proposed new wing with architect Henry Whittaker. However, his imminent retirement due to ill health precluded his continued participation. As well, the BCHIS now required quotes from three architectural firms before proceeding. Gardiner, Thornton & Gathe of Vancouver were awarded the contract in 1959 to do a survey of the hospital's needs.

Roger Strickland, chair of the board's building committee, approached the intermunicipal committee for support, receiving a favourable response from Victoria Mayor Percy Scurrah and his City Council, with a promise of endorsement for a fundraising campaign after the completion of the current campaign of the Royal Jubilee Hospital. Gerald Fitzpatrick Dunn agreed to chair the fundraising committee. This local businessman and accountant had been delivered into the world at St. Joseph's by Dr. James Douglas Helmcken in 1911. Though not a Catholic, he served on the board from 1953 to 1960, admiring the Sisters' willing work and commitment to help anyone regardless of religion, colour or station in life.[260]

Inadequate parking space, coupled with plans for future building, prompted the purchase in 1959 of Glen Court (to house interns) and two properties at the corner of Humboldt and Blanshard Streets in Victoria to complete the hospital's holdings of the entire block.

*　*　*

While the hospital was financially sound, the parochial schools in which the Sisters taught were in financial trouble and faced with possible closure in 1959. Since the schools filled the original reason for the congregation's formation, the Sisters decided to give one-third of their salaries from St. Joseph's Hospital and Mount St. Mary Hospital in Victoria and Mount St. Francis in Nelson (see Part Two and Three of this book) to the provincial administration to prevent such an outcome.[261]

The Sisters' generosity was mirrored by the staff of St. Joseph's, who designated July 22, 1959, as "F" Day in a tribute to Sister Mary Angelus's six years of service. Hospital employees assigned their day's pay to the building fund, making it the unofficial start of the fund drive. There were 675 employees at this time, with an average daily payroll in excess of $5,000.[262]

Thankful for the recognition, but also looking toward her next assignment as provincial superior, Sister Mary Angelus (Mary Barry) received a scroll from Vern Manson, marking her retirement from the hospital after six years as administrator. In her honour, all of the employees donated the day's pay to the building fund. SSAA P0258

In 1959 the estimate for building was $1.5 million. Federal and provincial grants covered $900,000, municipalities $300,000, leaving $100,000 to be contributed by the Sisters of St. Ann.

Donor lists for 1959 and 1960 covered a broad spectrum of the population. The business community was represented by the *Victoria Times*, the T. Eaton Company employees, Andrew Sheret Ltd., Yarrows employees, and BC Electric. The participation of such diverse charitable groups as the Khalsa Diwan Society, the Dart Coon Club and Shon Yee Benevolent Association truly reflected the diversity of the Victoria community in support of St. Joseph's.

Sister Mary Ann Celesta was named superior and administrator in July 1959. Sister Damian Marie had come the year before as bursar, and under the newly appointed assistant administrator, Patrick Blewett, set up the personnel department. Blewett was a former student at St. Ann's Academy in Vancouver and Nanaimo (the expansion of managerial staff aimed to meet the demands of the increasingly complex operation of a modern hospital). He had graduated from the University of British Columbia with a degree in hospital administration and worked at BCHIS for two years, which made him a valuable asset to the management pool, on top of lightening the administrator's workload.

The 1950s ended on a high note with a record number of interns, the introduction of a training program for orderlies, and Sister Mary Angelus's re-election as chair of the Catholic Hospital Association of British Columbia (CHABC). The operating year from July 1, 1959, to June 30, 1960, saw the hospital accommodate 13,629 in-patients, with

20,649 outpatients and 421 deaths. Statistics noted that 2,116 of the inpatients were Catholic, with the remainder of other denominations.[263]

Unfortunately, projected costs for building a new wing continued to escalate. In September 1960 the general council gave permission for St. Joseph's to proceed with a new five-storey wing to increase the number of beds from 448 to 480 and bassinettes from 48 to 65, and demolish the 1908 wing. Now the cost would be approximately $2.5 million, bringing the responsibility of the Sisters to $400,000. In December this estimate was raised to $3 million. Rome approved the request of Sister Mary Angelus, now provincial superior, for the Sisters to borrow $500,000 for their portion. The Sisters expected to repay the loan at the rate of $3,000 a month from their salaries. The public fundraising campaign's goal of $350,000 was reached in January 1963, with a donation of $5,000 from the diocese of Victoria and a bequest from former lieutenant-governor Randolph Bruce of $12,935. These amounts paled next to the rise in projected cost to $5 million two months later, with the Sisters' share now expected to be $1.5 million.[264]

While raising funds for the new addition, the hospital continued to improve the existing facilities by opening a six-bed intensive care unit (ICU), purchasing an encephalograph (equipment used to perform a medical test that measures brain waves) and installing an automatic switchboard. The city, wanting to improve traffic flow and safety around the site, replaced the wooden sidewalk on Blanshard Street. Amendments to the constitution and bylaws altered the makeup of the board, increasing the number of members to fifteen—with ten appointed by the corporation of the Sisters of St. Ann, one by the provincial government, one by the City of Victoria, and one by each of the municipalities of Oak Bay, Saanich and Esquimalt.[265]

Outside the hospital walls, the winds of renewal were blowing in the Catholic Church. Pope John XXIII had succeeded Pius XII, assuming the throne of Peter on October 28, 1958. He convoked the Second Vatican Council on December 25, 1961, but died on June 3, 1963, and so presided over only the first session of the council. Paul VI was elected on June 21, 1963. Four sessions attended by more than 2,600 bishops came to a close December 8, 1965. It was a momentous event:

The Council Fathers issued 16 landmark documents modernizing the liturgy, renewing the priesthood and religious life, enhancing the role of lay Catholics, opening dialogue with other churches and non-Christians, and identifying the Church as the people of God attuned to the problems and hopes of the world.[266]

Though religious women were not part of the formation of these documents, their lives were profoundly influenced by their content. Religious communities were called to re-examine the charism of their founders, to make themselves "relevant in a contemporary world."[267] The Sisters of St. Ann, as other communities, were free to experiment with clothing, prayers and community living in a more relaxed and informal manner. The deeply optimistic attitude of John XXIII informed their approach to living out their vocation in a changing society.

Visibly, the religious habit signified a woman's commitment; becoming a nun was known as "taking the veil." Any major change in garb would carry an emotional component. But the Sisters were also of a practical bent, and long before the 1960s had adopted some minor changes in clothing. As early as 1928 Sisters working in the operating room could wear white, and in 1938 Sisters on duty with patients were also permitted to wear white in a fabric that could be easily laundered. In November 1948, Sister Mary Druscilla exchanged her black habit, which she wore for her work in the laundry, for white when working on the women's ward. The general council in September 1951 authorized "Sisters employed in the kitchen of St. Joseph's Hospital, Victoria, to wear a white uniform as this concession seems to be legitimately required on account of the many government inspections to which the culinary and dietary departments are subject."[268]

The first major change in the habit's appearance was made to the headgear in the early 1960s. Mother General and her assistant demonstrated the proper way to wear the new headdress at the hospital in April 1963, and on August 13 that year 2,400 members of the congregation throughout Canada, the United States and the foreign missions donned the new look. The first picture to run in the *Bulletin* at St. Joseph's was of Sister superior—Sister Mary Ann Celesta—in this modified habit.[269]

Not long after, experimentation with wearing contemporary dress was allowed. Sister Mary Benedicta attended the University of Saskatchewan in lay clothing in 1966. Sister Mary Aquina (a.k.a. Sister Kathleen Cyr), who had graduated from Seattle University in 1963 with a B.Sc. in nursing, was the clinical instructor of psychiatric nursing in St. Joseph's School of Nursing (1965–67). When she set up a program of four weeks' instruction for each class at Riverview (Essondale) mental institution, she adopted lay dress because the habit could be a stressful symbol to some patients. To assist in the transition in 1969, a Mrs. Fraser, style representative for Woodward's store, gave the Sisters a brief, much-appreciated "charm class" to introduce them to modern fashion.[270]

Modelling the new habit for a 1963 edition of the *St. Joseph's Bulletin*, Sister Mary Ann Celesta, superior, (Sheila Griffin) foretells the greater changes to come in the wake of Vatican II—greater experimentation with dress, liturgy, organization, names and a drop in the number of vocations that will force the congregation to change how they carry out their ministry. SSAA P0316

Modification in dress was only an outward manifestation of a major change in thinking.

Desiring to live their vocation more deeply, the Sisters adopted a new plan for the hospital (and schools) whereby the one named superior would not also assume the role of administrator, since the qualities needed for both were not the same. Until now the superior/administrator had been the senior executive official of the hospital. As superior she had responsibility for the spiritual welfare of the Sisters assigned to her community. As administrator she had been totally responsible for the day-to-day operation of the entire hospital. It was recognized that even if one person possessed skills for both roles, there would be a kind of psychological tension within the individual that would cause one role to supersede the other. Sister Kathleen Moroney, provincial superior, announced to the hospital Sisters in January 1967 that Sister Mary McGarrigle—who had replaced Sister Sheila Griffin as administrator in July 1965—would soon be replaced by a layperson but retain the role of superior and attend solely to the Sisters' needs.

After a year of studying psychology at the University of St. Louis, Sister Kathleen Cyr was named superior at St. Joseph's (1968–72), not participating in the daily operation of the hospital, but assuring that the Sisters who lived in "Sancta Anna" on the fifth floor had a life together and were valued as individuals.[271]

At this time, many Sisters resumed their birth names.** For some this was easy, but others struggled with the changing mind of the church and its religious communities. When Sister Kathleen Moroney came to dinner in October 1967 to discuss the "future direction of the nursing apostolate," it was clear to all the Sisters that the future held new directions.[272]

*   *   *

Despite the upheavals, the Sisters continued to put patient care above all other concerns. At the instigation of Sister Catherine Moroney, St. Joseph's was one of the first four hospitals in British Columbia to participate in a professional activities study that started on July 1, 1961, though funding from BCHIS was still in question. The study was conducted by the Commission on Hospital and Professional Activities, a non-profit corporation sponsored by several national professional medical organizations, and situated in Ann Arbor, Michigan. A hospital discharge abstract prepared by each participating hospital's medical records department was sent to the commission. Within seventy-two hours the hospital medical records department received a complete index of diseases and operations, as well as a monthly analysis of hospital services and a semi-annual general summary. Code numbers for cases and physicians preserved anonymity. It is difficult in this computer age to imagine the time, effort and money needed for this exercise, but in the 1960s these reports provided comparative data related to other participating hospitals and indices that smaller hospitals would find difficult to maintain. These were essential for any hospital to secure

---

** From 1967 on, most of the Sisters reassumed their birth names. For example: Sister Mary Lucita became Sister Mary McGarrigle.

national accreditation. "They give the Administration a detailed idea of the type of patient care being rendered, and thus assist in the fulfillment of the hospital's obligation to maintain standards."[273]

Locally, the Victoria and district administrators' council had its inaugural meeting on August 13, 1964, in order to provide a formal setting to consider matters of mutual interest and of patient care. Sister Mary Ann Celesta was elected chair. Advanced education also remained of paramount importance. For example: Sister Mary Perpetua received her B.Sc. in nursing from Gonzaga University in Spokane, Washington, in May 1964; Sisters Mary Janita and Leanne Marie each received a B.Sc. in nursing from Seattle University later that May; and Sisters Mary Dolora and Joan Marie each completed a B.Sc. in nursing at Seattle University in 1966. Further, Sister Margaret Doris attained her master's degree in nursing administration from the University of Toronto in 1968 and became director of nursing service at St. Joseph's. Here she applied her many talents—which extended to being a woodworker, electrician, plumber and even welder.

As in the past, the Sisters were active members of the professional bodies guiding their particular area of expertise. In June 1965, for example, Sister Mary Justinian and Sister Mary Beatrice flew to Frankfurt to attend the International Congress of Nurses. The previous year, Sister Mary Ann Celesta had written exams and qualified as a member of the American College of Hospital Administrators.

The government-approved expansion of St. Joseph's Hospital began in 1964. Phase 2, completed in 1965, included creating a new linen service building; renovating the administration, admitting and emergency areas; and creating a new, centralized food service department. Continued improvements included the renovation of the laboratory and Annex (1966), the expansion and upgrading of the radiology department (1967 and 1968) and the opening of a new coronary care unit (1968). What didn't occur was the demolition of the 1908 wing, which still stands today.

The majority of employees were laypeople, but even in a time when women did not hold executive positions, the Sisters were the face of authority and leadership in most Catholic hospitals. Major changes in this stance took place at St. Joseph's in the 1960s. Maurice Cownden was hired as public relations director (1961), to aid with fundraising and to present a public image of the hospital to the community. Laura Foster replaced Sister Mary Benedicta as operating room supervisor (1963), Ardena Simpson became director of nursing service when Sister Mary Doris returned to studies (1966), and Lilian Knighton became director of St. Joseph's School of Nursing (1968) when Sister Ronalda McGauvran resigned.

As the Sisters divested themselves of management roles, the pivotal point was the appointment of Dr. Embert Van Tilburg as executive director of St. Joseph's Hospital. The Sisters knew he would understand and respect their values. Dr. Van Tilburg had emigrated from The Netherlands in 1955. During his years as a member of the medical advisory committee, he vetted the credentials of physicians seeking hospital privileges to make sure they were acceptable to the BC College of Physicians and Surgeons. Dr. Van Tilburg became medical director in July 1966, following the resignation of Dr. R.E. Adams, who had replaced Dr. Ernest Boettcher in

1962. Over time the hospital had become a much busier place, with more surgeries, more procedures done, more deliveries and a shorter length of patient stay. Dr. Van Tilburg's interest in these rapid developments prompted him to take a master's degree in the School of Public Health at the University of Toronto. This additional credential, including his thesis on medical staff organization, now qualified him to be hired as medical director—but not for long. With the resignation of Sister Mary McGarrigle, he was given the job of executive director in July 1967, thus beginning many years of planning for a new building while operating "a 450-bed hospital in a 250-bed chassis."[274]

A doctor and administrator the Sisters knew they could trust to lead St. Joseph's according to their values, Dr. Embert Van Tilburg's 1967 appointment as the first lay executive director of the hospital was a pivotal moment marking the Sisters' handing over of managerial roles. SSAA P0256

Nine Sisters of St. Ann attended an Institute for Religious

Women concerning mental health and communication in religious life that was held at St. Paul's Hospital in Vancouver in December 1965. This commitment to re-examining their life was soon followed—in February 1966—with discussion in their religious community, to "reach a deeper understanding of the mind of the Church in our Apostolate."[275]

They now began to fill needs outside their own hospitals. Sister Joan Brophy worked in White Rock, BC, as a medical record librarian (1967); Sister Joan Bell was nurse at a summer camp for disturbed children (1968); and Sister Anne Deas became director of nursing service at St. Boniface Hospital in Winnipeg (1972). They went where they saw a need, and because they had to have paying jobs.

The serious concerns of the day were leavened by many celebrations of special occasions over the years. For example: the Sisters hosted a welcoming Christmas banquet at the hospital for Bishop De Roo when he succeeded Bishop Hill (who died on March 29, 1962); when Dr. Doug Roxburgh retired after twenty-six years as the hospital pathologist, the five Sisters superior under whom he had worked over the years all arrived for his retirement tea (August 1964); Miss Hamilton-Smith, teacher in the classroom on the pediatric ward, arranged a tenth-anniversary celebration with the superintendent and representatives of the local school board; among eight golden jubilarians in 1965 were two still active at St. Joseph's Hospital—Sister Mary Gregory and Sister Mary Bertholde; the new spirit among the Sisters led them to host an open house in their new sixth-floor quarters, where they welcomed 750 visitors; and when the women's auxiliary donated $3,000 to the ICU in December 1966, the Sisters publicly thanked them for their devotion and untiring efforts. Of special note was the first "long-service dinner," held on May 11, 1967, to recognize employees who had worked for fifteen years or more and especially highlighting the fifty-two years of service by Sister Mary Gregory. Attended by sixty staff and their spouses, and with Mayor Hugh Stephen as speaker, the occasion was a great success.

Apart from the above, the contribution of a number of valued employees who were leaving or retiring were acknowledged at farewell teas, such as that in March 1968 for Ada McKenzie, who had been head nurse on maternity for twenty-one years and was a graduate of St. Joseph's School of Nursing (1929), and one in March 1971 for Patrick Blewett, who had been assistant administrator since December 1959.

Yet the serious concerns remained. The small number of women entering the novitiate naturally reduced those available for hospital training. The July 1967 financial statement showed a drop in revenue from Sisters' salaries due to fewer Sisters on staff. Half of the Sisters' salaries were going to pay the debt to the provincial council of $179,000, and since January 1, 1967, BCHIS had been charging $75 a month for each Sister's room and board.[276] These factors prompted a request that henceforth the provincial council keep all of the Sisters' salaries and that little community money be spent on hospital construction in the future, since municipalities were now expected to raise a share of the funds for capital costs—money that the community would have raised previously. By August 1967 the financial strain on the Sisters at St. Joseph's Hospital was such that the provincial council exempted them from paying $2,000 monthly on their building debt and in December 1968 cancelled the remaining debt of $175,000 on the recommendation of the provincial bursar, Sister Mary Annunciata.[277]

＊　＊　＊

A review of 1966 hospital statistics presented at the April 27, 1967, board meeting illustrated the hospital's growth and the breadth of its service. The number of paid staff in 1966 represented an increase of 54, or 7 percent, over the previous year's total of 827. The linen service department had processed 10,000 pounds, or 5 tons, of laundry each day, including that of the Gorge Road Hospital, Mount St. Mary and St. Ann's Academy. The purchasing agent, James Ashmore, and his staff had bought approximately $700,000 worth of supplies. The maintenance department had redecorated 152,000 square feet of walls and repaired 3,100 pieces of furniture.[278] All this contributed to the care of 13,677 in-patients—of whom only 2,291were Catholic—and 19,820 outpatients.[279] Clearly the scope of the work was beyond the capacity of the reduced number of hospital Sisters who could no longer contribute to the making of long-range plans.

Coupled with the Church's new thinking on the role of religious communities in the hospital apostolate, the Sisters believed they should be in a more active and direct ministry rather than in the administrative role their work had primarily become. With funding from the various levels of government, hospitals had moved from the dimension of charity to that of justice; every person was now entitled to proper health care. Professional standards had become more exacting and the social significance of the Sisters' work had undergone profound change. The larger community was more reluctant to put money into Catholic institutions. And in a major way, the Sisters felt that their duty and belief in protecting and fostering human life at all stages of development was being threatened. They began exploring other possibilities for their future.

Protection of the community's assets had been briefly addressed as early as 1959, when the provincial council had authorized the Sisters of St. Ann at St. Joseph's Hospital "to secure separate franchise from the Legislature of British Columbia under the corporate name of The Sisters of St. Ann, St. Joseph's Hospital."[280] Such legal incorporation would confine financial losses to the specific corporation, safeguard community property and limit liability for deficits. Even so, the application was soon abandoned, but protecting their assets remained essential. It is not surprising, then, that the hospital council suggested in January 1968 that they take steps to form a hospital society. Discussions continued. Sister Mary McGarrigle presented the proposed constitution and bylaws to the provincial council in June, and further revisions as time went on. But in January 1969 a committee of the board was asked to investigate such a formation since the minister of health had refused the proposal to form a society, with no explanation.[281]

A special meeting was held in February 1969 to discuss what shape this new society should take in order for BCHIS and Health Minister Ralph Loffmark to reconsider their earlier refusal. Of the reasons presented—no working capital; chronic deficit financing; and the unlikelihood of public money being put into a religious institution—the most likely to succeed was the fact that a society was needed in order to have a body to which the Sisters could deed the hospital. Throw into the mix the desire of the society to purchase the land of St. Ann's Academy for hospital expansion and the request made eminently good sense.

While the hospital continued to study options for future expansion, or even a move to another location, several revisions to the constitution and bylaws were put before the board. Finally, in November 1969, the health minister approved what was the seventh draft. The way was paved for the establishment of the South Vancouver Island Hospital Society (SVIHS). The regional hospital board was a stumbling block because it wished to hold title to the land and premises. Long discussions with the Sisters of St. Ann led to agreement on a price for the St. Ann's grounds and an acceptable proposal to the society. On November 13, 1969, St. Joseph's Hospital became a publicly owned institution with the establishment of the SVIHS.[282] At the first meeting, on November 18, 1969, Dr. Alexander Wood of the University of Victoria was named society president.[283]

This momentous move meant the need to investigate alternative housing for the Sisters living at St. Joseph's. Individual Sisters were consulted over varied options: join a local community in Victoria, join a small local community of hospital Sisters, or perhaps live in a pilot house. In the end, on August 26, 1970, the Sisters left Sancta Anna, their sixth-floor residence, and dispersed to Mount St. Angela (which the Sisters had bought in 1959 to accommodate sick or aged Sisters), Mount St. Mary Hospital (which had been built by the Sisters in 1941 to accommodate elderly people who needed minimal nursing care) or Queenswood House of Studies in Saanich (which the Sisters had created in 1967 as a study area and to provide residences for Sisters studying at the University of Victoria and elsewhere). One can only speculate on their feelings of leaving a home they and their predecessors had inhabited for almost one hundred years.

Leave-taking was not uncomplicated. Forming a society did not end the process. Prolonged negotiations with all parties concerned were grist for the newspaper mills of the day. The city contemplated extending Belleville Street through St. Ann's grounds, while the province, the regional hospital board and the SVIHS saw St. Ann's as the future home of the hospital. Eventually a proposal made by the society was agreed to on April 16, 1971, by the Sisters and their legal adviser, Gerald Sullivan, and the deputy minister of health and hospital insurance. Three days later, the board unanimously resolved:

> . . . that this Board approves in principle the proposals of the Minister of Health Service and Hospital Insurance and of the executive of the Capital Regional Hospital District for the acquisition from the Sisters of St. Ann of the St. Joseph's Hospital by way of a gift and, for the expansion of the hospital, of adjoining lands commonly known as the annex and St. Ann's Academy by way of purchase.[284]

However, nothing happened and, since the hospital and society boards were composed of essentially the same members, the future of the society was questioned when it had existed for three years and still had nothing to administer. Further complicating matters was the inclusion of extended-care bed allotments, which caused the joining of the boards from St. Joseph's and Mount St. Mary. The Sisters recorded:

> The early 1970s were difficult years as the Sisters sought to present the hospital they had established and maintained for almost 100 years to the citizens of Victoria. Indecision, political skirmishes, and administrative problems made even the giving of the $4 million dollar facility a frustrating procedure.[285]

On February 9, 1972, the historic document was finally signed, gifting St. Joseph's Hospital to the South Vancouver Island Hospital Society. Sister Margaret Doris and Sister Kathleen Cyr had completed the inventory of the hospital equipment and furniture. Sister Eileen Kelly, provincial superior, wrote on behalf of the Sisters of St. Ann to the medical and lay staff, to the auxiliaries, to Dr. Van Tilburg and to the public expressing appreciation for the co-operation, faithful service and friendly relationships during the ninety-six years the Sisters owned and operated St. Joseph's.

The hospital was immediately named Queen Victoria General Hospital, a very unpopular and short-lived name.

At a ceremony on September 26, 1972, Health Minister Dennis Cocke officially gave the facility the name by which it is still known, Victoria General Hospital. The *Victoria Times* carried the public acknowledgement and thanks to the Sisters of St. Ann of the BC government for the gift to the citizens of British Columbia, over the signature of Premier W.A.C. Bennett.[286]

All that remained for the transfer of ownership to the people of Victoria was the public handing over to the society. Standing on the front steps of the Humboldt Street entrance to St. Joseph's Hospital on February 16, 1972, Sister Eileen Kelly, dynamic representative of all her Sisters, gave Dr. Alexander Wood, chair of the society's board, the ceremonial key to the building, thus ending the ninety-six-year presence of the Sisters of St. Ann.

Though no longer administrators of St. Joseph's, the Sisters did not

Giving the hospital, in 1972, to the people of southern Vancouver Island, Sister Eileen Kelly, provincial superior, hands a ceremonial key to Dr. Alex Wood, chair of the Southern Vancouver Island Hospital Society. Back Row, l-r: Fred Norris, board member; unknown; Herbert Bruch, MLA; Sister Margaret Doris; Sister Kathleen Cyr; John Murray, comptroller. PHOTO BY JIM RYAN, SSAA P0269

lose their interest in pastoral care ministry. Victoria General operated at the St. Joseph's Hospital's Fairfield Road site until the 1983 opening of a new facility on Helmcken Road. The old hospital became the Fairfield Health Centre, housing extended-care beds for the elderly and various clinics and outpatient services for those with disabilities and diseases such as AIDS.

Enter Sister Ida Brasseur—recently retired after forty years in Alaska—who became a volunteer in the pastoral care program at the centre in 1988. She felt energized by knowing that "saintly pioneers and dedicated Sisters had ministered [here] among the sick." She rejuvenated the chapel from its use as a storeroom to an interdenominational spiritual haven that was rededicated on September 8, 1989. She felt fortunate to volunteer with Dr. Van Tilburg, the former medical director and executive director of the old St. Joseph's days. On November 15, 1990, Sister Ida Brasseur was presented with the Canada Volunteer Award Certificate of Merit, awarded by

In recognition of her pastoral care work at the Fairfield Health Centre, Sister Ida Brasseur is presented, in 1990, the Canadian Volunteer Award Certificate of Merit by C. Dupont, director of volunteers at the centre. Dr. Embert Van Tilburg, fellow volunteer and former executive director of St. Joseph's Hospital, is at the right. SSAA P0271

the federal government to recognize and encourage those who have made a valuable voluntary contribution toward improving the health and social well-being of their fellow citizens.

The curtain was drawn on the Sisters of St. Ann ministry at St. Joseph's when all the patients were removed early in 1994 and Sister Ida Brasseur withdrew.

The Sisters' commitment to serving the poor, the sick and the dying had encompassed the Victoria community through most of the city's history. As the population had increased, the hospital had expanded—several times—with the cost borne mainly by the Sisters. As advances in medicine were made, the congregation had sent its members to university to keep up their credentials and provided other opportunities for professional development. The Sisters witnessed the progression from private to universal medical coverage. This move to government-funded health care, as well as the decreasing number of nursing Sisters willing to staff St. Joseph's due to changing ethics and laws, culminated in the gifting of the hospital to the people in 1972.

Almost all of the hospital was demolished early in the twenty-first century to make way for the revamped, state-of-the-art extended-care Mount St. Mary Hospital, a facility that is still owned by the Sisters of St. Ann. As part of the sale, the remaining portion of St. Joseph's built in 1908 was transformed into seventy subsidized housing units and has the distinction since November 2007 of being Victoria's first police-certified crime-free multi-housing site. The Sisters would surely be pleased to see their ministry continued in this community-building program.

PART TWO

Expanding Horizons

Residents enjoying the fresh air in the back garden of Mount St. Mary. SSAA P0036

Chapter 7

St. Joseph's School of Nursing

St. Joseph's Hospital would be valuable "if only as a school for nurses."

—Dr. John Sebastian Helmcken

A quarter-century before St. Joseph's School of Nursing opened, Dr. John Sebastian Helmcken foresaw that it would have a strong future. At the laying of the cornerstone of St. Joseph's Hospital in 1875, he made the prophetic comment that the hospital would be valuable "if only as a school for nurses."[287] The school was formally inaugurated in 1900, under the competent direction of Sister Mary Gertrude of Jesus, after immigration and epidemics had fuelled the need for more nurses. Between 1875 and the turn of the century, teaching at St. Joseph's had been limited to older, more experienced Sisters mentoring the younger, untrained ones, with the hospital doctors obligingly demonstrating procedures, teaching anatomy and overseeing the nurses.

Gertrude Weimer—who would become the first of the teaching Sisters—was the eldest of nineteen children. She responded to Victoria Bishop Nicholas Lemmens' call at her parish church in Germany and left home in 1894 to enter the Sisters of St. Ann novitiate in Lachine. A year later she moved to Victoria.[288] After pronouncing her vows as Sister Mary Gertrude of Jesus on July 25, 1896, she worked first in the surgical service and then in all branches of the hospital—pharmacy, maternity, medical—acquiring theory from Dr. John C. Davie, Jr. and Dr. O.M. Jones by "listening to them intelligently, observing them closely, and obeying them

133

Originally from Germany, Sister Mary Gertrude of Jesus responded to Victoria Bishop Nicholas Lemmens' call for workers when the bishop visited her home parish. After gaining experience in all areas of the hospital, she founded the St. Joseph's School of Nursing in 1900. SSAA P0115

scrupulously."[289] She also took notes in lieu of the textbooks that were too expensive for the hospital budget. When it was time for a more structured training environment, Sister Mary Gertrude of Jesus organized the school of nursing, making "the art and science of nursing a sublime adventure for her students."[290] At the time of her death on July 4, 1914, at the age of forty, she had compiled three typed volumes of a nursing training manuscript and was preparing them for publication. She covered all topics, including a section on "How to Prepare a Room for a Major Operation in a Private House."[291] Her desire to equip the nurse with every tool led to some tension with other hospital staff, causing her to state:

> I am not trying to make the nurse a close competitor of the doctor. On the other hand I find it unjust to find fault with the nurse because she knows somewhat of the doctors' business . . . It is the duty of the physicians and teachers to fortify the nurse with knowledge of all those things which will serve her. This we must faithfully do, even at a terrible risk of teaching her a few facts more than is absolutely necessary.[292]

Unfortunately her early death prevented the publication of her manuscript, but her notes were distributed to the doctors for use in their teaching.

Nurses' training had always followed the apprenticeship model, a model that persisted into the late twentieth century, when education was moved to postsecondary institutions. Students were predominantly female, but contrary to this general rule a man, Anthony Williams, was the first St. Joseph's graduate. Williams had been a handyman in the early days of the hospital, cleaning floors at first, then holding legs during amputations, lifting patients and generally performing male nursing procedures. As reported in the *Daily Colonist* of June 1, 1975, Dr. Jones wrote a letter on March 2, 1898, attesting: "Williams has a good knowledge of his duties, is clean, sober and most reliable. He is well drilled in aseptic and antiseptic methods." His acquired skills merited him the first nursing pin dated June 21, 1901, and a framed diploma certifying that he was

An early student feeds an infant in paediatrics. No propped bottles for these babies. SSAA P0273

competent to nurse surgical and medical patients. This first male nurse was a blip in the statistics. From then until 1965—sixty-four years later, when two more men graduated from the school—all of the graduates were women.[293]

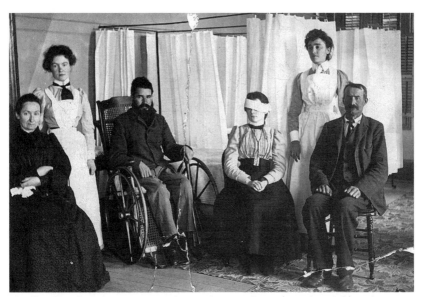

The first two female nursing students, Eleanor Allison (standing left) and Agnes Johnson (standing right) slept in available hospital rooms and learned on the job alongside the doctors and nurses. They graduated in 1902. SSAA P0274

The first officially recorded female graduates were Eleanor Allison and Agnes Johnson (who later married Frank Ellis) in 1902. When they first entered the two-year training program in January 1900, there was no set curriculum and no prescribed uniform. They slept in available hospital rooms and worked alongside Sisters and doctors over twelve-hour days to learn their craft, earning a munificent stipend of $5 a month. These two women were Protestant, an indicator that from the first, as in the hospital itself, creed was not a determinant of admission. In fact it was not until 1905, when Sister Mary Peter and two laywomen entered training, that there were any Catholic students. Race was also not a factor for admission, though, in reality, it was many years before different ethnic groups were represented in the student population. The February 1940 entry class of thirteen probationers welcomed the first Chinese student, the daughter of a Presbyterian minister.[294] The class admitted in 1952, the largest to enter training in the history of the school, included Rose Terry, an orphan from Kamloops, the first First Nations woman to attend and the recipient of

the prize as best clinical nurse at her graduation in 1955. Father Fergus O'Grady (later Bishop of Prince George) attended her graduation and proudly accompanied her to the so-called Father and Daughter Breakfast.

Mrs. Agnes Ellis (née Johnson) recalled fifty years later that she had had no formal classes but the doctors and Sister Mary Gertrude of Jesus had regularly quizzed them and given them oral and written examinations. They had also learned to be economical. They used only what was necessary and conserved equipment as best they could. Sea sponges were used, washed then reused, as were gauze bandages. Rather than waste

The first First Nations graduate (1955), Rose Terry (now Mrs. Rose Casper), received the prize of best clinical nurse in her class. The Rose Casper Healing Centre in Shalath, BC, is named in her honour as first aboriginal nurse in the province. SSAA P0303

electricity "the nurses were equipped with small coal-oil lanterns which they carried around and placed at different stations so as to light up the halls and bathrooms."[295]

The students were billeted in whatever rooms were available in the hospital but with the addition of the "A" wing in 1908, they moved to a more permanent dormitory on the fifth floor that sported one round window known to all as the "Bull's Eye." They slept in small cubicles separated by wooden partitions, with some privacy afforded by pulling down the starched, accordion-pleated curtains. Each small space contained a chair, washstand and two clothes hooks, with additional wardrobe space down the hall.

Sister Mary Anna succeeded Sister Mary Gertrude of Jesus in 1913, taking charge of the nursing students and combining their education with her other hospital duties. That year she expanded the program to two and a half years, increasing it to three years in 1914. She herself had not been trained formally, but had learned on the job. However, she was competent enough to be granted honourary status as a registered nurse by the Graduate Nurses Association of British Columbia.[296]

Enrolment at the nursing school fluctuated, but there was a gradual increase in the number of students during the years leading up to the First World War. New accommodation was needed. Sister Mary Anna supervised the move of thirty-four students to their new home in 1919 at Osborne Court on the corner of McClure and Collinson Streets, rented for $175 a month. Her students remembered her for her strict rule that uniform hemlines must reach the step when they stood at the bottom of the three-storey stairwell. This calm, tactful woman strove to instill in her students a love of duty and loyalty to their school.

Sister Mary Anna gradually implemented more hours of study and attempted to establish student rotation in the clinical areas. Unfortunately this was an uphill struggle, as some Sister supervisors viewed this change as detrimental to the patient, not thinking of its benefit to the students' education. Under the Registered Nurses Act of 1918, nursing education was now being monitored by the Graduate Nurses Association of BC, which administered examinations to those who wished to qualify for registration. For a period of three years after this act came into force a nurse could apply, pay the registration fee, and the association council, at its discretion,

A larger class reflecting the gradually increasing enrollment in the years around World War I, the class of 1919 is ready to face nursing challenges of their own.
SSAA P0279

could admit to membership without exam any person otherwise qualified who had graduated from a school of nursing before April 22, 1921. Prior to 1921 no provincial law governed the schools, leaving any hospital free to establish a school of nursing and conduct it in a manner best serving its purposes.[297]

While training nurses was the primary purpose of the school, soon after the First World War it adopted a more structured approach to teaching radiography and pathology. The School of Radiography that opened in 1919 prepared students to qualify for registration by sitting exams that had been set by the American Society of X-Ray Technicians. The Medical Technology School opened in 1921. Students in both programs lived in the nurses' residence and followed the nursing program for the first six months, after which they branched out essentially as apprentices for eighteen months. They graduated and received their diplomas with the nurses. This arrangement continued until the British Columbia Institute of Technology (BCIT) began training X-ray students in 1964 and medical laboratory technologists the following year. By 1969, when the practice of taking the platform with the nurses was discontinued, St. Joseph's had bestowed diplomas on 156 X-ray technicians and 127 medical laboratory technologists.[298] Four Sisters of St. Ann received their diplomas in radiography after completing their registered nurse (RN) training and six Sisters received diplomas in medical technology, two of them also having their RN status and three having completed a bachelor of science degree. In 1944 St. Joseph's was the first school in British Columbia to receive official recognition and approval of its laboratory technician program by the Canadian Medical Association.[299]

Many stories of these early decades enrich the history of the school. Sister Mary Patrick graduated in 1917, and for the next 17½ years she supervised the operating room (OR), often assisting the surgeon as anaesthetist, using very primitive methods of administering ether or chloroform. She watched her post-surgical patients closely as they were usually in shock from the length of their operations. Sister Mary Patrick was born in Prince Edward Island and nurses in the OR, including Sister Mary Faustina (graduate of 1932), remembered her "PEI Poke." When a nurse failed to anticipate the surgeon's needs, she would receive a poke in the back with long blunt forceps wielded by Sister, giving her instructions on how to

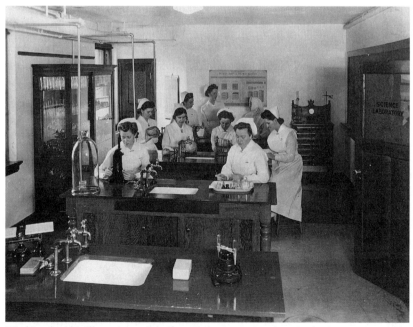

Working hard in the science lab, these late 1940s nursing students were part of a decade that saw great technological and medical advances which necessitated new facilities and a more robust curriculum. SSAA P0043

proceed. Since there were no recovery rooms, patients were wheeled back to their bedrooms, where heated stone ginger-ale bottles were used to warm them and their beds. The nurses always had to be conscious of the temperature so as not to cause a burn.[300]

*　　*　　*

Sister Mary Anna finished her term as school director in 1924, succeeded by Sister Mary Alfreda. In 1926 the school was blessed with another exemplary leader and its first full-time director, Sister Mary Gregory, also from Prince Edward Island. She had always desired to be a nurse. She graduated from the nursing school in 1918 and in 1922 became the first graduate of the School of Radiography. Her twenty-three years as director (served in three distinct stints) were broken only briefly by studies for her B.Sc. in nursing degree at St. Theresa's College in Winona, Minnesota, and her master's degree from Seattle University in 1941. Her students commanded her zeal and dedication. She was devoted to them, visiting each young woman at night to buoy her spirits, spending much time in counselling and guidance. St. Joseph's students acquitted themselves admirably in exams under the training school model. In 1929, Edith O'Brien came first in the RN provincial exams and Sister Mary Gabriella came second. Sister Mary Gregory's belief in advanced education for nurses led her to attempt an affiliation with Seattle University in 1939. She was able to set up a five-year program whereby St. Joseph's students would get a B.Sc. degree after two years of additional study in Seattle. This plan was short-lived, most likely due to lack of money, the beginning of the war and resistance to abandoning the traditional apprenticeship in-hospital model. Her former students demonstrated their regard and affection for her at the fiftieth anniversary celebrations in 1950 with a "magnificent gift" enabling her to visit "with my dear ones away back in Prince Edward Island."[301]

By 1930, twenty-three Sisters had completed the nursing course and received their diplomas. They lived together in separate quarters from the other students and did not go onstage to receive their diplomas at graduation but were presented with them later in a community gathering. Theirs was a tough, busy life, but one they had chosen.

They were up earlier in the day, often put in long hours on the wards, assumed more responsibility at an earlier stage (they became Supervisors almost immediately upon graduating) and generally had less time to themselves. They had their religious activities on top of the busy schedule of nursing students.[302]

The Sisters contended with clothing more cumbersome than the other students, although in the 1920s they adopted a lightweight white cotton habit with sleeves that they could roll up. The regular students' uniforms also changed over the years to reflect the thinking of the day, with the navy cape, lined in red, added at the time of a joint celebration of Thanksgiving and Armistice Day on November 11, 1929.[303] Black lace-up boots were worn until 1926, when the students asked Sister Mary Gregory if they could wear white oxfords to graduation, a change that was incorporated into the uniform from then on.

The first recorded graduation exercise was held at St. Ann's Academy auditorium in 1908. A 1912 photo shows red and white flowers bracketing the stage and red and white ribbons on the uniforms. A newspaper article in 1947 explained the significance of these colours: "red for courage 'mid earthly strife, white for the flower of a blameless life."[304] When the number of students graduating increased to forty-two in May 1940, the largest class to this point, the ceremonies were moved to the nearby Royal Theatre, rented for $60. The class made a stunning picture marching from the nurses' residence to the theatre. The celebrations extended in time to include a Father and Daughter Breakfast and a Mother and Daughter Tea. Lacking a parent to share the occasion, a girl would often enlist the willing company of one of the doctors under whom she had trained. In the latter years of the school, the event was moved to the uptown Victoria McPherson Theatre, but the final exercise in 1981 took place in the auditorium at the University of Victoria.

The increasing number of students in the 1920s demanded more and better accommodation. At early sunrise on April 26, 1929, the first sod was turned in preparation for building a four-storey grey brick home for 130 nurses on Rupert Street, next to the hospital. Father Emile Sobry blessed the site. The nurses vacated Osborne Court and moved to their new quarters in September that same year, with the official opening held

Built in 1929, the new residence next to the hospital provided much needed space, housing 130 nurses and providing additional classrooms. SSAA P0065

on February 8, 1930. Now there was space for classrooms and labs as well as a living room/lounge furnished by a generous benefactor of BC hospitals—Robert Randolph Bruce, lieutenant-governor of British Columbia

The method of educating nurses was being challenged in the late 1920s. In 1929 the Canadian Medical Association (paying a third of the cost) and the Canadian Nurses Association (paying the rest) jointly commissioned Professor George Weir, head of the faculty of education at the University of British Columbia, to prepare a report on the method and results of training nurses.[305] His *Survey of Nursing Education* was published in 1932, with many recommendations taking into account the advances in science and technology and the need for better-prepared nurses. He considered that there was more emphasis laid on the economic needs of the hospital than the educational needs of the students. Canada had too many small local schools of nursing, each following its own curriculum according to the perceived needs of the hospital. He made a personal visit to inspect St. Joseph's School of Nursing in April 1930, at which time he declared himself "well pleased at the efficient education" offered.[306] Certainly the congregation saw the urgency of having degreed Sisters in the hospital, as was evident in the number of them being sent to universities in Spokane, Seattle and in the eastern United States for studies in hospital administration as well as in nursing and other disciplines. Weir's survey was to reverberate down the years, but in the depths of the 1930s Depression, few of his recommendations were acted upon. Nursing schools continued to be run as part of the hospital budget, rather than stand-alone educational facilities.[307] A further study by the Canadian Nurses Association emphasized that there were too many small schools (many attached to hospitals with fewer than the one hundred beds that the association recommended). As a consequence, by 1945 twelve of nineteen schools in British Columbia had closed, leaving St. Joseph's one of seven larger schools still operating.

St. Joseph's School of Nursing was becoming known to the broader community. For the first time the graduation ceremonies of April 5, 1934, were honoured with the presence of not only Bishop Gerald Murray but also Premier Thomas Dufferin ("Duff") Pattullo and Mayor David Leeming. Writer John Murray Gibbon visited in August 1944 while compiling information on hospitals and nursing school statistics for his seminal book *Three Centuries of Canadian Nursing*.[308] Clearly the Sisters of St. Ann's contribution to health care and its operation of St. Joseph's School of Nursing was recognized nationally.

Professional bodies also recognized the skills and leadership of the Sisters. Sister Mary Gregory was asked to sit on the board preparing the provincial exams for the RNs and was appointed to represent the field of nursing on the editorial board of *Hospital Progress*, a journal of the Catholic Hospital Association of the United States and Canada (1936). Over the years several Sisters went to Vancouver to correct provincial RN exams. Sister Mary Beatrice (1929 graduate) was elected a councillor on the executive of the Registered Nurses Association of BC (1937). In May 1940, Mother Mary Mark, provincial superior, was elected the first president of the newly formed Catholic Hospital Association of British Columbia (CHABC).

* * *

The Second World War created a demand for more trained nurses. Both St. Joseph's School of Nursing and its counterpart at the other major hospital in Victoria—the Royal Jubilee School of Nursing—made efforts to recruit more students by visiting high schools and making radio appeals. In 1943 St. Joseph's took in two classes, on August 4 and September 8, hoping to alleviate the shortage.[309] The increase in applicants began to show the inadequacy of the nurses' residence. In July 1941 the mother-house in Lachine approved an addition to the school. BC Finance Minister John Hart gave the government's commitment to pay 25 percent of the total cost and to donate the services of the provincial architect Henry Whittaker, with Archie Sullivan as contractor. The total cost, including furnishings, was estimated at $75,000 and work began in October 1941. A wartime ban prevented the use of grey brick, so reinforced concrete was used for the five-storey building, which included thirty-eight private and fourteen semi-private rooms on the upper floors, with offices, class-rooms, lecture halls, a science and nutrition lab and an enlarged library on the ground floor. It was a building that Whittaker described as being "as bomb-proof as we can possibly make it."[310] Bishop John Cody, a pa-tient in the hospital at the time, blessed the new wing and chapel on July 24, 1942, and celebrated the first Mass on July 28. The formal opening took place on October 27 in the presence of three hundred guests. The students sang "There'll Always be an England" while Bishop Cody cut the crimson ribbon. The chapel was resplendent with red and white carnations and beautiful stained-glass windows donated by the alumnae in honour of Sister Mary Gertrude of Jesus and Sister Mary Anna. The always-generous contractor, Archie Sullivan, donated the altar and oak communion rail.

In the postwar years, dramatic advances in technology and medicine made it imperative for nurses and students to be relieved of their non-nursing responsibilities. Previously they had washed dishes, dusted and mopped, prepared special diets for the patients and completed the "ter-minal cleaning" after a patient was discharged or died. Now they were to be trained primarily in skilled patient care. Claire Harrington became the first clinical instructor in April 1943, covering all medical and surgical wards, using whatever space she could for a classroom—linen cupboards, sun porches, empty rooms. Students received more theoretical background before being thrust onto the wards for their practical experience. The block system of lectures was instituted, which, in the beginning, sometimes meant that practical experience came before the theory.

Advances in medicine and new views on training led the Registered Nurses Association of British Columbia (RNABC) in 1948 to propose having a central school of nursing aligned with the University of British Columbia, with the intention of obliging all student nurses to follow a first-year course at the university. Sister Mary Kathleen, the hospital superior, as well as Sister Mary Claire and Sister Mary Gregory had already been in discussion with the CHABC about the impact this would have on Catholic hospitals, since this program would be entirely separated from hospital control.[311] Though this step was not taken at the time, the discussion was a precursor to discussions in the future.

Ready with a smile, Sister Miriam Rita (Rita Downey) (1959) instructs students in the operating room. SSAA P0273

St. Joseph's celebrated the golden jubilee of the nursing school and the centennial of the congregation in 1950, with more than 400 graduates returning to celebrate with a picnic, a jubilee banquet, school and hospital tours, and a Sisters' anniversary supper. Early graduate Agnes Ellis (née Johnson, 1902) and Sister Mary Peter (1905) shared the spotlight. Thanks were extended to two "fairy godmothers," Mrs. Alex McDermott and Mrs. Angus Campbell, constant friends and benefactors of the students. Tribute was paid to the 102 St. Joseph's graduates who had served overseas in two world wars, and a Vancouver branch of the alumnae met for the first time. Gavels made from the mahogany staircase in the original building were presented to both alumnae groups. A spectacular showing of 700 geraniums on the hospital grounds marked the special occasion.

When a world-wide polio epidemic erupted in the early 1950s, St. Joseph's felt the impact. Nursing student Beverly Lake was diagnosed in September 1951, and moved to the isolation ward at the Royal Jubilee Hospital. She returned in November unable to walk and with a weakened right arm. After further nursing care at St. Joseph's, she was transferred to the Vancouver Rehabilitation Centre.[312] Subsequently she recovered and was able to graduate in 1954.

The Sisters regularly acquitted themselves well in exams. Back in 1936, Sister Marie Joseph des Anges was awarded the alumnae association's annual

To maintain standards and fulfil their mission, nursing Sisters underwent training alongside the lay students. Sister Mary Ludovic, provincial superior, is shown here in 1946 with the Sisters who had graduated from St. Joseph's School of Nursing to this date. SSAA P0277

bursary for obtaining the highest marks in the provincial RN exams. In 1955, Sister Mary Perpetua graduated with the highest average marks in the three-year program. By now the Sister students were taking the stage with the other graduates, so she was able to enjoy having her parents in the audience to see her receive this award.

The 1950s were years of concern in British Columbia, the Yukon and Alaska about the number of nursing Sisters, and particularly the number qualified to supervise. Not enough Sisters were in training. In 1952 this serious shortage led St. Joseph's local council to ask that more Sisters be trained as nurses and that one be trained as a qualified dietitian, a requirement from the RNABC for an accredited nursing school. Those who graduated in these years included Sisters Mary Ronalda (1951); Mary Perpetua (1955); Mary Anne Cecilia, Mary Doris and Rita Marie (all in 1956), Mary Benedicta (1958); Miriam Rita (1959); and Miriam Jude (1960). None, however, trained as a dietitian, though lay students did. Even though many Sisters went directly into supervisory roles, a shortage remained—a shortage that was felt until they relinquished control of the hospital.

Once graduated the Sisters continued, as their predecessors, to be on call twenty-four hours a day and their heavy workload remained, leaving little time for recreational pursuits while they continued their commitment to professional education. Sister Mary Doris and Sister Mary Ronalda, who had been in the novitiate together, completed bachelor of science in nursing (B.Sc.N.) degrees. Sister Mary Doris completed a master's degree in nursing administration at the University of Toronto (1968) and Sister Mary Ronalda received her master's degree from the Catholic University of America in Washington, DC (1965). Sister Mary Ronalda became the program co-ordinator for St. Joseph's School of Nursing, a position she loved, where her role was to encourage the students who had the ability to go on and further their education.[313] Sister Mary Aquina earned her bachelor's degree at Seattle University in 1963, studied psychology at St. Louis University and the University of Manitoba, then completed a master's degree in psychosocial nursing at the University of Washington in 1974. To repay a government student loan, she worked as a public health nurse in Ladysmith, British Columbia, for two years. When the University of Victoria inaugurated its school of nursing in 1976, she was one of the first three instructors to teach in the program.[314] Her nursing life came full circle when she accepted an invitation to join the advisory council to the school of nursing at the university in 2007 and went on to become its chair the following year.

Until 1968 a Sister of St. Ann filled the position of director of St. Joseph's School of Nursing. Sister Mary Gregory finished her long tenure in 1954, followed by Sisters Mary Lucita (1954–57), Mary Justinian (1957–59), Mary Ronalda (1959–62, 1966–68) and Sister Mary Doris (1962–66). As the Sisters moved toward withdrawing from the hospital, Lilian Knighton became the first lay director of the school in 1968. Each Sister who had been taxed with the administration of the school continued to remember her role as teacher afterwards, always emphasizing the patient as a whole person. Their students had arrived as naive girls and emerged as mature women. The students learned to comfort patients and their families, and to help patients cope with whatever situation confronted them.

In September 1961, St. Joseph's students obtained a five-day, forty-hour work week and the school of nursing reverted to taking only one class each year.[315] This move would stabilize teaching programs and avoid the repetition of classes for the usually small January intake. But the students continued to staff wards. In 1968 fear of an outbreak of Hong Kong flu led the medical director, Dr. Embert Van Tilburg, to acknowledge "student nurses could be placed on fulltime ward duty."[316] Nevertheless, strides were taken in expanding theoretical knowledge before placing students in the general hospital population. Sister Mary Doris made a successful effort in 1961 to admit male students, and two of them graduated in 1965. A total of ten men graduated from St. Joseph's School of Nursing during its eighty-one-year history, including Anthony Williams (the first, in 1901) and Rick Pascual (the last, in 1980).[317]

Catholic students had always been members of the Sodality,[318] a group providing them with special prayer and retreat opportunities to enhance their faith. Protestant students, though encouraged to attend the church of their own faith tradition, had no specific format in the school for practising their beliefs until the 1960s. Sister Mary Doris observed that two-thirds of the students were Protestant and some wished to have access to retreats, just as the Catholics. She promoted an "ecumenical first" policy. Father Edward Bader, CSP (Paulist Fathers), of Vancouver, who was preaching retreats for the Catholic students, wrote to Bishop Remi De Roo and Monsignor Michael O'Connell, vicar general of the Victoria diocese, advocating a joint retreat for student nurses with Anglican Canon Hilary Butler. Bishop De Roo replied favourably, although he stated there should be no "co-officiating at any religious ceremonies."[319] At Vernon Villa the Sisters had permitted an Anglican service once a month in the sunroom as a public service just as Catholics were permitted access to space to hold Mass in secular hospitals so this was not a completely new arrangement.[320]

The Sisters of St. Ann were committed to higher education for their nursing Sisters, but the nursing education system remained virtually unchanged even with George Weir's report reverberating down through the years. Two more major surveys—Dr. Helen Mussallem's 1960 report to the Canadian Nurses Association, *Spotlight on Nursing Education*, and the 1964 report of the Hall Commission on Health Services—finally made an impact in demonstrating that the old apprenticeship method was no longer adequate or economical. It was time to place nursing schools in "institutions whose *primary function* is education."[321] In line with this, in 1974 the school affiliated with the University of Victoria for the teaching of basic sciences. Nevertheless many girls were still attracted to hospital-based

Sister Mary Perpetua (Sheila Hughes), a graduate of the program herself in 1955 with the highest average marks, teaches skeletal anatomy to new students. SSAA P0321

schools. In 1973 there were nearly three hundred applicants for a possible sixty positions. The $235 fee for a three-year diploma program was much less than the cost to study at a university.[322]

Yet, a greater change was in the wind. St. Joseph's School of Nursing retained its name, its motto, its traditions and its alumnae when the hospital was turned over to the South Vancouver Island Hospital Society in 1972, but by the time of the seventy-fifth reunion in 1975 the future of the school was in doubt. Victoria General Hospital (formerly St. Joseph's Hospital) was planning to move to a new site and it was doubtful funding would continue for the school. The move did not take place until 1983, however, when Victoria General Hospital opened on Helmcken Road and the old building became Fairfield Health Centre, which was a geriatric centre offering day clinics, two rehab units and two residential floors for 160 residents. The number of residential beds and the use of the building declined until the old hospital and nursing building were deconstructed in 2000, making way for a new Mount St. Mary Hospital.

Many events marked the seventy-fifth anniversary from June 5 to 7, 1975, including a welcoming tea opened by Sister Mary Armella, sister of Sister Mary Gertrude of Jesus. More than 650 graduates returned, the oldest of them—Mrs. May Stewart (Davidson 1910)—arrived from California. Alumnae tours of the "Pioneer Log Cabin," the Royal BC Museum and the school were followed by tea at Government House, where memories shared became especially poignant since the demise of the school seemed not far off.

In reality the last class was admitted in 1978. The graduation of 35 women in 1981 marked the official closing of the school of nursing. Three hundred former graduates watched the ceremony at the University of Victoria Centre as the 1981 graduates received their diplomas. Since its inception the school had graduated 2,604 students—2,321 registered nurses, 156 X-ray technicians and 127 medical laboratory technicians. About 650 members attended the alumnae annual dinner.

This alumnae association had formed and met for the first time May 20, 1920, instigated by Sister Mary Anna, the second head of the nursing school, who instilled great loyalty and love of the school in her students and channelled this loyalty into the formation of the alumnae group. Sister Mary Bridget, former hospital superior, was named honourary president and fifty graduates attended with the intention "to promote high ethical standards in the profession and to unify in interest and affection the graduates of the School, the Sisters associated with the Hospital and the members of the School of Nursing."[323] In the ensuing years, the alumnae contributed greatly to the comfort of the students, providing bursaries, hosting graduation parties, dances and welcoming teas, and purchasing supplies and equipment—even paying for the delivery of the daily newspapers. In 1948 they started a fund to help graduates who found themselves in personal or financial difficulty, a fund that disbursed $7,000 before the school closed.[324]

With the closing of the school, the alumnae combined their bursary funds, named the new award the St. Joseph's School of Nursing Alumnae

Bursary in honour of the Sisters of St. Ann, and passed the administration of the fund over to the RNABC. It is still awarded today.[325] The alumnae association changed its structure to become a social group, in the hope that members could maintain the bond among graduates, and it still meets twice a year.

Sister Mary Justinian (1931 graduate), a student nurse at St. Joseph's, a

Having sent off its last graduating class, the nursing school closed in 1981. The prevailing educational philosophy of the time decreed that nursing training be more closely associated with institutions of higher learning. SSAA P0325

ward nurse, instructor, and later director of St. Joseph's School of Nursing (1957–59) spoke for many when she said: "My days at nursing school were full of fun." Sister Mary Justinian said her "happiest days were in the training of the nurses . . . they were very happy, fruitful days."[326]

She also summed up the school's ongoing influence with the words "St. Joseph's School of Nursing passes into history but a nursing heritage endures."[327]

Chapter 8

Mount St. Mary Hospital
(for Extended Care)

*Founded by the Sisters of St. Ann, we are a Catholic health
organization dedicated to continuing the healing ministry
of Jesus by providing compassionate, loving care to adults of
all faiths who require long-term support. We are committed
to meeting the physical, spiritual, intellectual, social and
emotional needs of all those we serve in partnership with
their families, friends and other health care providers.*
　　　　　　　　　　　　—Hospital mission statement

In the second decade of the twenty-first century, Mount St. Mary Hospital
has the singular distinction of being the sole health care facility in British
Columbia still owned by the Sisters of St. Ann. It operates under the aegis
of the Marie Esther Society as an extended-care hospital.[328] The state-of-
the-art building sits on the site once occupied by St. Joseph's Hospital and
its school of nursing. Mount St. Mary stands as testimony to the foresight
of the Sisters, who placed a covenant on the land when they gifted it to the
people in 1972, reserving it in perpetuity for health care.

Compared with some of the other health care institutions operated by
the Sisters of St. Ann in British Columbia, Mount St. Mary is relatively
new. The initiative that led to its presence a few blocks from St. Joseph's
Hospital came from Bishop John Cody of Victoria, who in 1939 informed
the Sisters of the pressing need for a Catholic institution for the "care of
aged and incurables" and offered the Sisters property owned by the diocese

at 999 Burdett Street for $5,000 plus the cancellation of a $15,000 debt owed by the diocese to the Sisters in Nanaimo. Not long before this the Burdett Street property had been assessed at $45,000. This new institution would be free from taxation if it were an annex to St. Joseph's Hospital and would relieve an overcrowding problem there. As a bonus, Bishop Cody promised to provide a chaplain for ten years at no cost to the Sisters.[329]

The property's long and interesting history dated back to its original purchase by the Anglican bishop of Columbia in 1864, who sold it in 1884 to one Tom Lubbe. In 1887, D.R. Harris, whose wife Martha was the youngest daughter of Sir James Douglas, purchased it. In 1890 they built a beautiful brick mansion surrounded by a handsome brick wall, which they called Easton House. But again in 1900 it reverted to the Trustees of Christ Church Cathedral located across the street. Alexander MacDonald, the Catholic bishop of Victoria, took possession of the site in 1914, thinking of it as a possible location for a new cathedral. But it became a white elephant, used variously as a residence for the Christian Brothers, a boarding house and, in 1918, as an improvised hospital where the Sisters of St. Ann cared for those who had been struck down sick during the Spanish flu epidemic. The building was gutted by fire shortly afterwards and the vacant property went to seed behind its walls until Bishop Thomas O'Donnell in the 1920s again offered it to the Sisters. They were unable to accept as they had neither the money nor personnel to operate another hospital.

When Bishop Cody again solicited their support in 1939, they were more receptive. Mother Mary Leopoldine and the general council in Lachine approved the project, agreeing to the bishop applying to Rome on their behalf to take a loan of $100,000 toward the approximate $200,000 cost of construction. They signed the deed to transfer the property on May 22, 1939.[330] St. Joseph's Hospital board of management, which would oversee the new hospital, also approved the project, confident of a $50,000 government grant. The minister of public works arranged for provincial architect Henry Whittaker and his staff to draw up plans for the facility.

* * *

Bishop Cody blessed the site and turned the first sod on October 4, 1939, in the presence of Mother Mary Leopoldine, Mother Mary Mark, the provincial superior, and many of the Sisters. It was said to have been a "dreary, drizzly autumn day. The place was a tangle of grasses and brushwood. The tall trees dripped cheerlessly—but the place was consecrated, God's work was begun."[331]

On this same day, Finance Minister John Hart promised a grant of $50,000 as long as building had commenced before March 31, 1940, the close of the fiscal year. Tenders were called and on March 25, 1940, Archie Sullivan, the Vancouver contractor who was building St. Joseph's Villa, was awarded the contract to construct the four-storey reinforced concrete building. To fulfill the stipulation of the provincial government, Sister Mary Alfreda, superior at St. Joseph's Hospital, hired a man with a scraper and horses to literally honour the requirement to break ground by March 31.

On April 1, bulldozers and shovels were at work levelling the solid rock foundation, taking care to preserve the giant oaks and cedars that lent an air of mature dignity to the site. During the summer and fall, as building progressed, plans expanded to add a partial fifth floor to provide sleeping space for Sisters, staff and maids. Bishop Cody imparted a solemn blessing,

On a drizzly autumn day in 1939, Bishop John C. Cody blessed and turned the first sod of Mount St. Mary Hospital, a new home for "the aged and incurables."
SSAA P0012

dedicating every nook and cranny on February 2, 1941. The first Mass was celebrated in the chapel on March 22. Furnishings arrived over the following month, and little by little the building and chapel took shape.

Miss Marie Stewart, a former city librarian, became the first resident on March 19.[332] As April started, nine seniors were making their home at Mount St. Mary. By then, the staff included Chong Hee, a Chinese cook from Canton who had already worked at the Sisters' Lourdes Hospital in Campbell River, BC (the subject of Chapter 9). The Sisters and many of the staff marked linens and blankets, washed dishes and put them away, made beds and hung pictures and crucifixes on the walls, all to prepare the new home. Gifts arrived from many sources—Lieutenant-Governor Eric Hamber included. When Walter Cross, a local meat merchant, presented his account for the first month, he stamped it "paid," adding another donation. Archie Sullivan and his wife contributed stunning stained-glass doors for the chapel, depicting St. John at the foot of the Cross.[333]

In May 1941 George Weir, now the provincial secretary, informed the Sisters that the government was prepared to enter into a contract with Mount St. Mary to provide eighty to one hundred beds for government patients who would require nursing and medical care. These "infirmary patients" would be paid for at a rate of $1.50 a day.[334] After signing the contract to accept these patients, the hospital completed the installation of equipment and furnishings to accommodate them. "Dr. Smith," a former St. Joseph's intern, was engaged for the new patients. He would visit the hospital every day and see every patient at least twice a week. The nursing Sisters trained fifteen girls as "practical nurses" and engaged two orderlies for regular duty.

Throughout July 1941, patients were admitted from the Marpole Infirmary in Vancouver. "Some of the men patients are quite crippled, and some of the women are very old and feeble—80 and 90 years old."[335] The first patient to die was Charles Johnson, who had arrived from Marpole on July 10 and lived only two days. At this time "the Mount"—as Mount St. Mary was affectionately known—also had twenty-three private patients. Some of these patients could pay their board, but others had been taken in as charity cases. In addition, the ailing mothers and fathers of Sisters would come to live at the Mount at no charge. Always frugal, the Sisters

On staff at Mount St. Mary, the Sisters of St. Ann standing at the front gate are, l–r, Sister Mary Liliose, Sister Mary Peter, Sister Mary Grace, Sister Rose Mary, first superior, Sister Mary Colette, Sister Mary Angelica and Sister Mary Malachy.

and other staff spent a great deal of time in the summer preserving fruits and vegetables to supply the table and keep costs down.

Sister Rose Mary was named the first superior in July 1941, with ten Sisters under her supervision. Before that, Mount St. Mary had been under the administration of Mother Mary Mark and Sister Mary Alfreda. Sister Rose Mary was the sister of long-deceased Sister Mary Anna, the well-known superintendent of St. Joseph's school of nursing. Sister Rose Mary had entered the novitiate relatively late, at the age of thirty-six, and she brought both maturity and astute business skills to the operation of the new hospital. One of those she supervised was Sister Mary Peter, who entertained the patients daily at the piano. The celebration of the sixtieth anniversary of her profession was a big event for the Sisters, staff and patients in 1942.

Erecting a new facility during the war years was an audacious undertaking. Many building supplies were restricted and many economies had to be practised, but Mount St. Mary emerged in a hybrid of modern art deco and machine-age art moderne styles. The Sisters had the expense of sewing dark navy curtains for all windows and openings and buying lanterns for all the floors to be used during the many wartime blackouts. They attended lectures on incendiary bombs and in many ways were kept very aware of war efforts. A pleasanter side of wartime included the Sisters serving breakfast, sponsored by the Knights of Columbus, to 150 servicemen in the auditorium at the nursing school, in addition to attending Mass in the chapel, or having their "guest-patients" entertained by the Air Force choir.

Generous supporters helped them through these years—donating a keg of beer, ice cream for two hundred from Palm Dairy, large hams from Mr. Cross's meat store, and crates of cherries, peaches and apples from Fred Nesbitt in Oliver, BC, where the Sisters also operated a hospital (the subject of Chapter 11). The government provided tobacco, cigarettes and pocket money for the infirmary patients and the Sisters made sure each resident received a gift on birthdays and Christmas. Joe North delivered one hundred baskets of fruit at Christmas, just as he did for the patients at St. Joseph's Hospital. Sisters Mary Colette and Mary Gerard Majella, like all Dutch Canadian citizens, received boxes of candies and biscuits from the Dutch Embassy when exiled Princess Julianna gave birth to a daughter in Ottawa in January 1943. When the Princess visited Victoria a year later, Sisters Mary Colette and Mary Armella were invited to Government House to greet her in her own tongue. Within a year of Mount St. Mary's opening, women who were old friends of the Sisters of St. Ann met to discuss visiting the "inmates" to provide companionship and assistance. By the mid-1960s a group called the "Pink Ladies" had formed as an adjunct to the "Friends" to regularly take around a mobile cart with notions to all the floors and wards. Thus began a long history of volunteers caring for patients' needs.

* * *

In 1944 the Sisters bought the adjoining property at 929 Burdett for $8,750 to provide accommodation for staff. The city put a "Quiet Zone" sign in front of the hospital to protect the residents from city noise, a practice that has long since been abandoned. They held the first bazaar on December 9, 1944, clearing $839, with the intent of raising funds to buy a station wagon in order to take patients on outings; that goal was finally realized in May 1947. During a transportation strike shortly after, the vehicle was used to ferry staff from home to work and back again. At the time of writing, the annual Mount St. Mary Bazaar continues to raise funds to provide comforts for the residents.

The residents did what they could from the beginning to help make the Mount a home. One man was ambulatory and ran errands and delivered trays; Mr. Cody, an arthritic patient, was a barber and gave residents a shave or haircut from his wheelchair; and Mr. Loftus lent his carpentry skills. By June 1943, Mount St. Mary had become a very busy hospital housing one hundred infirmary and fifty-seven private patients, of whom only forty-seven were Catholics. The hospital employed forty lay staff to supplement the Sisters' work.[336] These numbers remained stable for many years. As from their 1858 arrival, the Sisters welcomed all without regard to colour or creed.

Mount St. Mary was a care facility that, by its very nature, operated at a more subdued pace than an acute care hospital. The Sisters and staff came to know the residents very well and knew the inevitability of death. They endeavoured to make a real home for these patients during their final years. Two women who ended their days at the Mount had also begun their lives as orphans under the care of the Sisters. One was Mrs. Julia Apnaut (née Hamburger). Once orphaned and left with the Sisters in New Westminster, she returned in failing health to their care in May 1952 and died in November the same year. "She thought it quite wonderful that the Sisters who cared for her when she was a helpless child, should, generations later be the ones to make her last months on earth happy and peaceful."[337] Another associate of the Sisters died the same month. Joseph Euclid Bourgeois, one-time gardener at the motherhouse in Lachine and later in Victoria, could boast with pride that he had been one of the pallbearers of the venerated founder, Marie Anne Blondin.

Mount St. Mary operated as a private hospital from 1941 to 1965. By its tenth anniversary, in 1951, the hospital had admitted 548 infirmary patients and 373 private patients, and experienced 582 deaths.[338] Expenses increased every year. On November 8, 1954, the general council allowed the hospital "to spend three thousand five hundred dollars ($3,500) for the installation of a physiotherapy department and to pay this expense from the salaries of the Sisters."[339] These salaries continued to be reinvested in facilities and activities for the patients' benefit. Their salaries did not really reflect the amount of work that the Sisters did, since each one had several responsibilities and remained on call twenty-four hours a day. For example, Sister Mary Justinian in her 1965–66 term of office as superior and administrator, also took charge of domestic personnel, the maintenance program and the volunteers, and supervised the sewing room.[340] Sisters also participated in workshops, institutes and ongoing education pertinent to the needs of their particular type of facility. The year-end report and financial statements from auditors Ross, Touche & Company of December 31, 1959, showed the best financial results since 1949, but the building had depreciated and nothing had been spent on replacement due to lack of funds. Expenditures increased about 6 percent each year. The auditors advised that the Sisters could expect little or no profit by 1961 and from then on could expect increasing losses, thus they needed to ensure that revenue continued to rise. Salaries and wages amounted to 65 percent of expenses in 1959, but ten years later had risen to 81 percent of their total costs.[341] The 1963 financial report shows the hospital

Distinguished visitors, Eugene Cardinal Tisserant of France (front) and Victoria Bishop James Hill (back) toured Mount St. Mary in 1950. SSAA P0078

was receiving income from the provincial government for the remaining infirmary cases ($106,625.40), for social assistance patients ($73,626.20) and from private patients ($146,861.05). And there were some patients unable to pay. Coupled with the Sisters' salaries, there was still not enough to entirely cover expenses.[342]

BC Hospital Insurance Services (BCHIS) inspected private hospitals such as Mount St. Mary from its inception, though it did not fund them. In September 1965 two BCHIS accountants examined the office and administrative records of the Mount as the government now had plans to extend hospital insurance to non-profit hospitals and nursing homes. Mount St. Mary was officially designated as an extended-care facility by an Order in Council dated November 30, 1965.[343] On December 1, the Sisters of St. Ann took on a pilot program in which the extended care patient was defined as "eligible for hospital benefits by virtue of a demonstrated need for skilled 24-hour a day nursing services and continued medical supervision, which need not be provided in an acute or rehab hospital."[344] The Sisters were not convinced the layout and facilities of Mount St. Mary were adequate to meet the demands of extended care, but the need was so great, and "as the financial requirements in operating a private hospital were proving to be a definite burden, the Sisters agreed to accept."[345]

From the beginning of 1966, accountants for BCHIS and the hospital were back and forth adjusting the hospital books to fit BCHIS specifications, both groups helpful and eager to make the changes as painless as possible. The patients had to be assessed for eligibility but the Sisters did not feel pressured to transfer those who didn't fit the profile. "On the whole," wrote one of the Sisters, "the government men with whom we are dealing seem to be men of understanding and sympathy."[346] They began transferring some of their patients—boarding patients who did not qualify for extended care—to rest homes or private hospitals. Those eligible to remain were brought down to the nursing floors and the fourth floor was taken over by the Sisters for their private quarters. BCHIS began making regular payments for patients and gave an equipment replacement allowance based on plant needs at the beginning of 1966.

To fill the requirements of its new designation, the hospital formed a medical advisory committee of four physicians in 1966, with Dr. Vere

Stuart as its first chair. Twenty-six physicians accepted the Sisters' invitation to join the official medical staff. A board of management was named; it held its first meeting on March 2, 1967, and its constitution and bylaws were approved by the minister of health in 1968. The board would consist of nine members—six appointed by the Sisters of St. Ann, along with representatives appointed by the medical staff, the provincial government and the city. The first meeting was attended by Sister Mary Justinian, superior/administrator; Sister Mary Anne Cecilia, director of nursing service; Dr. Vere Stuart, medical advisory committee; Thomas Shorthouse, elected chair; J. Woolcock, chartered accountant, representing the city; Brigadier S. Mores; and D'Arcy McGee, who was a grandson of one of the Fathers of Confederation. (R.L. Sturgess was not appointed as the government representative until May.) On May 27, 1968, the board held its first annual general meeting. Sister Marguerite Lalonde, as assistant to the provincial, Sister Kathleen Moroney, attended this inaugural meeting to outline the "Role of the Board of Management in a Sisters' Hospital." She explained the vital role the board plays as policy maker, establishing and controlling standards in administering a hospital. Members, she said, were chosen "for integrity, rectitude, love and concern for others, business acumen, and with the knowledge that each member will uphold their position of trust and confidence."[347]

Events moved rapidly. The Hospital Employees' Union (HEU) was certified on October 11, 1966, and it obtained bargaining rights and negotiated a union contract with little controversy, bringing salaries at the Mount in line with those at St. Joseph's Hospital. Canada Pension Plan contributions commenced on December 1, 1966, and on January 1, 1967, municipal superannuation and CU & C (a non-profit health society) medical benefits for staff became effective. The board appointed John Stevens as the first business manager. The expense of operating Mount St. Mary was becoming exorbitant with all these developments. The hospital's commitment to fund employees' pensionable service prior to July 1, 1960, so they could obtain full past service benefits, meant it was paying down this debt until 1977. So serious was the financial problem that in December 1967 the Sisters discussed using the Mount St. Mary property as a residence for Sisters and boarders and asked the general council in Lachine to consider taking steps to withdraw from extended care under BCHIS "in order to safeguard our property so to avoid Community liability or deficits."[348]

Fortunately the congregation decided to continue this ministry. The business of running the hospital was always driven by consideration for the well-being of the patients. In Victoria the broader community planned events for their benefit. Freeman King, commissioner of the Boy Scouts, in 1948 delegated Scouts and Guides to push the wheelchair patients to the Victoria May Day Parade, an annual practice that continued into the 1980s. Who enjoyed themselves more, the patients or their helpers? The local multiple sclerosis

Sister Mary Angelica works with a resident in the late 1950s in what would become the Occupational Therapy Department in late 1968. SSAA P0039

and arthritis societies held garden parties and teas at the Mount. Birthdays were celebrated and Christmas was a very special time, with Salvation Army and Oak Bay High School bands entertaining. A part-time dietitian, Eleanora Van Tilburg, wife of Dr. Embert Van Tilburg, was hired in September 1968, filling a government requirement and enhancing patient services, and a new "diversional therapy" program—today called occupational therapy—was introduced that December. Activities included painting and pottery. The staff newsletter, the *Beacon*, printed its first issue on March 18, 1968. A particularly enjoyable time was "Wheelchair Night," which was initiated in December 1970 by Woodward's department store and gave challenged individuals the opportunity to Christmas shop with a companion/assistant when the store was closed to other shoppers. The first tea honouring volunteers was held on December 4, 1969, followed by the first long-service tea for three employees on December 9. Many events enlivened the days for residents and staff.

The spiritual life of the patient was most important to the Sisters. They strove to provide residents with attention from representatives of relevant faith traditions. They were ecumenical before it became more common in the 1960s. From the beginning they enjoyed a mutually warm and respectful relationship with their neighbours, the Anglican community at Christ Church Cathedral, whose pastor provided spiritual care to Anglican patients. Other denominations were invited to minister as well.

* * *

In June 1968 the provincial government engaged Agnew Peckham & Associates of Toronto to make a survey of Victoria's future health needs, a study to include extended-care needs. This report declared Mount St. Mary obsolete for extended care from a nursing and safety standpoint and recommended that a new 150-bed unit be built. Nothing resulted, so Mount St. Mary proceeded to upgrade fire protection, installing a good ramp-type exit and a new fire alarm system with smoke-proof doors and emergency lighting. Universal Appraisal Company was hired to determine the fair current-market value of the hospital, and appraised the land and buildings at $845,000 in November 1969. This report also noted evidence of "functional obsolescence." The hospital submitted to an accreditation survey in May 1969 in preparation for the setting up of an accreditation program for extended-care hospitals. Despite the earlier reports, the hospital was awarded full accreditation status in September 1971.

In the meantime the Sisters accepted the government's request to sponsor a new extended-care hospital to replace the old Mount, and the board met to study the design booklet from BCHIS. The booklet included the statement "It is essential that this facility provide a social, recreational, diversional and rehabilitative programme so that these patients may function to their maximum potential."[349] This point fit well with the Sisters' philosophy of care.

Economic realities meant the status quo continued, even though plans had progressed to the point of drawings being rendered for a new 150-bed unit. The government had other priorities. Members of the board attended the opening of the 300-bed public Gorge Road Hospital on January 31, 1973, and shortly 150 beds opened at another public institution, Glengarry Hospital. Then, as today, there was a need for ever more extended-care beds. Mount St. Mary struggled with its limitations. In 1975 the minister of health and the capital regional hospital district (CRHD) approved another renovation program, tenders were given and work began in September to upgrade the kitchen and other areas and to add another elevator.

So a new Mount St. Mary did not emerge during the 1970s and 1980s. These years were consumed instead with providing the best care possible, under continued financial restraint. Attempting to contain hospital costs and services with a constant occupancy rate of 99 percent was a challenge. The cost of food and commodities continually rose through the early 1980s, when there was an inflationary rise in the cost of consumer goods and a dramatic spiral in interest rates.[350] Where possible, generic drugs were used, good fiscal management practised and vigilance and control exercised, and throughout these years the hospital maintained its accreditation rating. The hospital also had to contend with bodies such as BCHIS, the ministry of health, the CRHD and the various unions.

At the end of June 1975, Sister Mary Justinian retired after ten years as administrator. This Irish-born woman excelled at nursing; Sister colleagues recalled that "later as administrator of hospital facilities owned by our Congregation she never let the management aspects of her role distract her from the primary purposes of these hospitals—the Christian care of the sick."[351] She was succeeded by Sister Mary Laurena (Sister Mary Powell), who had previously worked as director of nursing. Sister Mary Laurena held a bachelor of science in nursing education and diplomas in nursing and hospital administration.

Sister Mary Laurena remained as administrator until her death in 1989, except for a short break when Sister Thérèse Brousseau was acting administrator. The end of Sister Mary Laurena's long history in health care facilities operated by the Sisters of St. Ann also ended the full-time presence of a Sister as administrator at Mount St. Mary Hospital. Sister Thérèse Brousseau was made acting administrator again, until the first lay chief executive officer (CEO) was appointed September 1, 1990. Sister Thérèse Brousseau moved to Begbie House, a building purchased by the Sisters for use as apartments, general office space and to house their archives, on December 16, 1991, and Sister Mary Kevin to St. Ann's Residence, leaving the Mount with no Sisters in residence.[352]

Around this time, religious communities across Canada were putting their various facilities into separate societies. In October 1990 the Sisters had the Marie Esther Society incorporated under the BC Society Act as the registered owner of the real property of Mount St. Mary Hospital. The Sister directors of this society would appoint the board of management, vested with the management, administration and operation of the hospital's affairs. This model remained until June 24, 2008, when a change of governance was adopted and announced at the annual general meeting, at which time the congregation appointed one Sister and four laypeople as members to the society. The members continue to appoint the board of directors. There is no formal link between the hospital and the local Sisters of St. Ann, although they continue their interest and support.[353]

*   *   *

The BC government department responsible for hospital programs initiated extended-care reviews in November 1990, and conducted a comprehensive evaluation of Mount St. Mary. The hospital's strengths and limitations were reviewed and assessed; areas requiring change were identified, and among other things, recommendations were made for additions or reductions to funding allocations. Though the administrator, director of finance, director of nursing and the confidential secretary proved a strong management team, the review committee found each performed too many functions and wore too many hats. Additional staff were needed and it was suggested that a strategic plan would enhance service.[354]

> Under the leadership of volunteer boards and committees the hospital currently maintains a dynamic professional staff augmented in its efforts by sound principles of health care, contemporary theories of hospital administration, unlimited access to health care consultants, and extensive support networks among like facilities.[355]

With this statement, Mount St. Mary began the 1990s. A quality assurance/risk management committee was struck and began to give regular reports. Accreditation status was awarded again, and negotiations were ongoing with the unions. Various renovations and reorganizations were carried out to provide necessary care and a "community bathing program" was initiated to provide non-residents with access to safe bathing. The board held a retreat to establish a long-term strategic plan, and members of the ethics committee attended pertinent workshops. Externally the hospital maintained its membership in various professional bodies and associations, but suffered through the attempts toward regionalization in the capital regional district, which effectively halted any effort to planning new construction. J.B. McMahon retired as CEO in March 1996 and was replaced on April 1 by Colleen Black,[356] a woman able to contend with the complexities of dealing with the BC health care system as a new hospital was planned. When she retired in 2006, she commented that the previous ten years had been the best of her forty-four-year career because the mission of the Sisters of St. Ann was so close to her own. "I am proud to have been associated with the Sisters' mission," she said in a 2009 interview. "The Sisters have compassionate hearts."[357]

The need for a new facility was urgent. Talks ensued between the various bodies involved. City Spaces Consulting presented a plan, adopted in 2000, for subdividing and developing the former St. Joseph's property in the so-called Humboldt Valley. The Sisters' earlier condition that this site be used in perpetuity for health care now came into play. A final memorandum of understanding (MOU) concerning the Fairfield Health Centre (FHC) and Mount St. Mary redevelopment was signed by the health minister, the capital health region (CHR—now VIHA), the CRHD and the Marie Esther Society (MES) on June 9, 1999. It included the stipulation that the project would cover the costs for demolishing the old hospital and remediation of the site. All parties acknowledged the gifting of the Fairfield site by the Sisters of St. Ann, conditional on its use for health care purposes, and recognized that the current gross value exceeded $10 million. All of these parties would have the responsibility for the redevelopment, design and construction.[358]

A project building committee was struck, consisting of one representative from each group. The site was subdivided into three parcels:

- Parcel 1 was to be rezoned and sold for a use not yet determined.[359]
- Parcel 2 would be sold also. It would include the original "X" wing and chapel, to be retained as a significant heritage site.
- Parcel 3, where the school of nursing was situated, would be the location of the new multi-level, 150-bed care facility, financed by the BC government and the CRHD.

A 2001 painting by Robert Amos of the original Mount St. Mary Hospital on Burdett Street. This building was demolished and the property sold when the new hospital was built and opened in 2003. FROM THE MOUNT ST. MARY COLLECTION, WITH PERMISSION FROM ROBERT AMOS

As the new millennium began and the Sisters of St. Ann celebrated the 150th anniversary of their foundation and the 100th of the school of nursing, about a hundred former graduates gathered on the grounds on February 17, 2000, along with politicians, religious leaders and others before deconstruction of the hospital and nursing school began. Community archivist Sister Margaret Cantwell symbolically brandished the trowel used to lay the original cornerstone of St. Joseph's Hospital in order to recall the long history of the Sisters at this location. Ada McKenzie, the oldest living graduate, recalled her many years as a student nurse and later as head nurse on maternity. With the completion of the restoration at St. Ann's Academy and its grounds two years before, this property's rebirth became a testimony to the significant historical connection of the Sisters.[360] Environmentally friendly, respectful deconstruction took five months, removing reusable and saleable equipment. Fred Worthington, CHR director of support services, was quoted in the *Times Colonist* of May 16, 2000, as saying: "We sold industrial items such as washers, dryers, ovens and freezers. We donated beds to China and Bosnia. We didn't donate any risky or outdated equipment, or gear that could be misused."

The government's announcement in May 2000 of an increase in beds from 150 to 200 confirmed the hints given at the earlier ceremony. These extra beds were expected to add $5.3 million to the original cost estimate of $26.3 million. Jensen Group Architects designed a new model of multi-dimensional care, meeting with the staff design advisory group of Mount St. Mary as well as the residents' council, envisioning a new way of caring for residents in small groupings, with flexibility in lifestyle choices for residents of varying backgrounds and religious affiliations. The group was invited to suggest themes and names for the twelve "houses" in the new building.[361] The board approved them in May 2000:

- second floor, Nature
- third floor, History
- fourth floor, Saints
- fifth floor, Virtues.[362]

In June 2000 the cornerstone was removed intact from the "C" wing of St. Joseph's and was eventually placed in the new gardens. The time capsule, made of copper and sealed with lead, was found underneath the cornerstone and given to the Sisters' archives.

Government funding did not provide for a chapel or residents' garden. Considering spiritual care an integral part of residents' life, the Sisters took responsibility for providing these amenities. The funding campaign raised $500,000 in private donations to build the Blessed Marie Anne Blondin Chapel and Blondin Green. On Sunday, March

Salvaged from the original Mount St. Mary, this 1941 stained glass window, donated by the contractor Archie Sullivan and his wife, was re-installed in the chapel door of the new 2003 hospital. It depicts St. John the Evangelist and Jesus' mother Mary standing at the foot of the cross. SSAA P0011

23, 2003, Bishop Raymond Roussin, SM (Society of Mary), blessed the new chapel. He applauded the Sisters: "The hospital not only shows the sisters being faithful, but demonstrates the Church's ongoing respect for life and dignity we recognize in each person, particularly the elderly."[363]

Donor names are displayed on large shards of Italian Carrera marble from the altar of St. Joseph's Hospital Chapel, and more of the marble was used to make the new altar and the pedestals for the tabernacle and the statue of Our Lady. The stained-glass doors donated by Archie Sullivan in 1941 were transferred from the old chapel to the new, and stained-glass windows rescued from St. Joseph's and the school of nursing chapels were installed. More historical stained glass was installed throughout the main floor. Some of the arching windows from St. Joseph's frame archival display cases along the hall leading past the therapy areas to the administrative wing. Overseeing this hall hangs a large familiar portrait of Dr. John Sebastian Helmcken, remembered for his support of the Sisters' enterprise. Entry to the library is through doors salvaged from the school of nursing chapel, and the teak walls are from the Helmcken and Providence Rooms in the old St. Joseph's. Incorporating these historical artifacts into the new Mount St. Mary has given the building a feeling of rootedness and permanence that many modern buildings lack.

The official opening celebrations took place on March 24, 2003. Colleen Black, CEO, introduced various dignitaries, including Katherine Whittred, minister of state for intermediate, long-term and home care, who said:

> The new Mount St. Mary Hospital is an excellent example of the type of facility our government envisions for patients with complex care needs. Having seniors living in their own homes within a larger facility shows tremendous sensitivity and honours the need for a sense of community at this stage of life.[364]

Sister Marie Zarowny, province leader, presented a large golden key to resident representatives Mary Sangster and George McCaskill. Colleen Black had put out a request to the public for pianos. Within five days, sixteen pianos—one for each of the sixteen "houses" that existed by then—and a grand piano for the "village square" had been donated. Such a response from the community demonstrated the wide support Mount St. Mary enjoys.

Tours were available to visit the sixteen "houses" on four floors, each cued to house location by four colour schemes and the "house" name outside each "front door." Each so-called house has twelve or thirteen residents, who enjoy private rooms, each room having a bathroom ensuite, with shower; a ceiling-mounted lift; and a "memory box" at the door (a memory box could include favourite family photos and personal mementoes).

All that remained was to move in. On March 27, 2003, members of the military from the Esquimalt naval base wheeled residents up Quadra Street to their new $31-million home. Since the average age of the staff was forty-eight, the strong backs of these young volunteers were welcome. The staff had their opportunity to share memories and say farewell to the old hospital during a potluck dinner in the old building on April 5.

The good stewardship of all parties involved was acknowledged at a luncheon on August 3, 2004, when Sister Patricia Donovan, province co-leader, presented cheques to Don Amos, CRHD chair, and Rick Roger, CEO at VIHA, sharing 40 percent and 60 percent respectively of the remaining proceeds of the sale of properties on the Fairfield Health Centre site, for a total of $4,777,479.24. Sisters Ann Thomson and Sheila Moss, with Colleen Black, CEO of Mount St. Mary, members of the project building committee and Gwyn Symmons, head of City Spaces Consulting firm that drew up the plans for dividing the property, were also there to see the fulfillment of the commitment made in the memorandum of understanding returning the money for future health care purposes.[365]

The Sisters' pastoral care involvement continued in the new building. In the 1990s, a Sister would visit each resident once weekly, spending extra time with the newly admitted or the dying and their families. She would arrange ecumenical prayer services and lead memorial services for residents who had died recently. One or two would attend ethics conferences and Victoria Hospice workshops. Death was not their only focus. They took the opportunity to celebrate new life, arranging for staff and residents to bless expectant mothers who were on staff, as well as their babies.[366] Today Sisters Sheila Moss and Lucy DuMont carry on the ministry, serving on the mission team, and Sister Assunta Campese works as the pastoral care minister. Sister Frieda Raab, in her role as a member of the Marie Esther

Society, holds particular responsibility for the safeguarding of the mission of Mount St. Mary.

In March 2005 the Mount St. Mary Foundation was erected under the watchful eye of foundation CEO Mandy Parker. Government funding covered only a fraction of the cost of much-needed comforts, so private donations were solicited. An endowment fund called The Sisters of St. Ann Legacy Fund was inaugurated in April 2007. The Sisters' generous donation of $500,000 in January 2008 led the way for others to follow. One of their number, Sister Lucy DuMont—former pastoral care co-ordinator—had already launched into fundraising by setting herself the goal of walking in the October Royal Victoria Half Marathon (21.1 kilometres, or about 13.1 miles). She walked her first half-marathon in 2006, after which Councillor Chris Coleman accepted her challenge to walk in

Sister Lucy DuMont and her friend City Councillor Chris Coleman in the midst of walking the Victoria half-marathon, a now annual fundraising venture for the Mount St. Mary Foundation. In 2010 the "Marythoners" raised over $80,000. FROM THE MOUNT ST. MARY COLLECTION

2007 and again in 2008, when they were joined by other Mount St. Mary supporters sporting "We Love Lucy" buttons. The donations have risen every year—from $17,000 in 2006 to $25,000 in 2007, $29,000 in 2008 and more than $80,000 in 2010—with all proceeds used to provide special mattresses, commodes and so forth.[367]

Residents and their families often express appreciation for the dedicated care received in their new home. Janet Lowe, a former student of the Sisters whose father Dan Maloney was a resident in the old hospital and eagerly anticipated the move to the new, said her dad felt immediately at home in his new surroundings. "He loved the layout of the facility which encouraged socialization and a sense of community with the many activities offered."[368] And he spoke highly of the staff, who seem imbued with the same values of those who founded the Mount.

Sister Mary Ellen King, St. Ann's congregational leader visiting from Lachine, stated at the official opening in the new building: "We have a tradition of compassionate health care that is deeply rooted in this site."[369] The vision lives on.

PART THREE

Small Hospital Births and Deaths

St. Martin's Hospital, Oliver. SSAA P0300

Chapter 9

Our Lady of Lourdes Hospital, Campbell River

The ultimate goal of our care is to give those who are ill, through our care, a reason to hope.
                              —Joseph Cardinal Bernardin

Fifty years after opening St. Joseph's Hospital the Sisters of St. Ann accepted the responsibility of a second BC hospital, in the small settlement of Campbell River, 185 miles north of Victoria. The citizens had appealed to Bishop Thomas O'Donnell to secure the services of the Sisters of St. Ann and, with the approval of Mother Mary Leopoldine, the superior general in Lachine, three Sisters embarked on this new mission: Sister Mary Mark, past administrator of St. Joseph's Hospital; Sister Mary Gerard Majella, provincial bursar; and Sister Mary Leo, a registered nurse. The Sisters sailed from Victoria to Vancouver, and from there on the *Princess Beatrice* to Campbell River, which they reached on February 11, 1926, the anniversary of the first appearance of Mary to Bernadette Soubirous (who would become Saint Bernadette) at Lourdes, France. It was a fitting beginning for a hospital that would be named Our Lady of Lourdes.[370]

At this time Campbell River consisted of a vacated hospital, a general store, hotel, garage and post office and about twenty homes. The village took its name from the nearby river, which in turn had been named after Samuel Campbell, assistant surgeon on the surveying vessel HMS *Plumper* from 1857 to 1861. The village began July 1, 1904, when Charles Thulin opened Willows Hotel on the bank of the river to serve fishermen and loggers. By 1914 the Thulin family owned all the private businesses and land in the downtown area. Charles Thulin and his wife Mary donated land on a hillside overlooking Discovery Passage and helped raise funds to build a hospital that opened on June 6, 1914.[371]

The First World War, the Spanish flu pandemic and Prohibition (1917–20) adversely affected the Thulins. Many individuals owed them money, and the hospital itself was in debt to them for more than $3,000. When the Credit Men's Association foreclosed on these debts on behalf of the Vancouver wholesalers in 1923, it was a huge economic blow. The hospital was not sustainable and its doors closed in 1924.

The three Sisters arrived in 1926 to complete negotiations for the financial and legal transfer of the Thulin property and to reopen the hospital under the auspices of the Sisters of St. Ann. They met with the former hospital board to reach an agreement on the terms and though the board was willing to authorize the transfer, the Sisters wished the local community to be consulted. A public meeting held March 10, 1926, drew two hundred representatives of the town, the logging companies and their workmen, as well as C.H. O'Halloran, the Congregation of the Sisters of St. Ann's lawyer from Victoria. A resolution was passed to convey the property—valued at $10,000—to the Sisters and they were presented with the title deed. They now assumed responsibility for any immediately needed repairs. There was much to be done.

Previously the Sisters had a written guarantee from three major logging companies to deduct 25 cents a week from the pay of their approximately seven hundred workers, as well as provide further financial aid if required. In return for 20 percent of these workers' fees, the two doctors in Campbell River—W. Richardson and R. Ziegler—agreed to take care of all medical cases without further charge. All accident cases would be looked after by the BC Workmen's Compensation Board at a rate of $2.50 per day. The hospital seemed to be financially well secured once there was the expectation of other logging companies joining the plan and the formation of a board, consisting of five Sisters of St. Ann, three representatives of the logging companies and one government-appointed member (a provincial government requirement in order to receive government funds).

Though the hospital had been closed for two years, it was still quite clean and orderly, with curtains on the windows, linen stored in cupboards and a supply of pharmaceuticals on hand. However, there was some flooding because of a combination of leaking water pipes and radiators having been left open, so everything was damp; this meant fires had to be kept going day and night for several weeks in order to dry the place out. Repairs began with rebuilding the kitchen floor, upgrading the plumbing, placing the cottage on a foundation so it could be used as a morgue and providing accommodation for an orderly. Excavation of the basement began in July, to extend the main building's foundation in order to provide suitable quarters for staff, space for a chapel and additional space for the existing kitchen and pantry.

Things moved quickly, though. The first three patients arrived on February 21, all of them with broken bones. The majority of Lourdes patients came from the logging camps, often with horrible injuries. On June 21, 1926, for example, a logger was admitted after being injured in a dynamite explosion, and ended up having to have his left hand and part of his right amputated.[372] A patient with a badly broken leg developed gas gangrene and died. The lack of a completely equipped operating room did not prevent the success of an appendectomy in October 1926, and in early January the next year the two doctors successfully performed the first new

Our Lady of Lourdes Hospital in 1929. Not having the funds to maintain a hospital themselves, the people of Campbell River asked the Sisters of St. Ann to take it on in 1926. SSAA P0071

bone technique on a patient with two breaks in one leg, installing a silver plate to unite and keep bone fragments in place.[373] Aside from surgical problems, many medical conditions developed. The staff treated typhoid fever and infantile paralysis (polio), and even put up a tent in the woods to isolate a smallpox patient. The hospital was so busy that space was at a premium. The Sisters were on call twenty-four hours a day, and at times one of them was getting up from a bed just as another was ready to fall into it.

Sister Mary Alfreda came as superior to replace Sister Mary Mark in July 1926. She supervised the repairs to the home on the adjacent Carruthers property that had been purchased in June 1927 to provide housing for the Sisters, nurses and a chaplain, as well as a permanent chapel. Bishop O'Donnell forwarded $600 that had been donated to the Catholic Church Extension Society by F.W. Dobell to furnish a chapel dedicated to Saint Teresa of Lisieux in memory of his wife.[374] This chapel was the first Catholic church in Campbell River, and would remain so until St. Patrick's parish was built on land donated by Ann and Roderick Haig-Brown and blessed by Bishop James Hill on May 12, 1957. In October 1927 the cottage was ready and the Sisters and lay nurses moved into the refurbished "Floracita Cottage."

Clearly more space was needed. Sister Mary Osithe came in August 1928 to work on plans for a new wing. That October, Twizel & Twizel of Vancouver were chosen as architects, and in June 1929 the plans for the new wing were examined and approved by the board and the contract awarded to Archie Sullivan for $54,000. Previously the hospital had purchased Dr. Ziegler's house, as well as a small piece of land in front of the hospital and another adjacent property, and received the provincial government's promise of a $17,000 grant. On May 29, 1929, Father G.R. Quinlan turned the sod for the new wing with the same spade that had been used to turn the first sod at St. Joseph's Hospital in Victoria, and by 5 p.m. that day excavating had begun. Father Quinlan blessed the new chapel and other rooms in the new wing on December 12. The official opening was held the next day, attended by one hundred guests despite a howling blizzard. Those present included Mother Mary Dorothy, provincial superior; Sister Mary Mildred, superior of St. Joseph's Hospital; Sister Mary Mark, who had opened the hospital in 1926; and A.S. Lamb, operator of Lamb Lumber Company, representing the government. A four-piece orchestra

To relieve crowding in the hospital, in 1927 the Sisters purchased the adjacent Carruthers property as a residence for the Sisters, nurses and a chaplain. It was known as "Floracita Cottage." SSAA P0072

from Cumberland provided entertainment and refreshments were served by the women's auxiliary.[375]

The new wing increased the capacity of the hospital to forty-two beds. A wide veranda running the length of the new addition afforded a magnificent vista of Discovery Passage, with a view of the ships bound for Alaska and coastal British Columbia. Donors included Robert and Jennie Butchart of Victoria, who furnished the sunroom; the Hudson's Bay Company, which gave complete furnishings for the parlour; and Archie Sullivan and his wife, who furnished another complete room. The total cost of building was $95,937.49, of which $68,981.86 had been borrowed from the bank and other sources.[376] The hospital was now able to fill the medical needs of the largest centre of logging operations in British Columbia.

*　*　*

Many in the logging industry supported Lourdes hospital and the Sisters. One who stood out was Roger Cobb, manager of the International Timber Company, a company whose assets were acquired by the Elk River Timber

Company just before the Depression. Cobb donated $5,000 to help with the initial repairs, sent a high rigger to paint the flagpole and floated a boom of seventy-two logs to the hospital with a winter supply of wood in September 1934. After a one-day stay in hospital, he personally donated more money and continued to send a yearly supply of wood from the camp. Twice he donated shingles—once to repair the roof of the original building and a second time in 1939 to fix the roof of the newer section.[377] At a time when the companies were faced with a downturn in the market, the rise of unionism, the Depression, a reduction in the number of employees and a salary drop of the loggers from $4.50 to $2 a day,[378] the hospital experienced a drop in revenue but still flourished with support from the community.

Supporters included the Anglican community of Quathiaski Cove, on the southwest corner of Quadra Island, whose pastor—a Rev. Green—for years delivered an abundance of fruit and vegetables from the community's fall fair. The local game warden brought deer meat that had been confiscated from illegal hunting and local aboriginal people gave salmon in gratitude for care received by their family members. The Sisters owned a cow and chickens themselves, to provide milk and eggs. Other friends donated "crates and crates" of produce, which was preserved at canning bees.[379] From the beginning a grotto dedicated to Our Lady of Lourdes

Built in 1933 in honour of the appearance of the Virgin Mary in Lourdes, France, the grotto became a favourite "haven for contemplation and solitude." SSAA P0123

had been a dream. It remained a dream until 1933, when B.B. Bryan, another grateful patient, visiting from New York, donated $300 specifically for this purpose. A man who had been hired to build a chimney was contracted to build the grotto with the help of the hospital handyman. These men asked each other, "Do you know anything about building grottoes?" and decided between them that it was "sort of like an upside down boat cut in half."[380] They built three models before hitting the right shape. The resulting "haven for contemplation and solitude," with statues of Mary and Saint Bernadette in niches, was apparently a delight to everyone.[381]

The town's support was reciprocated by the Sisters. In appreciation for the builders of the new wing, they prepared and served lunch to all the workers. Following the disastrous Sayward forest fire originating at the Bloedel, Stewart & Welch timber camp, which raged for six weeks in the summer of 1938, destroyed 74,495 acres, threatened a number of timber camps and the town itself,[382] the Sisters celebrated a Thanksgiving Mass for those grateful for being spared.[383] Throughout the Depression years and beyond, they made charity visits to local poor families. They held an open house on the annual Hospital Day in May, welcoming visitors to enjoy their hospitality, tour the hospital and ask any questions they might have. When the Red Cross sponsored home nursing classes in 1940, Sister Mary Kathleen and Sister Mary Grace taught them in the hospital. On Mother's Day that same year they held services for those mothers whose sons were at war. On Hospital Day in May 1942 they sponsored a memorial service in tribute to the nurses of Canada who had sacrificed their lives in the service of their country in both world wars, and flew the

(l–r) Sister Mary Martha, Sister Mary Freda and Sister Mary Kathleen pose for a picture in front of the hospital in the late 1920s. SSAA P0120

flag at half-mast.[384] Always, they welcomed all visitors with warmth and generosity.

Even in the far reaches of the British Empire, small hospitals such as Lourdes were remembered on the occasion of the Queen's coronation in 1953. On Coronation Day—June 2—the governor general offered silver spoons to all babies born that day. Lourdes Hospital delivered four Coronation Day babies, all of whom were born within the space of just nineteen minutes—twin boys and two girls.[385]

Fluctuation in bed occupancy led staff to perform other than their normal duties. Orderly Dupré was able to paint the wards and halls when the patient load was down. And the Sisters filled in wherever help was needed. If the basement flooded, the Sisters were in there bailing with everyone else. In December 1928 a huge storm blew smoke back down the kitchen chimney, causing the stove to smoke and making it necessary to prepare meals elsewhere. When the storm abated, Sister Mary Kathleen and the orderly took the pipes down, cleaned them—covering themselves in soot in the process—and put the pipes up again.[386]

Many of their patients came as the result of emergencies. On October 8, 1935, there was a locomotive accident involving many of the crew at the Campbell River Timber Company camp. The Sisters' archives reveal the difficulties of that day:

> From 8 o'clock, when the first load of battered humanity arrived, till 11:30 the ambulance sped back and forth bringing its burden of injured but bravely smiling men. Only the most seriously hurt were brought to the hospital, dozens being treated at camp for minor injuries. Doctors and nurses worked steadily all day setting limbs, cleansing and binding wounds, striving to alleviate pain, and still there was work for the morrow.[387]

One who nursed such patients was Irene Wheldon, a young woman who had trained at St. Joseph's School of Nursing then arrived at Lourdes as a nurse in 1927 where she worked under the mentorship of Sister Mary Alfreda and lived in the Floracita Cottage next door. In 1934 she entered the novitiate in Victoria, much against her mother's wishes and as Sister Miriam Theresa she returned years later to nurse. She noted in an interview that the patients were mainly the victims of logging accidents, many of them needing to be transferred to Vancouver accompanied by a nurse, a duty she sometimes performed.[388]

Further evidence of the urgency of the cases comes from Bob Langdon, a pilot for BC Airlines who arrived in Campbell River in 1946. As the book *River City* notes:

> His clippings tell of endless daring rescues in gale-force winds and zero visibility, transporting injured loggers, farmers and pregnant women from the outlying islands and inlets to the Lourdes Hospital . . . Langdon and his crew made an average of four flights a week for stretcher cases, 90 percent of them from logging camps where time can mean the difference between life and death.[389]

Throughout its life Lourdes hospital struggled financially, the Sisters and staff doing the best with what they had and enduring hardships uncomplainingly. It was November 1944 when the first elevator was installed, which meant an end to much hauling and climbing up long corridors and stairways. Some logging companies and the BC Workmen's Compensation Board were slow to pay their accounts and when patient revenue was down, the hospital would borrow in order to make the monthly payroll.[390] A Royal Canadian Air Force pilot downed in an accident in the river swallowed a great deal of water and gasoline. The hospital had not been able to afford to have an iron lung on hand, so staff were forced to apply artificial respiration manually for three hours. Some patients were cared for over many years without paying. One woman died in February 1948 after being a patient since September 1941.[391] The hospital suffered from an erratic water system until August 1948, when pipes for a municipal water system were laid. In February 1952, the hospital accountant reported uncollected accounts receivable of $22,000. No wonder they had trouble meeting expenses.

* * *

In 1952 local people felt the hospital was inadequate for the needs of a population that was expected to double within a few years after the June opening of the Elk Falls Mill. A committee was struck, which resulted in the formation of a hospital society to study the needs and discuss plans for a new hospital. On October 9, 1953, Lourdes' board met with members of the newly formed hospital society to be informed of the society's plans for a new building. On October 21 Mother Mary Luca, provincial superior, met with both groups and announced that the Sisters of St. Ann would be unable to finance a new hospital. They discussed opening Lourdes as a home for the aged, but this did not materialize.

The new Campbell River and District General Hospital opened on September 7, 1957. On Saturday, September 21, a constant stream of friends arrived at Our Lady of Lourdes Hospital to say thank you and goodbye to the Sisters who had served them for thirty-one years. The chamber of commerce presented a scroll expressing gratitude to the Sisters. Representatives of the women's auxiliary that had organized teas and other fundraisers throughout the years hosted this final tea. Mary Thulin, now ninety-two years old, recalled the beginning of the auxiliary when she was its first president in 1926, and Mrs. Ann Haig-Brown, the last president, expressed the sorrow of all that the Sisters were leaving.

The municipality purchased the property in 1958. During the long interim between the transfer of patients to the new hospital and before the sale to Campbell River, the Sisters of St. Ann maintained a caretaker and paid the taxes, the cost of heating the building and other maintenance expenses.[392] At last municipal offices moved into the addition in 1960, and shortly afterwards the old section was torn down. Lourdes Hospital was demolished in 1982.

Chapter 10

Bulkley Valley District Hospital (Sacred Heart Hospital), Smithers

All who have been involved in the work of the hospital are
certainly entitled to the reward promised by Christ when
He said: What you do for the least of mine, you do for me.

—Sister Mary Colombe-de-Jesus
speaking to Smithers Rotary Club

"Smithers accepted," proclaimed the telegram. In this brief exclamation Mother Mary Leopoldine, the provincial, received permission from the motherhouse in Lachine to develop a new hospital in the interior of British Columbia in March 1933. This would be the Sisters of St. Ann's third health care mission in British Columbia.

Smithers and the Early Years

Smithers, a picturesque oasis located in the shadow of the majestic snow-topped Hudson Bay Mountain, deep in the fertile Bulkley Valley region of British Columbia, was originally the home of the Carrier First Nation, who called it the Watsonquah Valley. The first non-aboriginal exploration of the area came in 1864 during a survey by Colonel Charles S. Bulkley—formerly a communications expert with the Union Army during the American Civil War[393]—for the ill-fated Collins Overland Telegraph line. However, Smithers' strongest and more permanent roots lie in the development of another communication link, the Grand Trunk Pacific Railway (GTP).

Smithers was founded in 1913 as the divisional point of the GTP, which was nearing completion of 3,000 miles of main line from Winnipeg, Manitoba, to Prince Rupert, British Columbia. Despite its grandiose plans, which included a line of coastal steamships based in Prince Rupert, the GTP did not realize its expected revenue and declared bankruptcy soon after the First World War began.[394] The Canadian government assumed control of the railway in 1919 and merged it with the Canadian Northern Railway to form the Canadian National Railways. During the GTP's active years in the Bulkley Valley, the board chair was a British citizen, Sir Alfred Waldron Smithers (1850–1924), whose heritage is reflected in the naming of the village.

In anticipation of the railway, the Bulkley Valley, with its magnificent pristine landscape, attracted immigrants from Eastern Canada and from as far away as Europe, most notably Switzerland. The area was rich in mineral and forest resources and its land attracted farmers, including some who started dairy operations. With this growth came an increasing demand for medical services. Dr. Horace Cooper Wrinch (1866–1939), who had trained in Toronto, came to British Columbia as a medical missionary for the Methodist Church, and served the Bulkley Valley's medical needs from his home in Hazelton that sometimes doubled as a hospital. As well as serving the medical needs of the community, he was the local member of the Legislative Assembly from 1924 to 1933.[395] In the early years, because he was the only doctor within a 100-mile radius, he was often unavailable.

With this need, as well as concerns over the unsanitary conditions of the drainage ditch that ran through the centre of the village, the arrival of the first permanent doctor was welcome news. Dr. Cecil Hazen Hankinson (1890–1949), a graduate of Montreal's prestigious medical school at McGill University, set up practice on July 19, 1919, to serve a Bulkley Valley population that had increased from 1,000 to 1,500 by 1920. Despite agitation for a local hospital since 1915, the community did not have one so Dr. Hankinson set up practice above the J. Mason Adams drugstore on Main Street, a location that Dr. Wrinch had used on his weekly visits to Smithers, but he soon moved his practice to the community hall. Ten years later, in 1929, he moved to Prince Rupert and later served as president of the British Columbia Medical Association from 1941 to 1942.[396] Both Drs. Hankinson and Wrinch advocated the introduction of health care insurance, a universal benefit not realized until the late 1940s. Little more than a year after Dr. Hankinson arrived, the Smithers Citizens Association established the first hospital, with a recognized hospital board, in a former private home located on the southwest corner of King Street and Second Avenue not far from Main Street. On September 1, 1920, the hospital, with a capacity for a dozen patients, was officially opened at a cost of about $6,000.

Not until December 1921 did Smithers become an incorporated village, but the area continued to develop throughout the 1920s. One of the major land promoters was Francis Mawson Rattenbury, the architect who designed the BC legislative buildings and the Empress Hotel in Victoria. His Rattenbury Land Company was one of a few major partners in schemes to settle the valley. New farmers arrived with modern equipment such as milking machines and tractors, and a cold-storage plant was built for meat. The increasing population meant the area had more medical needs.

By early 1933 the Depression and local problems caused by the destruction of many businesses by fire meant the hospital board found it impossible to carry on. Board members looked farther afield to find some group able to build and manage a new facility. Having heard of the work of the Sisters of St. Ann in Victoria, the hospital board appealed to Bishop Émile-Marie Bunoz, OMI (Oblates of Mary Immaculate), who was bishop of the vicariate of the Yukon and Prince Rupert, to petition the Sisters of St. Ann to build and operate a new hospital. The French-born bishop arrived in British Columbia in 1891 shortly after his ordination and quickly learned the Chinook language so he might communicate with the aboriginal people of the coast. The board assured the Sisters of their confidence and support and that of the Smithers community. They proposed that the estimated $24,000 cost of the new hospital should be shared equally among the Sisters of Saint Ann, the Village of Smithers and the Province of British Columbia.[397]

*   *   *

The Sisters moved quickly. Within two weeks of receiving Bishop Bunoz's request on March 6, 1933, Mother Mary Leopoldine had gained approval from Lachine to build this new hospital. Bishop Bunoz was delighted with the news, which he joyfully described as "one more brilliant unit added to your numerous and glorious undertakings on the pioneer line."[398] Father P. Cozanet, OMI, pastor of St. Joseph's parish in Smithers, also rejoiced and hastened to assure the Sisters that, "if there is some little opposition on the part of a few, their opinion does not carry any weight."[399] As the hospital board had initiated contact with the Sisters it would seem that the citizens generally approved of this move. Indeed, Mayor S. Mayer of Smithers[400] informed the provincial secretary in Victoria, whose portfolio included health care, that the Sisters of St. Ann would be taking charge of the new hospital project and would have the authority to deal with the ministry in Victoria.

The support of the townspeople took a practical form. Despite the Depression, individuals, businesses, charitable groups and government came forward with much material to help furnish and equip the new hospital. J.B. Kirby donated three lots to complete the block to be occupied by the new hospital. The women's auxiliary, which had so long supported the original Bulkley Valley District Hospital, agreed to continue its work with the new hospital. The members welcomed the Sisters and honoured the departing matron, a Miss Ballantyne, with a tea and presentation of gifts as a way of marking the transition from the old to the new.

When Mother Mary Leopoldine and Sister Mary Ludovic, superior of St. Joseph's Hospital in Victoria, visited Smithers to see the situation first-hand and to conclude negotiations, they were filled with hope for the success of this newest endeavour to save souls and serve the people of God. On her return to Victoria, Mother Mary Leopoldine expressed a "Deo gratias [Thanks be to God]" for the favourable conditions surrounding the new hospital, which included the "good will of the forty Catholic families" and pleasure at the location and donation of the property for the new facility. On May 5, 1933, the hospital board and the Sisters of St. Ann signed an agreement to transfer all the current hospital holdings to the Sisters. For their part, the Sisters agreed to build the hospital for not less than $25,000.[401] This proved to be a gross underestimate of the cost, which later rose to $60,000. The Sisters were to carry this extra financial burden for a long time.

Construction work began immediately under the supervision of Sister Mary Osithe and Sister Mary Francis of Jesus, provincial bursar in

Victoria. Sister Mary Osithe, who was already renowned for her varied artistic skills and was essentially a self-taught architect, sketched out the plans. While in the novitiate in Lachine she had studied under Sister Mary Helen of the Cross, William Raphael (1833–1914) and Edmond Dyonnet (1859–1954). Sister Osithe had made her religious profession on July 12, 1894, and came west in 1897 to head the art department at St. Ann's Academy in Victoria, a position she filled for almost forty years—the only gap being the eighteen months she served as superior at Little Flower Academy in Vancouver.[402] Her talents extended to oil painting, watercolour, china painting,

An artist and self-taught architect, Sister Mary Osithe designed a number of buildings for the Sisters, including the new Smithers hospital. SSAA P0327

calligraphy, photography and architecture. Her reputation grew beyond the convent and drew many Victorians, mainly women, to her art program, where she taught students, recorded their efforts and sold necessary art supplies. In 1912 Sister Mary Osithe began doing architectural plans. She designed the gymnasium for St. Ann's Academy in Victoria; drew up plans for a new laundry at the convent in Nanaimo; and designed an addition to St. Joseph's Hospital in Victoria and for Little Flower Academy in Vancouver, built in 1931, which was the most ambitious and satisfying of her projects. With such illustrious credentials it would seem natural to ask her to put the vision of a new Smithers hospital into concrete form.

From her plans, BC government architect Henry Whittaker and his assistant, a Mr. Hargreaves, drafted the final design without extra charge to the Sisters. Archie Sullivan of Vancouver was awarded the contract to build the new hospital in August 1933. He had proven his capability of delivering quality work in time to meet deadlines with the construction of both the Little Flower Academy and Our Lady of Lourdes Hospital in

Campbell River. Since preparation of the land had begun immediately after the Sisters had agreed to come to Smithers, the foundations were in by the end of August. Sullivan felt strong ties to the Sisters and their endeavours. He donated the chapel altar and a tabernacle with a door of gold. On discovering that he shared his birthdate, April 18, with Mother Mary Ann, the founder of the Sisters of St. Ann, he sent mother provincial large quantities of hyacinths and snapdragons to celebrate the occasion.

Once the foundations were laid, Sisters Mary Osithe and Mary Francis of Jesus went to Vancouver to begin purchasing some of the items that the new hospital would need. En route back to Smithers after a thirty-nine-hour sail they stopped in Prince Rupert, where Bishop Bunoz showed them some of the sights and the Sisters of St. Joseph who ran the parochial school provided hospitality. Then the two Sisters boarded the overnight train to Smithers. Mrs. William Duff, who had earlier hosted mother provincial and Sister Mary Ludovic, provided them with accommodation in Smithers for a week, until they were able to rent and outfit a small cottage, very similar to the 1858 pioneer cottage of the first Sisters of St. Ann in British Columbia. Their expenses for groceries were minimal as the local people kept them supplied with both perishables and non-perishables. Now they were ready to jump in with both feet and commence their ministry in this beautiful location that Sister Mary Osithe's artistic sensibility had once seen as a crater as she described the volcanic region for visitor Father Bernard Hubbard, SJ (Society of Jesus), known as the "Glacier Priest."

Work advanced rapidly on the new hospital, which was situated on an elevation overlooking the town on property the size of a town block. Planning began for the ceremonial laying of the cornerstone, an event that the Sisters, the citizens of Smithers and the surrounding area, and all the workers and officials involved in the building eagerly anticipated. After their arrival on October 28, Mother Marie Dorothée, superior general, Mother Mary Leopoldine, provincial superior, and Sister Mary Geraldine went immediately to the church for Mass and to offer prayers of thanksgiving. Bishop Bunoz arrived from Lejac bearing gifts for the new chapel. Sunday, October 29, 1933, the feast of Christ the King, dawned sunny and mild, illuminated by the light reflecting off the foot of sparkling snow that blanketed the ground. Still, festivities could take place outdoors. It seemed auspicious that this event was taking place in Smithers in the year that the Sisters of St. Ann celebrated their diamond jubilee—seventy-five years of service in British Columbia. The historical importance of this occasion led the Sisters to consider what to include in the cornerstone. A copper box measuring 3 by 10 inches contained an official record of the proceedings; a copy of the October 25, 1933, edition of the Smithers newspaper, the *Interior News*; sacred medals and pictures; postcards of Smithers and the Catholic church; as well as current coins and bills. This copper box was inserted in the middle of the 18- by 24-inch cornerstone bearing a cross in each corner and the inscription:

J.M.J.A.[403]
PRO DEO ET HUMANITATE
BULKLEY VALLEY DISTRICT HOSPITAL
Erected 1933

The Smithers Band entertained at the ceremony, and the St. Joseph's Church choir added to the impressive occasion. The band later contributed much—in pleasure and in funds. It played for the patients at Christmas and special holidays and gave public concerts from which it donated all or part of the proceeds for the improvement of the hospital.

Local residents continued to support the hospital. At the laying of the cornerstone, Dr. R.B. Brummitt, "Exalted Ruler" of the Elks lodge, presented a cheque for $4,000; Rev. L.J. Hale, the minister of St. Stephen's Anglican Church, was present to support the Sisters and in the future he and his parishioners frequently supplied fruit and vegetables from their fall fair and other extras for the patients and staff. Throughout the winter individuals and groups continued to seek ways to assist the hospital by furnishing a room or donating needed items. The donors could select these furnishings or objects from a catalogue and mother provincial would purchase them in Vancouver or Victoria. Touchingly the children of the local public school donated a magazine rack in memory of seventeen-year-old Danny Foster, a young man who had died of an undiagnosed illness earlier in 1933. The *Interior News* wrote that his loss threw "a pall of gloom over the town and district where he was so well known and so highly admired by all." Thus did the community make the hospital part of their lives.

Work continued on the inside of the hospital. By the feast of Our Lady of Lourdes on February 11, 1934, Sisters Mary Francis of Jesus and Mary Geraldine were able to move in. They prepared accommodation for Sisters Mary Henrietta of Jesus, superior; Mary Itha, nurse; and Mary Angelica, who was to be cook. Less than a month later the first patients were brought from the old hospital to the new—a man and a woman, both Protestants, and a Catholic man. The next day, with the transfer of "a Catholic and a charity case . . . the good work begins."[404] One of the first men remained a patient until his death on February on 13, 1935, almost a year after his admission. This was a portent of the future as the hospital had to deal not only with acutely ill patients but also with those requiring long-term care, a costly endeavour.

The Sisters had agreed to build a hospital for not less than $25,000, but costs had escalated to $60,000. On February 25, 1934, Sister Mary Francis of Jesus, the provincial bursar, asked George M. Weir, provincial secretary, for an additional sum to bring the government contribution up to one-third of the cost, its usual policy. To meet the added costs, the Sisters had borrowed $17,000 from the Oblates at an interest rate of 4.5 percent.[405] Although the Oblates waived the interest of $425 that was due and payable on November 3, 1935, because of the Sisters' "straightened [sic] circumstances consequent upon depression and in view of your services to the Oblate Fathers,"[406] the weight of the debt greatly concerned the Sisters. In dealing with the government the Sisters had the support of E.T. Kenney, the local MLA and a supporter of the Liberal government of Premier Thomas Dufferin ("Duff") Pattullo. In November 1935, Kenney urged the government to pay the one-third cost of the hospital construction. The Sisters made a second appeal early in 1936, when the hospital was unable to pay the interest on the money it had borrowed, and only then did the provincial government send a cheque for half the requested amount. In a covering letter, P. Walker, the deputy provincial secretary, entreated the Sisters to keep the matter personal and private, writing: "It would be very unfortunate if there were any public discussion or dispute about this matter."[407] Happily, the government paid the other half in two instalments in April 1937.

On March 22, 1934, the hospital secured a chaplain, the legendary Father Nicolas Coccola, OMI, an Oblate priest of Corsican birth who had worked for many years as a missionary priest to the aboriginal people of British Columbia. After he had spent eleven years ministering in the First Nations reserve of Lejac, he came to be chaplain at Bulkley Valley District Hospital at the age of eighty, and he remained there until his death on March 1, 1943. For well over half a century he had travelled the northern parts of the province serving various aboriginal groups in a dedicated and often courageous manner. His memoirs illuminate the hardships, difficulties and joys experienced by missionaries and the population of these areas.[408] Credit reflected on the hospital when he and Sister Mary Henrietta of Jesus were chosen for the district to receive the

First chaplain of the Bulkley Valley District Hospital, Father Nicolas Coccola, OMI, arrived at the age of eighty, after a long and legendary life among the aboriginal peoples of northern BC. SSAA P0141

King George V Silver Jubilee Medal for outstanding citizenship, presented at a public celebration in Alfred Park in May 1935. Father Coccola's earlier experience in 1882 as chaplain to the Sisters of St. Ann at their school in Kamloops made him feel especially comfortable to serve them in this capacity at their newly opened hospital in Smithers. One of his first joyful acts, on the first Friday of April, was to bless the statue of the Sacred Heart, a gift from the mother general in Lachine, which was placed in the niche prepared for it, facing the entry to the hospital. Henceforth the hospital, though legally named the Bulkley Valley District Hospital, was known to the Sisters as Sacred Heart hospital. Dedication to the Sacred Heart of Jesus imbued all their activities with an elevated purpose.

Although patients had been moved into the new building in March 1934, the harsh winter meant that little could be done about finishing the stuccoing of the building or laying out the grounds. Once spring came, E.T. Kenney and Mayor Mayer arranged to have the government superintendent of public works—a Mr. Cotton—supply the gravel and employ relief men and government machines to do the landscaping and roadwork. By providing jobs, this in turn helped the local economy.

All was in readiness for the official opening of the hospital June 8, 1934, an event eagerly anticipated by the Sisters, the people of the Bulkley Valley and so many others who had been instrumental in the planning and completion of the hospital. Inauguration day was a half-day holiday for the schools and businesses due to the excitement and involvement of so much of the village and surrounding areas. Dignitaries arrived and took their places. The speeches began. Henry Whittaker, the provincial architect, declared the building second to none in all of British Columbia with 90 percent of its material manufactured within the province and 98 percent within the British Empire. J.G. Stephens, "Exalted Ruler" of the Elks, turned over a clear deed to the X-ray and sterilizing equipment. Father Cozanet spoke for the Sisters, extending their gratitude to each individual and group who had contributed to the success of the hospital project. He finished his speech with the Sisters' wish, "May the Giver of every best gift and every perfect gift be most bountiful to all our friends."[409]

With pride, Mother Mary Leopoldine observed what had been accomplished in such a short time since the receipt of the telegram from the motherhouse authorizing the congregation's commitment. When it came time for Bishop Bunoz to bless the hospital he spoke of his great appreciation for the co-operation shown between the public and the Sisters of St. Ann. He repeated earlier commitments made that the new hospital was "a public institution and was for the service of no particular faith nor for any particular school of thought, but was dedicated to the work of alleviating human suffering."[410] That commitment continued throughout the years the Sisters devoted to the Bulkley Valley District Hospital.

To loud applause, E.T. Kenney clipped the ribbon, the band played and the crowd of roughly four hundred entered their hospital to enjoy tea served by the women's auxiliary and to inspect the new facility. The care of patients continued throughout. As if a sign of continuity, the birth of a baby at this very moment completed the joyful celebration.

Gratefully the Sisters expressed appreciation for the generosity of benefactors such as Bishop Bunoz and the Oblates, who donated an equipped private room; Sullivan, the contractor and friend, for the altar; and the women's auxiliary for a beautifully furnished private room; as well as the Girl Guides, the sodality (a lay ecclesiastical organization), the Girls' Athletic Club, the Hudson's Bay Company and all the individuals and businesses who gave so that the hospital might provide health care comparable to the best of the day. Ironically, on one occasion the straitened financial circumstances meant it could not accept a donation. In 1939, Lord Duffield of England offered an iron lung, used for the treatment of polio patients, to all hospitals in the British Empire. Regretfully the board of management turned down this offer because the hospital did not have the income to guarantee transport and to provide the three nurses who would need to be in constant attendance, or to keep an engineer available for maintenance. Fortunately, patients requiring such treatment could be sent to larger centres.[411]

The busy life of the hospital had begun and Sister Mary Henrietta of Jesus and her Sisters found themselves immediately immersed in all the activities particular to this life. They dealt with the government through a hospital inspector named McCrae, who examined the books, especially the admission and dismissal rates, and a Dr. McQuarrie who consulted with hospital officials on the care of First Nations patients. Government officials could also be generous. E.M. Straight, the superintendent of the Dominion Experimental Farms in Saanichton who had visited the previous summer, sent forty-five dozen red tulips.

While the Sisters cared for the physical well-being of their patients, they were also concerned about their souls. Daily records mention patients who made peace with God or returned to the Church before dying. Numbers of baptisms celebrated in the hospital chapel, conversions, numbers of Catholic and non-Catholic patients as well as totals of in- and outpatients were chronicled annually.

Sister Mary Henrietta of Jesus, who served as superior and administrator as well as director of nursing, had proved herself during her first obedience at St. Joseph's School of Nursing, where she completed her nurse's training in a language that had previously been foreign to her. Sister Mary Henrietta of Jesus had been raised in Alfred, Ontario. After attending St. Ann's boarding school at Rigaud, Quebec, she followed an aunt and several cousins into the community of the Sisters of St. Ann, professing her

The hospital's Chapel of the Sacred Heart, which came to be widely used by the Bulkley Valley community as well as by the Sisters. SSAA P0133

vows on July 23, 1908, in Lachine. After twenty-three years at St. Joseph's Hospital in Victoria, she was named administrator of Lourdes hospital in Campbell River. Less than two years later she was posted to Smithers, where she remained until August 1937.

One of Sister Mary Henrietta of Jesus's more pleasant associations was with the women's auxiliary, a group that retained the role it had played in the original hospital. The auxiliary met first on September 7 with Mrs. C.J. Kirby as acting president.[412] It raised money for equipment and supported the administration, board and staff in many ways. Sister Mary Henrietta herself devoted hours of her "free time" to making beautifully embroidered items and crafts for sale at fundraising bazaars.

Essential to the operation of any hospital is a strong and supportive board of management that reflects the needs of the community it serves and maintains a mutually supportive relationship with the administration. Smithers was blessed with many citizens who gave generously of their time in this capacity. The Board was comprised of representatives of the Catholic, Anglican and United churches; the provincial government; the women's auxiliary; a district member; and two members of the Sisters of St. Ann, one of whom was the superior/administrator. At its first meeting on January 23, 1935, the board adopted the constitution and bylaws. It elected Sister Mary Constantine as secretary. The board elected as its chair John W. ("Happy") Turner, of whom it has been said that he was "one of the Bulkley Valley's best loved pioneers" and that, "No matter what happened, his great gift of laughter saved the day."[413] A member of the first hospital board, he continued on the new one, setting an enviable record of service and remaining as Chair until his death in 1956. His hospital responsibility was a top priority. While holidaying in England in 1954 he dropped in to British Columbia House in London, where someone suggested he contact Sir Waldron Smithers after whom Smithers village was named. Sir Waldron invited Turner to his home in Seven Oaks for tea. Not one to miss an opportunity, "Happy" invited Smithers to furnish a room in the new wing to be added in 1955.[414] Ultimately his offer was not accepted.

In 1935, the first full year of operation, changes were already needed. The noisy laundry machinery disturbed the rest of patients and took up space that could be put to better use. Consequently an extension was built on the back of the garage that had been constructed in 1934 in combination with a root cellar and morgue. In 1938 the laundry had to be renovated and insulated as it was too cold to work in during the frigid winters. By the end of 1935 a new greenhouse, to supply all the tomatoes needed for a year— fresh and canned—had risen on a concrete foundation. Most years, the hospital chronicles noted when the tomato seedlings were set and how many pounds were produced. Adding to the usual sounds on the

A Sister working in the garden to produce vegetables for the hospital— about 1936. The greenhouse was built in 1935. SSAA P0134

hospital grounds was the clucking of chickens that had been raised for several years to provide eggs and chicken dinners for the patients and staff.

The patient population reflected the type of life led by the majority of residents of the valley, a life of physical labour. The accidents were severe, but the injured could expect the best of care at their Bulkley Valley District Hospital. Guns were *de rigueur* in a community where people hunted and fished to supply their needs, and accidental gunshot wounds were common. In December 1937, William Duff had "the great misfortune of shooting Mr. Cook accidentally while out hunting" (Cook died). In January, MLA Kenney advised Duff that he was at liberty, the incident having been adjudged accidental.[415] The railroad, lifeline to the area, also claimed victims. In May 1939, a man was run over by train flatcars and despite surgery and the amputation of his arm, died within a few days. Recreational accidents also took their toll. In January 1938 a patient was admitted after a ski penetrated his thigh, causing the chronicler to suggest it was enough of an injury that "some may want to avoid [it] by giving up ski-jumping."[416]

There were positive outcomes too. A success story in April 1941 illustrated the skills of the nursing staff. A man identified as M. Kwantes of Houston, British Columbia, had cut off one foot accidentally and injured the other with a chainsaw. The resulting gangrene should have killed him, but successive amputations controlled its spread and Kwantes survived.[417]

The Sisters had always expected to provide nursing care to the First Nations population. Aside from the desire to evangelize them, caring for their bodies and their souls, the Sisters had come to need the income provided by the federal Department of Indian Affairs in this regard. One of their very first patients was a First Nations man identified as a Mr. Joseph. Over the years so many tubercular patients, adults and children, came for assistance that in 1944 the board considered building a separate TB wing for First Nations patients (though they never did). Mothers would accompany their children and remain with them throughout their illness. A young First Nations boy whose foot had been frozen was a patient for two weeks before his foot had to be amputated.

Relations with Indian Affairs were not always smooth. Most of the inspection visits from departmental agents were positive, with agents approving the care and accommodation afforded to First Nations patients.

The Sisters had understood when they took over the hospital that First Nations peoples from surrounding reserves would patronize the hospital and since the Department of Indian Affairs paid for their care, this would help with the upkeep. The promised numbers, however, did not materialize, apparently because the hospital was inaccessible to many potential First Nations patients. On August 4, 1939, the provincial superior asked the BC government to reopen the road between Babine and Smithers. An unsigned note with this letter states that 27 miles of this road led to Cronin mine and $15,000 would make it passable. If it were classed as a mining road, Ottawa would pay two-thirds of the cost.[418] To realize the importance of this assured government income, it is necessary to remember that patients themselves were expected to cover hospital costs and, unfortunately, this led to many bad debts that went uncollected.

There was always a separate billing for items purchased for the care of First Nations patients, and in 1944 the per diem rate paid by Indian Affairs was raised from $2.75 to $3 a patient day and $2 a day for patients with tuberculosis. At the time, other patients were charged $3.75.[419] Indian Affairs continued to pay less than the accepted hospital rates for in- and outpatient care, therefore the hospital board, at its October 31, 1951, meeting, passed a resolution that "hospitals will no longer accept payment for Indian outpatient X-ray service except it be at the rates as established by the member hospitals."[420]

Tending souls was an integral part of the care for all patients. In the case of the First Nations peoples, the Sisters were particularly attuned to their special saint, Blessed Kateri Tekakwitha, "Lily of the Mohawks," often storming heaven with prayers for her intercession. A novena was offered in her honour, asking for an increase in First Nations patients. One Sister "pinned (a) badge of the Sacred Heart and a relic of Kateri Tekakwitha" on an acutely ill post-operative patient awaiting a second operation, "asking them to cure her without surgical means." It was recorded that the patient had improved by the following day and continued to do so until her discharge three weeks later.[421]

The Sisters maintained contact with the First Nations people of Lejac and Moricetown (which today is about 30 km from Smithers) throughout the year, particularly at Christmas, when they would visit. When Sisters Mary Mercy and Mary Angelica made such a visit in 1935, they were serenaded with Christmas hymns in the local Carrier language at the priest's home.[422] The Sisters often took visitors to Moricetown to see the exciting spectacle of the First Nations peoples fishing and preparing their catch for the winter, as they had been doing for at least four thousand years in this Bulkley River canyon. To see the sockeye leap high out of the water, light flashing from their iridescent flesh, was an inspiring glimpse of life in the wild. The fishermen's tenacity and perseverance reflected that of the Sisters who came to observe them. Since fishing in Bulkley canyon was reserved for aboriginal peoples only, a gift of fish from them or the game warden was a treat indeed.

*　*　*

Sister Mary Henrietta of Jesus, with her patience and kindness, had guided Sacred Heart hospital through its early growing pains. When she was posted again to Lourdes hospital in Campbell River in the summer of 1937, her successor in Smithers was Sister Marie Anne de Sion, a Franco-Canadian woman who had received her nursing diploma from St. Joseph's School of Nursing in Victoria in 1923. Sister Marie Anne de Sion believed that true science and holiness were compatible, and demonstrated this belief by studying for diplomas in pathology, X-rays, hospital administration, obstetrics and radiology. Her natural love of order and organization suited her admirably for her role as administrator, though working in her second language was difficult.

Sister Marie Anne remained only a year in Smithers and was succeeded by Sister Mary Patrick, a native of Prince Edward Island. Although Sister Mary Patrick (Teresa McLeod) was of Scottish descent, her feast day was celebrated in Smithers with a chapel full of shamrocks. Sister Mary Patrick functioned as superior, administrator and head nurse with immense responsibilities to keep the hospital operating smoothly. She even qualified as a certified steam boiler operator![423]

Sister Mary Patrick shepherded the hospital through most of the war years. Remote as Smithers might seem from the furor of war, it nevertheless experienced many war-related events. Father Godfrey Eichelbacher, OMI, was to be named chaplain of Sacred Heart hospital in 1944, almost a year after the death of Father Coccola, and he relayed news of conditions in Germany on his way home from Rome in February 1939.[424] Fears were realized when England and France declared war on Nazi Germany on September 3, 1939.

Smithers was strategically located as an air base and transport hub for soldiers. Soldiers were brought to the hospital for treatment of a variety of ailments, including five who were hospitalized with measles in March 1943 and two badly burned Royal Canadian Air Force men rescued from a plane that burst into flames while taking off. The Sisters were on the receiving side when Captain Dr. Hogg of the RCAF assisted the severely overworked Dr. L.M. Greene in surgery. In December 1944 the hospital received a large supply of food, including items that were difficult to get in wartime—meat, syrup, butter, eggs—when soldiers who had been doing mountain-climbing practice left town.

Among the original Sisters in Smithers, Sister Mary Patrick (centre) served as superior, administrator and head nurse, and led the hospital through the war years. Sister Mary Constantine served as the first secretary of the board. SSAA P0136

The Pacific war especially affected the Smithers hospital. Sister Mary Ignatia who was named as superior to Smithers in August 1944, had been repatriated in 1943 from internment in Japan, where she had served with four other Sisters of St. Ann at a mission established in 1934.[425] Canada, of course, had removed its Japanese residents from the coastal areas beginning less than three months after the Japanese attack on Pearl Harbor and the declaration of war on Japan by Canada and the United States. However, Smithers was inland so the Bulkley Valley District Hospital was able to hire a Japanese Canadian man named Z. Utsunonmyia as gardener in 1943. What an asset he was to the hospital, coaxing real production from the soil. "The result of his labor—170 lbs of peas, 100 lbs of radishes, 50 lbs of spinach, 50 heads of cauliflower, 2000 heads of lettuce, 400 heads of cabbage, 230 cucumbers."[426] Their own Victory garden. He remained at the hospital until 1947, when he left saying he was "too tired."[427]

Out of bad things may come some good. The Second World War saw many advances in medical and surgical fields. Of exceptional importance was the advent of penicillin. It was used for the first time at Sacred Heart hospital for a ninety-year-old man, halting a case of osteomyelitis of the foot (though not before the appendage had to be amputated).

Normal activities of a hospital carried on. A new X-ray unit was installed after MLA Kenney obtained $5,000 from the BC government. The first twins born at the hospital were to Mr. and Mrs. F. Johnson of Terrace, who invited two staff members to be godparents to Jean Ann and Robert Noel, their tenth and eleventh children.[428] Premier John Hart paid a visit, and was said to be very pleased with the well-equipped hospital. Sister Mary Colombe-de-Jesus received a licence to drive. There was an influx of First Nations patients from Moricetown presenting with measles, mumps and pneumonia. Hospital Day was celebrated each May with a tea, sometimes a shower, and always gifts and donations to contribute to the well-being of the hospital and its patients. The Sisters kept long hours, often working all day only to sit up at night with a very sick patient. Smithers had no undertaker, so at the sudden death of board member John Gray the Sisters went

A welcome visit from Premier John Hart in 1943 to the hospital in Smithers.
SSAA P0139

to his home, laid him out for the family and transferred him to the hospital morgue until burial.[429] Finally, on May 7, 1945, it was recorded that

> The great news of the cessation of hostilities in Europe reaches us at 7:30 a.m., while at 11 a.m. the sirens and whistles boom out their joy. At 1 p.m. we have Benediction of the Blessed Sacrament in the Hospital chapel and sing with full hearts a glad Te Deum.[430]

In the celebrations prompted by VE (Victory in Europe) day in May and VJ day (when Japan stopped fighting in the Second World War) in August, there was much thanksgiving, tempered by the sorrow for those who would not return and the death of long-time friend Bishop Bunoz on June 3, 1945.

However, another Oblate priest, Anthony Jordan, was shortly named as vicar apostolic (and also ordained a bishop and went by that title). He led the vicariate for ten years in a time of rapid postwar growth, and established many new churches and two new schools. Like Bishop Jordan, Ellen Parker—who had made profession as Sister Mary Ignatia in 1921—had been born in Britain but had come to Canada at a young age. Unhappy as a teacher, she had happily transferred to nurses' training, then to staff nurse at St. Joseph's Hospital, Victoria. Her years in Japan had honed her administrative and nursing skills. Her frugal stewardship extended to the minutiae of hospital life. She had a window installed in the laundry so that the natural light would save on electricity; she ordered a new brick stove for the greenhouse to increase the produce that could be grown. She wrote to Mother Mary Mildred, provincial superior, that "work is made easier when everyone works harmoniously together as we do here. The spirit is excellent, mutual relations friendly, helpful and sincere."[431] Her premature death at the age of sixty-one in 1963 in a car accident near Whitehorse was a heartfelt loss to her congregation.

Not long after Sister Mary Ignatia had arrived in Smithers, the *Interior News* declared: "We cannot commend the Sisters of Bulkley Valley District Hospital for using the best private rooms at the hospital for patients other than those for whom they were intended." An opportunity now arose for the Sisters and their supporters to reiterate the credo on which they had opened the hospital eleven years previously. Eight First Nations patients had arrived needing urgent care. Only six ward beds were available, so two of these patients were treated in a private room. This offended some. Dr. Greene, now medical superintendent, replied: "The sick shall be cared for in the Bulkley Valley District Hospital to the best of our ability irregardless of their race, colour or creed." J.W. Turner, board chair, echoed that "the Sisters were operating the hospital for people of every race, creed and color, without distinction." He affirmed that no one who suffered would be turned away for lack of money, and that all patients with communicable diseases were properly isolated, and impeccable cleaning techniques were followed. And by the way, the hospital would be very happy for financial aid to build a new wing to alleviate overcrowding.[432]

Obtaining enough nurses to staff the hospital was a chronic problem. Normally, married nurses were expected to look after their own domestic concerns. During the war, however, the hospital called on local married graduate nurses to fill the gaps caused by severe shortages of nurses. The Sisters were so grateful for their assistance that late in 1944 they inserted a thank you in the *Interior News*:

> We extend to the married Graduate Nurses of Smithers and vicinity our heartfelt thanks and sincere appreciation for professional services so generously contributed, particularly during this past year, when the shortage of trained nurses on the staff was keenly felt. You have helped vitally to keep the "Home Fires Burning" at the Hospital, and this in spite of the demands of home duties. You have proved yourselves a credit to the high ideals of the nursing profession: *Non nobis solum.*

Another solution to the nursing shortage had been the issuing of temporary permits to nurses who had qualified elsewhere and whose qualifications had been investigated, but these permits were cancelled at the end of the war even though the shortage of nurses continued as the demand for their services rose.[433] Another problem was pay inequity from one location to another. In 1939 a nurse's salary in Burns Lake, BC, was $66 a month, for example, while Smithers was trying to raise its rate to $50 a month. A far cry from Sister superior's report to the board in 1938 that "the Nurses were satisfied, and... there was no need of increasing their wages."[434]

Though there were not enough nurses, those who did work were

A staff photo in 1944 before the beautiful Hudson Bay Mountain, (l–r) Sister Mary Anne D'Aurey, Sister Mary Albert (Lavinia Richard), Sister Celine Marie, Sister Mary Colombe, Sister Mary Patrick and Sister Mary Lidvina; standing on the right is Dr. L.M. Greene, with hospital staff behind. SSAA P0138

housed in the hospital, taking up precious space that was needed to care for the increased number of patients. A nurses' residence became a pressing matter. Eight patient beds could be freed if the nurses had their own separate quarters. As well, the hospital rented rooms elsewhere for night nurses, since they could not sleep in the hospital with its attendant daytime noises. In pressing her case with mother provincial, Sister superior mentioned that the needs in Smithers might be insignificant next to St. Joseph's planned addition in Victoria, but the need was as great. Building material was scarce immediately after the war, but Sister Mary Ignatia hoped to buy an airport structure that the Air Force no longer needed. The War Assets Corporation rejected the Sisters' offer of $2,000 twice, indicating it would take not less than $4,000. Sister Mary Ignatia exploited the Oblate connection in Ottawa and asked Father Plourde to intercede with Ian Mackenzie, the federal cabinet minister from British Columbia. However, no luck there, and the buildings were sold to local businessmen, the Billinkoff brothers, who then sold some of the materials to the Sisters at a discount and supplied the rest of the necessary material from Prince

George, where they had also purchased some army barracks. The Sisters did buy "a very nice morgue table" and other medical equipment from the War Assets Corporation office.[435]

The Later Years

In 1948 the federal government authorized the spending of $30,000 a year for the coming five years to aid in building new hospitals or additions to existing facilities, on the basis of $1,000 a bed. George Pearson, provincial secretary, promised a grant of approximately one-third of the cost of the nurses' residence, up to $25,000. The final third of the cost was to be met by the people of the district. Hallelujah, construction could begin.

Archie Sullivan was too busy with St. Joseph's Hospital in Victoria to give time to Smithers, so a local tradesman, a Mr. Adomeit, contracted to build the residence. It took him about four months, and was based on the plans of Henry Whittaker—an addition 45 feet by 26 feet facing Queen Street. Father Godfrey blessed the ground on August 15, 1948, the BC public works ministry donated the use of a bulldozer to level the earth, and construction began on August 21. Many local groups—including the women's auxiliary, the Legion and the Graduate Nurses Association of Smithers and Vicinity—and many individuals contributed furnishings for

Thanks to postwar government spending on new hospital facilities, the Sisters were able to build a new residence for the nurses in 1948. L to r—Father Godfrey Eichelbacher, Sister Miriam Claire, Sister Mary Barbara, Sister Mary Thomasina, Sister Mary Ignatia and Sister Mary Lidvina. SSAA P0131

the new residence. At the official opening on May 21, 1949, board chair J.W. Turner related the history of the hospital, reminded the citizens that they would be expected to assume one-third of the expense for the nurses' building, revealed the extraordinary statistic of nearly one hundred births in 1948, and invited all present to enjoy afternoon tea in celebration of the building.

* * *

The routine work of the hospital continued. The Sisters worked their regular shifts, and frequently were up through the night for extra duty. At no time did they receive extra remuneration for these hours. Hospital work was particularly demanding when floods on the Skeena and Bulkley Rivers in 1948 cut off rail, telephone and telegraph service and made it impossible for staff to reach the hospital. Because only one nurse was on general duty, Sisters Mary Ignatia and Mary Barbara had to be the duty nurses from 7:30 a.m. until 11:30 p.m. for several days. And when Prince George Hospital asked in September 1955 for suggestions about replacing X-ray technicians on holidays and weekends, Sister Mary Kathleen responded, "This problem in Sisters Hospitals was taken care of by the Sisters themselves who are always on call for any emergency."[436]

Care of the sick, body and soul, enveloped their whole life. This life was not without risk, as evidenced when Sister Mary Ignatia "suffered a blow on the cheek from an insane patient which fractured her jaw. Reverend Father Godfrey and Miss Miller, a nurse, also received facial injuries."[437] At one point the Sisters tended to four sisters who had been forced to jump from their second-floor apartment to escape a fire, sustaining injured backs and fractured vertebrae. Caring for such patients was strenuous work that required a strong back to do much lifting. Especially painful, though, were cases of suicide. When one man, a "fallen-away Catholic," put a bullet through his head, he was anointed and given conditional absolution. As had been his wish, he was buried from the United Church, yet he left $5,000 to the Sisters in his will.[438]

Despite an exhausting schedule, time was made to celebrate. Christmas was a joyful time, with gifts being given to each of the patients and music being made welcome, and New Year's Day was usually spent quietly as a day of reflection, unless patient needs intervened. In the early days of the hospital, hymns were sung in French on New Year's Day, to reflect the French-Canadian roots of the Congregation of the Sisters of St. Ann and the heritage of many of the Sisters. When Sister Mary Gustave's golden jubilee was feted, it was recorded that, "in spite of the tension caused by overwork, everyone does her utmost to make the day a happy one for Sister."[439] Weddings were held in the chapel, including those of two Polish "DPs" who worked for the hospital.[440] To celebrate the centenary of the Congregation of the Sisters of St. Ann in 1950, the Sisters decorated the chapel with snapdragons, gypsophila and delphiniums in pink, blue and white, with matching vigil lights.

Professional development was important for all staff. Sister Mary Beatrice came to give instruction in the operation of the X-ray machine. A provincial government nutritionist advised on dietary matters for patients. One or two Sisters attended the regional meetings of the hospitals of northern British Columbia and the provincial hospital meetings in Vancouver to keep abreast of current advances in administration and health care. Exemplary standards were expected from all and it was rare that a nurse would be dismissed. One was, shortly after arriving, as she "does not prove to be the kind of a nurse we need in our hospitals."[441]

Practising medicine in a rural area also gave the local doctor a broad range of experience. Dr. Greene performed procedures that he would never have been called to or allowed to do in a larger centre. He gave his own blood to a very ill young mother of three children and performed an emergency appendectomy on his own five-year-old son, Billy. Wishing to work to the highest professional standard too, he expanded his credentials by spending six months in Scotland doing surgical studies to become a Fellow of the Royal College of Surgeons (FRCS) but he moved to Powell River in 1949.[442]

There was also a change in the hospital's administrator. Sister Mary Ignatia was assigned to Campbell River and Sister Mary Kathleen succeeded her. By then, seven other Sisters were serving at Smithers. For the next five years much of Sister Kathleen's energies were focussed on plans for a new addition. At one point 22 of the beds in the hospital were occupied with flu patients. Sister Mary Thomasina declared: "PATIENTS PATIENTS, everywhere! 72 of them in this 45 bed hospital."[443] The district had almost doubled in population and patients were overflowing into corridors and closets.

*   *   *

In the 1950s, Smithers was prospering along with the rest of the country. It was no longer a backwater village and the hospital kept up with modern times. A registered nurse named Ferne Trout came from Vancouver to present an educational program to the staff, including a very modern topic, "nursing aspects in atomic bomb and chemical warfare."[444] Miss M. Kerry, RN, the editor of the *Canadian Nurse*—a publication of the Canadian Nurses Association with a national readership—came looking for case studies, news and stories from Smithers. Because blood supplies had to be flown from Prince George, the hospital began keeping O-negative blood, the universal donor, on hand, and maintained a list of local donors of other blood types who could be called on if the need arose. The increase in the northern population initiated the division of the Regional Hospital Association into Northwestern, to cover hospitals from Prince Rupert to Burns Lake, and Northeastern, to include all hospitals from Vanderhoof to Williams Lake. Even patient transport was evolving with the times. The day came when Dr. Prouse returned by helicopter from the Cronin–Babine mine with a miner suffering a broken back. The dust flew as the helicopter approached for landing, with the patient strapped on one side and the doctor, face down, on the other. It was a photo opportunity not to be missed.

Prosperity may have seemed the norm, but money issues continued

As administrator of the Bulkley Valley Hospital, Sister Mary Kathleen was a persistent campaigner in the early 1950s for new additions, including an elevator. SSAA P0126

to plague health care in British Columbia. The board noted how a special general meeting of the British Columbia Hospitals' Association on June 21, 1952, had unanimously confirmed its "support of the compulsory hospital insurance of British Columbia."[445] Perhaps this prompted Eric Martin, health and welfare minister in the new Social Credit government, to advise hospitals that "the people of the Province are disturbed at the increasing cost of providing hospital care to our population."[446] Universal coverage would help hospital budgets and relieve some of the concerns caused by bad debts. The year before, the British Columbia Hospital Insurance Service (BCHIS) had cut $17,000 from the Bulkley Valley District Hospital grant while cutting Hazelton's hospital by only $2,000, though the two hospitals were comparable in size and operation. In 1954 the Smithers hospital had the second-lowest per diem rate in British Columbia, the lowest being in Williams Lake. These inequities in treatment were as frustrating as they were inexplicable. Sister superior attended a special meeting in Vancouver in December 1952 because the BCHIS, the government agency responsible for hospitals, had announced the freezing of hospital allowances for the coming year. The hospitals felt they would not have sufficient money to operate without compromising patient care. People with chronic-care needs, today called long-term care, were often admitted to the hospital though the government paid nothing for their care. Where else would they go? In addition, it seemed impossible to get the Department of Indian Affairs to pay the per diem rate charged to other patients.

Nevertheless, Sister Kathleen, a woman of strong determination and trust in God, pursued her goal of enlarging the hospital. Mother Mary Dorothea, provincial superior, and Sister Mary Gladys, provincial prefect of studies, came to Smithers to discuss the possibility of a new wing. A federal architect named Langmeade, who had worked on the new Smithers Post Office, drew up tentative plans and estimated it would cost $127,000 to add sixty-two beds. However, BCHIS preferred a steel and concrete building, which would permit only thirty-five extra beds if it were to keep within budget. G.H. Beley, the government representative on the board, flew to Victoria to discuss these plans with A.W.E. Pitkethley, the hospital construction manager of BCHIS.

The public was aware of these negotiations. Yet the goodwill that the community had expressed toward a Catholic hospital run by women religious was under challenge. In response to some criticism of the Memorial Wing fundraising appeal, J.W. Turner, as board chair, wrote to the *Interior News* to point out that while the hospital might be operated by a group of Catholic Sisters, five of the six lay board members were not Catholic. The chair himself was a member of the United Church. Since four of the current members had been on the board of the original hospital, they recalled the difficulty they had encountered keeping it open and all had welcomed the Sisters "when they came to relieve us of our burden." The hospital was open to all in need, at all times. He noted, too, that experience had shown that more staff would materialize if they could work in a "well provided" hospital. Clearly the Sisters and their operation were appreciated and supported by the majority of the residents. The Legion, which had seen the congestion in the hospital, sponsored a $15,000 drive toward its expansion. Thermometers were put up on Main Street to record the progress of the campaign, and the members distributed collection cans throughout the village. Other denominations concretely supported the Sisters. Choirs came to entertain the patients. The United Church minister's wife played the organ while Canon Hinchcliffe of the Anglican Church directed a choir composed of members of all persuasions. The choir of the Dutch Reformed Church also gave concerts in the hospital chapel.

Throughout, Sister Mary Kathleen continued to press her cause with the congregation and the provincial government. By November 1953 the architect of the original building, Henry Whittaker, who was now in private practice in Victoria, estimated the cost of the new addition at $128,334 based on 118,000 cubic feet at $1.25 per cu. ft. He had come to Smithers while Mother Mary Luca, the new provincial, and Sister Mary Gladys were there to make final plans and decisions for the new wing. Mother Mary Luca stressed that the overall cost was not to exceed $150,000. A month later Archie Sullivan, the original contractor, estimated the cost would be $168,000, which was $18,000 more than the Sisters had agreed to. The fact that BCHIS now would pay 50 percent of all construction costs would help allay this cost overrun.

Sadly, on returning from a Victoria trip in February 1954, Sister Mary Kathleen suffered repeated heart attacks. Once she was back on the job in late May, she engaged in an extensive correspondence with Mother Mary Luca, A.W.E. Pitkethley of BCHIS and Whittaker, as changes in the architect's plans and questions of an escalating budget were addressed. Pitkethley wanted to see how the existing building would be integrated with the new; wanted bathroom doors to open out, not in, for access if someone should fall while in there; and a call button in each bathroom for safety. The Sisters felt that financial restraints might force them to wait to bring the old building in line with the new. However, it seemed expedient to do this work at the same time since BCHIS would grant 50 percent for the work if done now, as opposed to a possible 33.3 percent if it were delayed. Whittaker went over the plans with Sister Mary Kathleen, writing to mother provincial emphasizing the necessity of this new addition since the beds in the corridors and sunrooms made it very difficult for staff to carry on their duties. He noted that fortunately the fire marshal was ignoring this fact for the moment. Because patients often lived at great distance from the hospital, doctors often admitted patients who might otherwise have been outpatients. Pitkethley advised that a few last adjustments to the plans were expected as we "cannot compromise on what we consider reasonable standards."[447]

On June 15, 1954, BC Health Minister Martin officially approved a thirty-bed reinforced concrete addition and permitted Whittaker to call for tenders. The building was to include an emergency operating room to comply with a condition of the federal government grant. This was a tonic to Sister Mary Kathleen. Now they awaited approval from Lachine. Sister Mary Kathleen feared that since no one at the mother-house was familiar with hospital projects, it would be difficult for the council to understand the escalating costs. Even so, Mother Mary Luca had already been given permission to extend the financial limit up to $170,000. Tenders were read in Victoria on July 12 and the contract given to the lowest bid of $215,000, which had been made by Ward Construction of New Westminster. This was $45,000 over the estimate, but the minister agreed to increase the provincial grant. This formality taken care of, Whittaker suggested to Martin that if he could convey this news on July 26, Saint Ann's Day, the Sisters would be deeply appreciative. He did, and naturally, they were. Lachine's endorsement came two days later with the proviso that costs were not to exceed $215,000. The breakdown was approximately:

BCHIS $107,571

Dominion Government $36,000

Donations $8,000

Sisters of St. Ann $63,571

Total $215,142

On August 5, 1954, the red-letter day, Dr. Max Weare turned the first sod for the new thirty-bed addition. Construction started immediately. The good news continued when Mother Mary Luca and Sister Mary Cornelius signed the contract on September 1. A sad note, however, was the death on November 9 of Sister Mary Seraphina, who had been working in the office and dining room, after a short illness.[448]

As in the past, the local community came forward generously to furnish and equip the new wing. In solidarity with Rotary Clubs all over the world celebrating their golden anniversary, the Smithers Rotary Club furnished a four-bed ward, at a cost of about $700. The following summer the district governor of Rotary, M. Chapman Robinson, visited the new wing and the Rotary ward, admitting that because he was blind he could "only see it spiritually."[449] The women's auxiliary, now boasting a membership of sixty, furnished a three-bed ward. Ladies of the Royal Purple, the Women's Institute and countless individuals wanted to be involved.

Work progressed rapidly enough for the long-anticipated installation of Smithers' first elevator. Sisters Mary Kathleen and Mary Peter proudly took the first ride in this Otis Fenson elevator on January 26, 1955. One can only imagine how much easier life became for staff (let alone patients), who had been carrying food, supplies and patients up the stairs since the hospital's beginning. The elevator was a great novelty, attracting the attention of all visitors and those who attended the opening later in the year. For Sister Mary Kathleen it was a great boon since she was not allowed to climb stairs. Now she could join the others for meals in the dining room. After the appropriate inspection the elevator was handed over and Sister Mary Kathleen signed the letters of acceptance. A Mrs. Rossberg, a maternity patient, wandered into the new wing and was the first patient to travel in the elevator. After the blessing of the elevator in February, a man named Yok Tong May, of the Smithers Bakery, had the dubious honour of being the "first corpse to be taken down in our new elevator."[450]

215

* * *

"It was a beautiful day for the opening Wednesday, with a warm sun shining down from an azure blue sky, studded with occasional fleecy white clouds."[451] What an auspicious sign for the formal opening of the new Memorial Wing of Bulkley Valley District Hospital on March 30, 1955. Many dignitaries attended, attesting to the importance of this now modernized hospital in the life of valley residents. Bishop Anthony Jordan, OMI, dedicated the building to the use of the Sisters of St. Ann. G.H. Beley, BC government agent and board member, read congratulatory telegrams from federal Health and Welfare Minister Paul Martin, as well as T.A. Mainprize, the Smithers division Superintendent of the Canadian National Railway, Skeena MLA Frank Howard, Lieutenant-Governor Clarence Wallace, BC Premier W.A.C. Bennett and others. Mother Mary Luca read words of praise from the superior general, Mother Mary Liliane, for those who had contributed to the building. Representatives of a variety of government agencies and groups connected with the building of the new wing added their congratulations and expressed their best wishes. BC Health Minister Martin accepted the traditional brass key from Don

In 1955, Sister Mary Kathleen unveiled a plaque on the new Memorial Wing, commemorating those who had fought and died in the world wars. SSAA P0148

Wagg, representing the architect, and declared the new wing open. Martin was lavish in his praise of the Sisters' selfless dedication and their generosity in spending $75,000 on this Memorial Wing. All was done in the presence of a hospital staff that might have represented the United Nations. Sister Miriam Anne had been born in England, Sister Mary Lidvina in Austria and Sisters Mary Peter and Mary Noemi in the United States; other Sisters hailed from various Canadian provinces, and there was a chaplain from Germany and an aide named Cecilia Hidber from Switzerland.

The most important speech of all belonged to Mother Mary Luca, provincial superior, who reiterated the foundation on which the hospital was built:

> There is only one reason for the existence of a hospital and that is the care of the sick and their restoration under God to complete health. Each hospital has its own purposes, objectives and philosophy. In a Catholic hospital such as this our objective is to serve Christ in the persons of the sick and the afflicted. The Sisters of St. Ann have been called to Smithers to administer to the sick and under God to bring them health and peace of soul and body.... Be assured that we are ever at your service.[452]

On September 11, 1955, Sister Mary Kathleen unveiled a plaque on this new Memorial Wing commemorating those who had fought and died in the world wars of 1914–18 and 1939–45.[453] The curtain rose on another part of the journey. The facility was now up to date and anticipated filling the growing needs of an increased population. When Martin visited Smithers that summer he expressed growing alarm at the escalating costs of all hospitals, a 74-percent increase from 1949 to 1954. In 1949, he explained, "there were 147 employees for every 100 patients, last year (1954) there were 170. Wages have gone up 95 percent since 1949. The average cost per capita per annum for patient care in hospitals in the province was $24, compared to a national average of $14."[454] Alarming statistics indeed, but this was scarcely news to the administrators of Sacred Heart hospital. Not only had the number of hospital days soared from 1,042 in 1934 to 17,427 in 1954 but the cost per hospital day had more than doubled from $4 to $8.40.

The demands of patient care and hospital administration placed considerable stress on the usual exercise of spiritual life for the Sisters. Sisters working in the hospital often found it difficult to arrange time to make a retreat in Victoria. Trying to enter into a private retreat while living at the hospital was often a futile exercise as the needs of patients often interrupted meditation and prayer. However, the presence of one on retreat was considered a blessing to the hospital. Sister Marie Joseph des Anges was seen as a "living vigil light" for eight days while she prayed near the tabernacle in the chapel.[455] When making her official visits, the provincial superior encouraged the Sisters in remote areas and reminded them of their connection to their whole religious community who continually kept them in prayer.

The arrival of any new Sister, adding to the nursing contingent, was eagerly anticipated, but on one occasion the new nursing sister came as a patient. Due to the rolling motion of the ship that was taking her to Prince Rupert, Sister Mary Fintan lost her footing and fell, breaking her nose in the process and sustaining two black eyes. What an arrival! Things went from bad to worse for her as she contracted a severe staphylococcus aureus infection while she was languishing in bed with a high temperature and swollen glands, an event Dr. Weare diagnosed as mumps. Mumps was the disease of the day—many adult patients and staff were down with it in these pre-vaccine days. To complete Sister Mary Fintan's afflictions, a deviated septum necessitated her return to Victoria for surgery. Sacred Heart hospital was left short-staffed again.

Professional behaviour was expected at all times, even though this forced the Sisters to defy the bishop. Bishop Fergus O'Grady, who succeeded Bishop Jordan, initiated a movement called the Frontier Apostolate in which he began to recruit hundreds of young people from all over the world who would help in schools and hospitals for no recompense. Over thirty-five years about four thousand people served in this work.[456] When the bishop suggested that his Frontier Apostolate nurses serve at Sacred Heart hospital with their salaries going directly into the program, the Sisters held their ground, insisting on keeping to their standards which required all nurses from other countries to be properly qualified and registered in British Columbia.

In the case of one doctor, although his credentials were acceptable he was not. In December 1954 the board gave hospital privileges to a doctor who had practised in Saskatchewan after graduating from the University of Zagreb in Yugoslavia. There were soon many complaints of his failure to abide by hospital rules and regulations. He failed to write up patient histories and other reports unless he was paid. A nurse related how he had admitted a family of four at 5 a.m., none of whom was an emergency patient. When the doctor did not live up to the expectations that the board outlined for him in a registered letter, the Sisters invited Dr. Armand Brunet, medical superintendent of St. Joseph's Hospital in Victoria and a former member of the Joint Commission on accreditation standards covering both Canada and the United States, to attend a board meeting to render advice. Dr. Brunet reminded the board of its responsibility of confidentiality and of the need for a physician to provide good medical records. After reviewing the situation and interviewing board and staff, he recommended revoking the doctor's hospital privileges. When the offending doctor received the board's letter informing him that he would not enjoy hospital privileges after June 30, 1956, his reaction confirmed the wisdom of this decision. He stormed into the hospital at 10 p.m., delivered letters to his patients and "instantly discharged them." When the registrar of the College of Physicians and Surgeons asked if the Sisters and the board wished to make a formal complaint, they declined since they understood the doctor would be leaving the province.[457]

A much happier and more positive relationship existed with Dr. Max Weare, a graduate of the University of Western Ontario in London who had interned at Vancouver General before setting up a practice in Terrace, BC. The Smithers board gave him hospital privileges and he moved there late in 1952. Sister Mary Kathleen had enough trust in Dr. Weare to appoint him chief of medical staff in 1956 and have him as her personal physician. He attended her when she had a heart attack and accompanied her, along with Sister Mary Agnes Claire, when she had to be moved to St. Vincent's Hospital in Vancouver.

Since there was no veterinarian in Smithers, the hospital staff was sometimes called on to be Saint Francis to animals in need. Once, while Dr. Weare was working in Houston, Sister Mary Benedicta, a 1959 graduate of St. Joseph's, found herself doing surgery on a dachshund to remove a fish hook from his lip. His leathery skin made it impossible to inject a needle to freeze the area, so she just made an incision and took the hook out. Several dogs with broken limbs were X-rayed and had casts applied in the emergency room. One can only speculate on the feelings of a patient who found a dog in the emergency bed in the next cubicle.

Following Sister Mary Kathleen's incapacitation, Sister Mary Velma assumed her role as administrator/superior in August 1956. She had worked only in education and wrote to Mother Mary Luca that she found it "a new world and a new language."[458] But she did not stay long, as she was called to Lachine to serve as fourth councillor on the general council at Lachine. Mother Mary Ludovic returned to the west to replace her effective November 22, 1956. All were overjoyed to learn she was returning as superior, since her roots with Sacred Heart hospital went back to its very conception when she had travelled with Mother Mary Leopoldine to Smithers to choose its present site. Upheaval again. At the age of seventy-seven, and with increased frailty, she felt it necessary to resign this arduous office within a year of taking up her position.

A more stable atmosphere emerged with the appointment and arrival of Sister Mary Lucita in the summer of 1957. Coming on the heels of her experience as director of nurses at St. Joseph's School of Nursing in Victoria, as well as a course in hospital organization and management, Sister Mary Lucita had the confidence and calm demeanour to take on the management of a very busy acute-care hospital.

This stability was needed in a time of increasingly complex governance and care protocols. The provincial council of the Sisters of St. Ann in Victoria worked out a revised set of bylaws and a constitution for all their BC hospitals, all of which were approved and signed by Eric Martin in 1957.

The Canadian Arthritic and Rheumatic Society (CARS) sent a doctor to assess the need for physiotherapy in Smithers. Modern equipment was arriving on the medical wards and modern conveniences such as heated tray carriers and a large deep freeze eased the workload in the dietary department. General Electric X-ray Corporation installed a miniature Photoroentgen unit for routine chest X-rays, which were now required for all patients over the age of three admitted to BC hospitals. These X-ray plates were sent once a week to a Dr. Wilfred Thorleifson, a radiologist in Vancouver who had been interpreting the hospital's X-rays since the early 1940s. During those years he received a flat fee of $20 per month, which increased to $35 in the late 1950s, by which time the number of X-rays to be read had multiplied. In the next decade Dr. Thorleifson visited the hospital, taught staff how to get the best results from up-to-date equipment and was very pleased with the excellent results. The amount he was paid for his reading of the X-rays was increased after he requested such consideration. He was being paid $200 a month when the BC Hospitals' Association and the BC Medical Association recommended that a "specialist's fee" be set at 20 to 30 percent of the cost, to be paid to the specialist by the hospital. At the time, Kitimat for one was giving the radiologist 28 percent and Bulkley Valley offered him $300, which he deemed satisfactory, asking only that in the future the hospital use Air Mail Express to deliver the plates to him in Vancouver. This practice continued as long as the Sisters were in charge.

The board and the hospital staff were keen to earn accreditation as confirmation of their professionalism. With an eye to attaining this status, Sister Mary Kathleen had appointed Dr. Weare as chief of staff in 1956 and Dr. D'Amico as secretary. She appointed two Sisters as medical records librarians, with Sister Mary Laurena being given responsibility for keeping

The Sisters pose in the hospital entrance in front of the statue of the Sacred Heart of Jesus, 1957–58. Front row l to r—Sister Mary Colombe-de-Jesus, Sister Mary Lucita, superior, and Sister Mary Agnes Claire. Back row l to r—Sister Mary Noemi, Sister Mary Yolande, Sister Mary Bernice, Sister Miriam Claire, Sister Marie Elie Anicet and Sister Mary Stanislaus Kostka. SSAA P0147

the cross-index of operations, and Sister Mary Perpetua, the cross-index of diseases and patient diagnoses. Sister Mary Kathleen began meeting on the third Wednesday of each month with the medical staff, the hospital council and a Sister nurse. Ongoing education would keep the Sisters current in hospital procedures and processes. Sister Mary Stanislaus Kostka attended a course in food management in St. Louis, Missouri, sponsored by the Catholic Hospital Association of the United States, then attended a dietetic supervisory course annually for three years to attain a certificate in principles of dietary management. While Sister Mary Lucita was superior, she continued summer courses studying hospital administration at Xavier University in Cincinnati, Ohio. Sister Miriam Rita attended Seattle University to work on her bachelor of science in nursing. Other Sisters and nursing and support staff upgraded their skills regularly with workshops and courses. Unfortunately some of the criteria for accreditation were difficult for a small rural and remote hospital to fulfill. The hospital would need to perform a certain number of autopsies and have adequate facilities to do so. Moreover, Sister Mary Lucita found it impossible to have at least three members on the active medical staff and to supply continual surgical coverage.

It seemed no time after the opening of the Memorial Wing before more building plans were considered. In 1957, Sister Mary Lucita asked Whittaker to sketch plans for an addition to the nurses' residence that would include ten single rooms and five double rooms for aides and maids. She wrote to Pitkethley, manager of the constructions division of BCHIS, that the hospital's average daily census might be fifty-one, but sixty to seventy or even more patients often occupied beds. The nine rooms the hospital was using for live-in nurses could be freed up for patients if the nurses' residence was expanded.

The hospital seemed to have a perennial problem of nurse shortage. A dozen married women in Smithers could work part-time, but this arrangement was unsatisfactory and "in general cannot be relied upon," Sister Mary Lucita wrote to Pitkethley. "It is most difficult to make out time-tables when one has to phone individual nurses to cajole them into working a week at a time," she wrote.[459] Unfortunately, in January the following year Sister Mary Lucita had to withdraw her request for funds from BCHIS as the Sisters of St. Ann were unable to assist financially in the cost.

*   *   *

Every new decade brought new directions. The 1960s exploded with new technology, new thinking and new characters on the world stage. All Catholic hospitals were trying to adapt to changing times and financial constraints. This was the background to Sacred Heart hospital's life and the ministry of the Sisters of St. Ann. By the early 1960s new building plans were in order as the original building and equipment became dated. Expansion meant the need for more property. The Sisters asked Smithers to close 9th Avenue between Queen Street and Columbia Drive, as well as the T-shaped lane in the Block 138 property behind them. The property they had purchased in 1947, 1958, and 1959 and further negotiations with Smithers allowed the possibility of expansion.

On August 2, 1961, Sister Mary Lucita advised mother provincial that the heating system had disintegrated in the past four years and questioned the wisdom of putting new oil stokers in old boilers at a cost of $40,000. She was reluctant to install gas heating, feeling it would be safe if one were trained in its use, but "some holy nun deciding to skip down to the laundry to press her habit on the gas-heated presser and pop!" would be

The Bulkley Valley District Hospital in 1962, at a time when it needed extensive upgrades of equipment and infrastructure. SSAA P0142

disastrous. The hospital and the nurses' residence converted from coal to oil heat. Sister Superior was able to sell eighteen tons of the remaining coal to Smithers Fuel Company, but held back six tons in case the new boiler was out of order and the old coal-heated boiler had to be put into service. This was a salient point since there was no laundry service in the village. The fire marshal alerted them to the need of sprinkler systems, upgraded wiring and a new water tank. Even the office equipment seemed archaic. Staff welcomed the change to a modern telephone system when the "dial system" came into effect, and none were sorry to see "cranks" eliminated.

On the administrative side, the cost of a newly instituted superannuation plan for employees had to be accounted for in the budget. Most hospital staff employed in 1960 were eligible for the new plan, though it was not compulsory to participate. Part-time employees were not eligible. A shorter, forty-hour work week meant more nurses were needed in order to cover all shifts. In 1959 the board had agreed to take part in the province-wide bargaining for nurses. Malpractice insurance rates were escalating. Bad debts plagued the bottom line. A modern development was the desire of the younger nurses to have their own apartments rather than live in a residence, a desire which, when realized, might free up a few of the hospital beds now allotted to staff.

Sister Mary Lucita asked mother provincial to change the bylaws for Catholic hospitals to provide for automatic rotation of membership on the boards of management and shift the onus from administration to remove any member who might wish to remain ad infinitum. Bulkley Valley District Hospital wasn't the only facility to find itself in the awkward position of trying to oust a well-meaning but ineffective hanger-on whose presence on the board prevented the administration from appointing a more appropriate member who would bring a fresh perspective and talent to the table. A change to the bylaws would impose a mandatory term for every board member. Each of the hospitals run by the Sisters of St. Ann would adhere to the same guidelines.

Times were changing. The days were fast disappearing when fire marshal Hayward could gather a group of volunteers and install a parking lot in a day as he had done in 1959, or to expand a parking lot as in 1960. The intimate relationship of the village and the hospital was embodied in the participation of the Sisters and other hospital staff in local events such as bazaars and fairs and the willingness of local people to be involved in the upkeep of the hospital. Lacking funds in the early years to hire a certified engineer for their laundry machines, the Sisters had relied on some Canadian National engineers, Percy Davidson in particular. Sister Mary Colombe-de-Jesus related how "I used to go for him at the early morning hour of 5:00 o'clock so that he could start the steam and after two hours of hard work he would report for his regular duty at the C.N.R. station."[460] A local farmer named McMillan invited Sister Mary Lucita and helpers to dig up and bring home a generous supply of vegetables. These relationships forged a strong bond of mutual respect between the Sisters and the community.

In September 1961, Mothers Mary Velma and Mary Angelus arrived in Smithers to discuss long-range planning, recommending that the general council give permission for Don Wagg to prepare such plans and for the Sisters and the board to look into establishing a so-called improvement district. Representatives of the communities served by the hospital would meet to outline the boundaries and to prepare and present a plebiscite to put to the electors once the provincial government approved the formation of a hospital improvement district. An improvement district would help the Sisters to finance any future expansion through a small increase in property tax in this unorganized region. The federal and provincial governments would provide two-thirds of the necessary funds, while the Sisters would provide the remaining third, but would only have to provide one-sixth if an improvement district was formed. In March 1962, the general council in Lachine agreed with the plan "to establish an Improvement District in view of future expansion of the hospital, in order that part of the cost will be a public responsibility."[461] The board had recently sent a letter to various district organizations that stated: "It is becoming increasingly evident that the facilities of Bulkley Valley District Hospital are inadequate to serve the growing needs of the area, and that some positive steps must be taken immediately to overcome this deficiency." They met with civic and benevolent groups, who agreed to form a committee whose mandate would be to consider instigating an improvement district.

The Sisters and the board had hoped that forming a hospital improvement district would alleviate their financial concerns. Once the committee had made its recommendations, a plebiscite was to be held to garner the support of the district. The Sisters had agreed to pay for this plebiscite from their own resources. When the plebiscite was held in Smithers School District No. 54 on November 2, 1964, a total of 461 voters said yes and 403 said no. Unfortunately, a 60-percent vote in favour was required to pass the bill. Ironically, negative votes came from Telkwa, Houston and Quick, which had provided forty-one, twenty-three and four patients respectively in September 1964. Mr. C.M. Goodacre, chair of the organizing committee, told the board that Telkwa always voted against referendums on principle, Quick was comprised of scattered farmers afraid of taxes and Houston expected to build its own hospital. This was small consolation, as the negative outcome of the vote meant the Sisters or Smithers alone would have to absorb the whole one-third non-government-funded share of the cost of any new building. When chief electoral officer M.F. Hurley, sought the payment of $561.77 for the expense of the plebiscite, the board quickly voted to look for a way to repay them, which they did from the so-called plant fund late in 1965.

Meanwhile, the architect's preliminary estimate for the new building was $250,000. At this time figures were based on a cost of $20,000 per bed. A new wrinkle in the Sisters' relationship with the architect arose from the desire of BCHIS to see a formal agreement between the principal and the architect. Don Wagg presented a standard form designed by the Royal Architectural Institute of Canada to serve as his contract with the Sisters after years of working with an unwritten understanding. By August 1964 a new estimate for building was presented at $750,000. In June 1966 the projected expense had skyrocketed to $1,268,820 plus the cost of furnishings. Now the expense of building was based on $40 per square foot rather than a per-bed cost. On February 13, 1967, a letter was sent to Pitkethley at BCHIS, "outlining a revised building programme as prepared by Mr. Wagg at the request of the Hospital Board by the Regional Hospital District representative; this indicates $3,000,000 would be required."[462] Escalating costs indeed.

Decisions were postponed in the spring of 1963 since a new superior would be named in the summer. Sister Mary Lucita was leaving, to be succeeded by Sister Mary Colombe-de-Jesus, who had served the Bulkley Valley District Hospital for many years in other capacities. After profession at the motherhouse in Lachine in 1935, then teaching for seven years in Quebec, Sister Mary Colombe had expressed a wish to serve in the west, where she had been sent in 1942 to be the bookkeeper at the Smithers hospital before moving to other hospitals in British Columbia.

Sister Mary Colombe-de-Jesus took over as administrator just as Pope John XXIII died and Paul VI took office. The reign of Pope John XXIII and his convening of the Second Vatican Council had opened the door to broader lay involvement in the Church, but also caused great upheaval in the Church, which led to much deeper changes for the congregation than the dropping of the Holy Habit and the adoption of a "new look" in their costume, a change that attracted many favourable comments. Sister Mary Colombe's kind, gentle and sympathetic way would steer the Sisters, staff and patients under her care through the turbulent 1960s.

Though the hospital consumed most of the hours of the Sisters' day, they managed to sustain their prayer life and fill other commitments. They had continued their ministry to the aboriginal population, and in 1963 Sisters Mary Dolora, Mary Epiphane and Mary Aquina were honoured to attend the installation of Peter Alfred as the new chief at Holy Rosary Church on the Moricetown Reserve. They also had opportunities for regular rest and relaxation after the congregation approved the purchase of 16.4 recreational acres on Lake Kathlyn (twenty minutes north of Smithers) in 1963 and the construction there of a cottage in 1965. This would save the cost of trips to Victoria for vacation and allow Sisters a retreat for some rest occasionally during the year.[463] In fact, when hospital beds were over census, the Sisters contemplated moving their lodgings to Lake Kathlyn to provide more beds for patients. The purchase of this retreat seemed to indicate that the Sisters expected to be in Smithers for many more years.

A picturesque snapshot of Hudson Bay Mountain and Lake Kathlyn. In 1965 the Sisters built a cottage on Lake Kathlyn, 20 minutes north of Smithers, a place where they could enjoy rest and recreation. SSAA P0144

And so the work of the hospital continued without firm plans to replace the now inadequate original building. The Sisters worked with what they had, doing piecemeal repairs and improvements if they became necessary. Care was exemplary. Sister Mary Janita, who worked in Smithers from 1964 to 1966, recalled in a 2005 interview how a university student working on a summer job was injured when a helicopter tipped over on a mountain. The nursing staff worked diligently to stabilize this young man and keep infection at bay until he could be moved to Vancouver for further treatment. When he was stable enough to be moved a week later, Sister Mary Janita accompanied him, in an unpressurized plane for part of the trip, keeping the intravenous drip going and managing his pain. At the Vancouver General Hospital the doctors expressed appreciation of the excellent care the patient had enjoyed. Though both his legs had to be amputated, he eventually was fitted with artificial legs and even skied again.[464]

*   *   *

The local community had concerns about having only one medical practitioner, a concern that prompted the Smithers Chamber of Commerce to draw the attention of Eric Martin to this in 1964. They emphasized that this one doctor had "to serve an estimated area population of 8,000 persons, young and old, and the 84 bed modern Bulkley Valley District Hospital, covering distances of more than fifty miles radius from his office in Smithers."[465] This chronic shortage of doctors was not unique to Smithers. The BC College of Physicians and Surgeons attributed this problem to the small number of doctors being trained in British Columbia and the general trend of the professionally trained to move about the country and the world. The college sent a memo to rural and small-town British Columbia ("undoctored areas") suggesting an externship program that would send third-year medical students to remote locations, not to have them provide full medical assistance, but "to introduce potential practitioners to practice in the areas." Sister superior found the program helpful to the Smithers hospital and the board approved subsidizing these students.

Between 1962 and 1968, letters crossed among government offices, the Sisters of St. Ann, the architect and the hospital board. No firm decisions were made and the frustration was obvious. Smithers needed a larger and more modern facility, but no plans reached fruition. Though permission was given in some instances to upgrade the original building, it became apparent that constructing new administrative offices, a laundry, kitchen and cafeteria should form the nucleus of a completely new hospital and permit the abandonment of the 1934 building.

The Sisters were increasingly concerned about soaring costs and the declining availability of religious staff. Consideration was being given to relinquishing control of the hospital in Smithers. Painful decisions were being made. Changing demographics in the lay world were evident in the amalgamation of the afternoon and evening chapters of the women's auxiliary. Women were working outside the home and their volunteer capacity was dwindling.

When the provincial council met in Victoria in November 1968, discussion focused on the Sisters' future in Smithers. They had learned that some medical staff there would prefer to see the Sisters withdraw because they did not want the Sisters to force their "moral issues" on the doctors and their patients.[466] The Sisters also felt that the civic community would prefer to have a general hospital rather than one operated by a religious group. Not surprisingly, they requested permission from the general council in Lachine to withdraw from Smithers.

Thus Sister Kathleen Moroney, provincial superior, wrote on January 13, 1969, to Health Minister Ralph Loffmark, the mayor of Smithers and T. Forsyth, secretary of the Bulkley-Nechako Regional Hospital District, that the Sisters of St. Ann desired "to withdraw from the operation and ownership of the hospital," effective June of the same year. Two days later she wrote to Bishop O'Grady, now situated at Sacred Heart Cathedral in the newly created Diocese of Prince George, explaining and outlining their inability to continue at Sacred Heart hospital in Smithers and Sacred Heart School in Prince George. As the first bishop of this new diocese he was disappointed to learn that he would be losing the support of these willing Sisters in what was still considered a missionary territory.

The board soon asked BCHIS for direction and instruction relative to the proposed withdrawal. They wished to know how the Sisters would be reimbursed for their equity in the hospital and were advised by the deputy minister that "any price negotiated with the Sisters of Saint Ann . . . would be a local charge."[467] The minister responsible, along with regrets at the withdrawal of the Sisters, suggested that an informal body be formed of lay board members, representatives of citizens' groups, the town council and service clubs. The board called a special meeting "to form a committee to discuss and make proposals relative to the ownership and operation of the Bulkley Valley District Hospital, Smithers, B.C."[468]

As this process proceeded, the newly minted Town of Smithers proposed a special resolution:

> NOW THEREFORE BE IT RESOLVED that the Council of the Town of Smithers convey to the Sisters of St. Ann their sincere appreciation for the dedicated service they have rendered to the care of the sick of this town and district over the past 35 years with a devotion to duty that is unsurpassable.

This approbation was a balm during the difficult days and months the Sisters spent winding down years of service in this rural community. They had witnessed its growth from village to town. They had ministered to those in need, from birth to the end of life.

Sister Mary Colombe-de-Jesus was invited to speak to the Rotary Club shortly after Smithers attained the status of Town in 1967 on "What the Sisters of St. Ann Have Done for This Town." In recounting their purpose of coming as nurses, cooks, bookkeepers and clerks to "work without financial gain," she also gave credit to the people of the district: for their "generosity, labour and dedication" that had "been a temporal as well as moral support for the Sisters" in helping them to "fulfill the purpose of an institution such as this; to alleviate human suffering." She also gave credit to her Sisters for often working without pay and, when finances permitted, drawing a salary and using it "to pay the interest on the loan." She illustrated the burgeoning growth and responsibilities of the previous thirty years: In 1935, there had been 217 admissions; in 1965, 1,943. In 1935, 9 babies had been born in the hospital; in 1965, 181. The annual payroll had risen from $2,752 to $250,940 and the food budget from $2,217 to $24,000. These statistics painted the picture clearly. What indeed had the Sisters of St. Ann done for Smithers!

When the Bulkley Valley District Hospital Society was formed, negotiations began for the transfer of the assets to the new society.

Universal Appraisals of Vancouver worked under an urgent timetable. The Sisters retained Bernard Fahy of the accounting firm Thorne, Gunn, Helliwell & Christenson, also in Vancouver, to represent their interests. Misunderstandings were bound to occur, which slowed the process somewhat and prevented a complete handover on the desired June date. When Sister Mary Colombe-de-Jesus left in August, Sister Mary Angelus came to fill her vacated role until an agreement was reached and the legal documents of transfer were executed. Sister Mary Angelus attended the board meetings as late as October 15, under the new administrator, K. Knight. The Sisters were leaving due to increased government participation in hospitals, a shortage of personnel within their congregation, and an increase in the number of lay people willing to assist and work in the hospital environment. It remained for Sister Kathleen Moroney, as provincial superior, to write September 29, 1969:

> to confirm that we offered our entire interest and equity in all the assets and liabilities of the Bulkley Valley District Hospital to the Bulkley Valley District Hospital Society for the sum of $165,000. This offer was on an "as is where is" basis and excludes only the Sisters' personal effects, the farm property, and the cottage and property situated on Kathleen [sic] Lake.

The formal and public celebration of the transfer of ownership—the handing over of a cheque, the deeds and a symbolic key—was held in a lawn ceremony on October 30, 1969, with as many staff and patients attending as could be managed.

But the real farewells had taken place in June. A new director of nursing service, Betty Roberson, had arrived from Vanderhoof to take over Sister Leanne Marie's position as director of nursing service. As well as Sisters Leanne Marie and Mary Colombe-de-Jesus, four other Sisters witnessed the end of ministry in Smithers: Sisters Mary Veronica, Mary Rosalia, Maureen Ann and Mary Antonia of the Sacred Heart. They recalled the many years of devoted service to the community and all who needed medical treatment under their care. The people who had benefited expressed their gratitude. Many goodbyes occurred throughout June. Some of the most poignant were those spent with Sisters of other congregations. They had supported each other in this far country for many years. Sharing a meal with the Sisters of the Holy Cross in their home they recalled many other occasions of happy recreation and joint celebration of feast days. Retreats and hospitality had been shared with the Sisters of St. Joseph in Prince Rupert and all congregations who had travelled and joined in religious celebrations in the northern area.

The Catholic Men's Club and the Catholic Women's League feted them along with the Holy Cross Sisters and some of Bishop O'Grady's lay apostles, giving a souvenir spoon to each of those departing. The town council, not to be outdone, held a banquet at which mutual thanks were expressed, while the board and staff of the hospital gave a farewell supper, with a gift of money to each Sister in a parting gesture.

Archbishop Douglas Hambidge of the Anglican Church told years later of the good relations that existed among all the churches in Smithers, a situation not repeated in many small towns in British Columbia. The people had basic values of friendliness and supportiveness, accepting everyone. The people warmly regarded the Sisters, and pastors regularly visited patients in the hospital, no matter their denomination. Archbishop Hambidge expressed disappointment that one of the first actions taken by the new board was to remove the Cross from the building.[469]

These pioneers were leaving the hospital where their concern for the young, the old, the suffering, had led to many healing encounters and growth in a caring community. They had thrived on the challenge, calling on the intercessory power of Mother Mary Ann to solve problems that seemed far beyond their own strength. The Duff family welcomed the Sisters into their home when they arrived in Smithers in 1933, and it seemed most appropriate that the Sisters said their farewells at a tea held at the home of William Duff's son and daughter-in-law thirty-six years later.

Chapter 11

St. Martin's Hospital, Oliver

Charity is a unifying principle because it embraces all.
—Bishop Martin Johnson

The pioneering hospital work of the Sisters of St. Ann in British Columbia took another step forward on April 18, 1941—Mother Mary Ann's birthday—when the general council in Lachine approved the erection of a hospital in Oliver. The Sisters had had a presence in Oliver since July 1937, when Sisters Mary Joseph Edward and Mary Alacoque first conducted two-week summer catechism classes there for Christ the King parish children, a practice that would continue for a total of thirty years.[470]

Oliver, located in a glacial valley in the shadow of the Cascade Mountains, took its name from Liberal Premier John Oliver (1918–27), who was responsible for an irrigation system known as "the Ditch" that turned the South Okanagan from an arid desert into verdant, lush ground suitable for agriculture. In 1918 the BC government purchased 22,000 acres in the South Okanagan for $350,000 and proceeded to develop an irrigation system that was "designed to convert some 8,000 acres of desert land, on each side of the Okanagan River, into viable agricultural land and make the land available, at a reasonable cost, to the returning soldiers from World War I."[471] Soon orchards and fruit farms prospered enough that Oliver became known as the Cantaloupe Capital of Canada.

The closest hospital to this community was in Penticton, 25 miles away. But prosperity brought growth to the Oliver area, and that in turn

233

created the need for a closer hospital to provide medical care and to keep a doctor in the community. In 1937 representatives of the Oliver Board of Trade met with Health Minister Dr. George Weir and Deputy Provincial Secretary P. Walker, to ask for aid in erecting a hospital. Percy Ward, inspector of BC hospitals, surveyed the area and recommended that Oliver form a hospital society and draw up bylaws. Thus the Oliver–Osoyoos Hospital Society began at the end of 1937, with plans to organize a popular subscription drive, gain government approval and assistance and solicit a non-profit group to operate the hospital.

A board of directors was elected at a public meeting on July 6, 1938, but the BC government seemed unwilling to appoint a representative. Finally, after a fifteen-month delay, the government appointed Oliver resident E.A. (Allan) McDonald, thus allowing a first sitting of the full board on October 17, 1939. Because the society board believed that even with a government grant the community could not financially support a hospital with paid staff, it looked for a non-profit agency or religious community to consider taking the responsibility.

Bishop Martin Johnson of Nelson, whose diocese included the Okanagan Valley, lent his weight to the appeal to the Sisters of St. Ann to consider operating a hospital in Oliver. He visited Mother Mary Mark, provincial superior, in Victoria in 1938 to emphasize his support. Also anxious for the Sisters to assume the task was Dr. Norbert Ball, a young graduate from the University of Toronto who had arrived in Oliver in 1933 at the age of twenty-eight after his internship at St. Paul's Hospital in Vancouver.[472] His devotion to his practice was evident, but he needed a hospital in closer proximity to his patients. He told the Sisters that the Oliver–Osoyoos district's population of roughly three thousand would support such a hospital. Two gold mines, a large lumber mill and box factory, seven fruit-packing houses, the government maintenance depot and a nearby First Nations reserve guaranteed the project would succeed.[473]

Mother Mary Mark wrote a non-committal letter to the society in 1940, mentioning the stress of getting Mount St. Mary up and running in Victoria, the lack of available Sisters to staff another institution, and the need to consult higher authorities.[474] When the society had not heard definitively from her for almost a year, it asked on January 20, 1941, for a definite statement of the Sisters' position. Mother Mary Mark relented and accompanied her request for approval from the general administration with a letter from Bishop Johnson. When the approval was granted on April 18, negotiations began, the Sisters insisting on ownership if they were to run a hospital. A Crown grant for the land was dated November 7, 1941, to the Sisters of St. Ann. Plans were then submitted to BC government architect Henry Whittaker for approval, and Archie Sullivan was again given the building contract for an institution of the Sisters.

Mother Mary Mark chose the name St. Martin's Hospital in recognition of Bishop Martin Johnson's continued interest. On April 9, 1942, Father John LaBrake blessed the hospital site and Fred

A strong supporter of the Sisters of St. Ann, the Most Reverend Martin M. Johnson, Bishop of Nelson from 1936 to 1954, was instrumental in bringing the Sisters to Oliver and Nelson. SSAA P0160

Nesbitt, president of the hospital society, turned the first sod and then presented the spade to Mother Mary Mark and to Sister Mary Kathleen, inviting them—and then all present—to turn the sod as well. A meeting of the nine-member board with the contractor and the Sisters followed.

Mother Mary Mark returned to Oliver on August 24 with Sister Mary Dositheus and Sullivan in order to commence daily supervision of the work, the Sisters staying as guests of Mrs. Mary O'Hara. Already the residents were generous in supplying them with gifts of eggs, fruit and tomatoes. Mother Mary Leopoldine sent trunks of altar linens and other gifts from the general administration. The women of Oliver planned canning bees for the benefit of the hospital, putting up peaches and plums by the gallons in September. By November the Sisters were busy setting up

Father John LaBrake, with Mother Mary Mark (left), Sister Mary Kathleen (right), and community members, blesses the grounds in 1942 and turns the first sod for the construction of the new hospital in Oliver. SSAA P0153

beds, washing windows and marking blankets. The installation of electrical power occurred just one hour before they moved in on November 5.

These months were important also for the formation of groups that would provide constant and valuable service to the hospital. The women's auxiliary held its first meeting on October 14 in the Elks Hall.[475] On October 31, the board of management held its first meeting in the hospital by lantern light as electricity had not yet been connected. Even though the hospital wasn't open for business, Mother Mary Mark and Nesbitt represented it at the British Columbia Hospitals' Association meetings in Victoria.

★   ★   ★

The last Sunday in November of 1942 began in the hospital with Bishop Johnson offering Mass in the new chapel, then walking through the entire building, blessing each part of it. A more formal opening took place at

2:30 that afternoon, when BC Agriculture Minister Dr. K.C. MacDonald opened the front door with a ceremonial gold key. Bishop Johnson spoke: "Charity is a unifying principle because it embraces all. In this hospital all shall benefit whether poor or rich, attractive or repulsive, native or new Canadian."[476] One man came to realize this after stating that he would rather die in the gutter than go to a Catholic Sisters' hospital. He was taken seriously ill, required surgery and was so appreciative of the care given him by the Sisters that for years afterwards he sent them a dozen fresh eggs regularly from his farm.[477]

The first baby arrived not long after the opening. Baby boy Barney was born at 2 a.m. on November 30 and baptized in the hospital on December 9. The first operation, a skin graft, was performed on December 10.

Many from the community toured their new hospital, a T-shaped building of cream stucco finished with black trim of Tudor-like design standing on rising ground west of the town and facing east. The main floor had business offices, private and semi-private rooms and a surgery. The lower floor contained an isolation unit and a separate section for First Nation patients as required by the federal government of the time. The Sisters and nurses occupied the upper floor. The chapel was also located on the top floor, the altar and communion rail again a gift from Archie Sullivan. At completion of the hospital the Sisters had contributed almost 90 percent of the $120,000 expense that the Congregation of the Sisters of St. Ann expected to recover from profits, but the only way

Named after Bishop Martin Johnson's patron saint, St. Martin's Hospital was erected in 1942 to serve the growing population of the Oliver–Osoyoos district.
SSAA P0149

to show a profit was for the Sisters to work for nothing. The pioneer staff members were Sisters Mary Mark, former provincial; Mary Dositheus, RN; Mary Constantine; and Mary Dunstan.

Before and after the opening, donors continued to give—the Canadian Legion, the Women's Institute, the Oliver Board of Trade, local sawmills, the Elks' Lodge and many individuals. Anthony Walsh, a well-known Catholic teacher on the local Inkameep Reserve, donated his excellent library to the hospital when he joined the army.

Through the years, participation by the local community continued as they visited on the annual Hospital Day, entertained the patients, held bazaars and teas and donated and canned the fruit for which the Okanagan is so famous. In 1944 an Egg Week sponsored by the auxiliary brought in more than 300 dozen eggs, which were stored "in water glass for future use."[478]

The hospital instituted its own insurance plan, charging $16 per "contract" per year. Five days in maternity cost $32 without a contract and $23 with; the general ward charge was $5.50 a day and $10 per

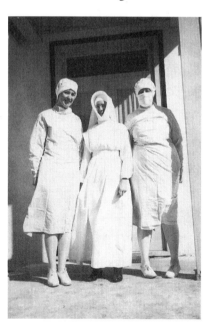

newborn day.[479] "The first year's report showed a total of 407 patients with 4,129 patient days, 79 babies born, 187 X-rays, and 178 operations."[480]

The type of patients treated once again reflected the main occupations of the community residents. Many miners were admitted with lung infections caused by the dust they had inhaled while working in the mines. In the summer, hospital staff dealt with many patients from among the fruit pickers who suffered strains and sprains from climbing trees and lifting, or broken bones from falling out of trees or off ladders—an occupational hazard. The operation of the

One of the original Sisters at St. Martin's Hospital, Sister Mary Dositheus poses in 1943 with two nursing staff. SSAA P0157

board was also influenced by the seasons, as meetings could not be held during harvest time in the orchards.

Newcomers in the early years included Sister Celine Marie, a graduate of St. Joseph's School of Nursing (1934), who arrived in 1946 as nursing and operating-room supervisor and X-ray technician, and stayed until 1957. She had earned a B.Sc.N. at Seattle University in 1940; after receiving a diploma in hospital organization and management in 1965 from the University of Manitoba, she returned to St. Martin's Hospital until 1968 as administrator and superior during the difficult years when Oliver and Osoyoos citizens were at war over the site of a possible new hospital. During her career she served in each of the six hospitals operated by the Sisters of St. Ann in British Columbia.

Maintaining the plant was frequently a problem. Only months after the hospital opened, the weather was so cold that frozen water pipes burst in the main hall. A more serious incident occurred in January 1950, when twenty-eight water pipes froze and burst along with the radiators, shortly followed by a hot-water pipe bursting between the walls, causing flooding in the rooms below. Again in December 1964 the frozen pipes burst, cascading water into the nurses' quarters. Adding insult to injury, fire broke out on the lower floor when the plumber was thawing the pipes with a torch. Insufficient insulation also meant the upper floors where the Sisters lived became particularly unbearable when summer temperatures reached as high as 110 degrees Fahrenheit.

In those days an elevator was not a given in any new building, which meant a lot of hauling of materials, equipment, laundry and food. In 1948 Sister Mary Agatha, the administrator, conferred with the government in Victoria and with Whittaker, the government architect, about the installation of an elevator. She also hoped to build a nurses' residence in order to free up beds for the heavy influx of patients. In March that year every bed was occupied and two patients had to be refused.[481]

An elevator remained a dream until 1955. A. McCulloch, architect, submitted the final designs for remodelling and the alterations necessary for installation. The government agreed to a grant, tenders were submitted and a contractor was chosen. Finally in September history was made when the equipment for a new Otis elevator, the first in Oliver, arrived. The official introduction of the elevator on November 30, 1955, was a milestone for the hospital and all the board members and their wives, as well as the executives of all the organizations who had sponsored furniture and equipment for the hospital, got together to applaud and then enjoy tea.

Recognizing that the long hours and pressures of operating a hospital were taking a toll on the Sisters, the general council gave permission for the purchase of a recreational property. In January 1966 the Sisters took possession of lakeside property and a house on Vaseaux Lake, purchased from H. Bailey for $21,500. They enjoyed many relaxing and happy times here.

St. Martin's was often full to capacity, the overcrowding making patient care more difficult. The Sisters and the board discussed this situation frequently. In March 1966, Health Minister Eric Martin gave approval in principle for a new hospital to serve the South Okanagan. But the wheels moved slowly. By the end of 1967 the minister of health announced that the new hospital would be built in Oliver, a very unpopular decision with the citizens of Osoyoos. The Oliver–Osoyoos Hospital Society struck a committee to meet with the architect and individual groups as detailed

The staff of St. Martin's Hospital in 1957. Front row l to r—Sister Mary Doris, Sister Rose Mary, Sister Mary Bertholde; back row—Sister Mary Odila, Sister Mary Ann Cecilia, Sister Mary Martinus, Sister Mary Walter, Sister Mary Albert (Lavinia Richard). PHOTO BY NAN DEWICK, SSAA P0154

planning got underway. But the fire marshal cancelled a meeting of the society when 1,500 people tried to crowd into the Osoyoos Elementary School. It was recorded that "a very unfortunate animosity exists between the two communities over the site of the new hospital."[482]

On March 19, 1970, the regional hospital district announced in Penticton that it had been given responsibility for planning and construction of the new hospital. The government gave formal approval in July 1971 for Kenyon Company of Penticton to construct the new hospital.

Thus on December 20, 1972, Sister Margaret Doris reported to the board that (1) letters of termination had been sent to all the staff, (2) all suppliers had been advised of the imminent closing of St. Martin's Hospital, and (3) the date had been set for the transfer of patients.[483] On January 12, 1973, twenty-three patients, including four newborns, were transferred within 1½ hours to the new South Okanagan General Hospital, thus marking the official closing of St. Martin's as an acute-care facility.

*   *   *

To Sister Sheila Griffin, administrator since the summer of 1968, fell the onerous task of determining the future of the old building. Many interested parties, including the local community and the BC government, weighed in with opinions. The hopes had been that St. Martin's could see new life as an extended-care unit or personal-care facility. But on March 14, 1972, the manager of the construction and inspection division of the British Columbia Hospital Insurance Service (BCHIS), stated that the building was not suitable for an economically sound operation as an extended-care unit. The final decision came in a letter from Denis Cocke, minister of health in the newly elected New Democratic government, that the "hospital is not operationally suitable for health care."[484] Cocke personally toured the building on April 25, 1973, and confirmed that the government could not find a health-care use for it. Sister Margaret Doris announced at the final meeting of the board on June 27 that the Sisters would be leaving St. Martin's the next day—Thursday, June 28, 1973.

The community could not see the Sisters leave without acknowledging their contribution. On January 27, 1973, at the annual banquet of the

Oliver–Osoyoos Rotary and Chamber of Commerce, they had received recognition of their thirty years of service. The 250 people attending heard:

> It is surely a fitting tribute to the Sisters of St. Ann that the two communities who argued so long and bitterly over the location of the new hospital . . . set aside their differences and joined together in a mutual expression of appreciation for the work of the Sisters in the South Okanagan.[485]

They were presented with the Civic Achievement Award and a framed scroll expressing the people's gratitude.

Further recognition came with the dedication of the west wing of the South Okanagan General Hospital to the Sisters of St. Ann in 1975 and the installation of a plaque to honour the Sisters' contribution. Victor Casorso, past chair of the St. Martin's board, stated at the ceremony: "By their deeds they will be remembered and may their light forever shine."[486]

The original St. Martin's Hospital building was demolished in 1981. At the corner of the property stands a plaque mounted on a large boulder commemorating this original building. It bears the words, in part:

Site of St. Martin's Hospital

1942—1973

Operated by the Sisters of St. Ann

Chapter 12

Mount St. Francis, Nelson

*Mount St. Francis welcomes everybody regardless of
denomination or religious affiliation. The clergy of every
denomination or sect are encouraged to visit their members.*
—Sister Mary Dositheus

On a visit to the motherhouse in Lachine on November 7, 1946,
Martin Johnson, bishop of Nelson, asked Mother Mary Leopoldine,
the superior general, for the services of the Sisters of St. Ann to open a
facility to care for aged men of the Kootenay area. By then he was already
familiar with the Sisters' work at St. Martin's Hospital in Oliver, and felt
that the postwar revival made this an appropriate time to propose such an
undertaking.

Nelson sits in the midst of the Selkirk Mountains on the west arm of
Kootenay Lake in southeastern British Columbia and has become known
as the Heritage Capital of BC since the restoration of many of its buildings in the 1980s. It was named in 1889 after Lieutenant-Governor Hugh
Nelson (1887–92) and incorporated as a city in 1897, when its population was three thousand,[487] It had come to life in 1886 with the discovery
of rich silver deposits nearby. Nelson became the regional supply centre,
situated as it was on a major transportation corridor with two railways
running through it. One of these was the Canadian Pacific Railway that
brought together its Kootenay mining and smelting operations in 1906
to form the Consolidated Mining and Smelting Company,[488] a company
that was to form a strong bond with Mount St. Francis in the hospital's

inaugural days. The city was fortunate in the distinctive architecture of its main buildings, built from the 1890s to the 1920s. Many of its large brick and stone Victorian structures still stand, their solid construction having helped them escape the kind of fires that decimated the early buildings of so many other towns in the Kootenays. Today they are a major tourist attraction.

When Martin Johnson became the first bishop of Nelson at its formation as a diocese in 1936, he saw the need to provide for the care of the area's early pioneers, many of whom were now pensioners and mainly former miners. His overtures to the community met with success and local businessmen gathered at the bishop's home in 1946 to discuss plans. Following his approach to the Sisters of St. Ann on November 7, Mother Mary Mildred, provincial superior, and Sister Rose Mary, superior at Mount St. Mary in Victoria, visited Nelson from November 26 to 29 to survey the 37-acre McKim estate that the diocese had recently purchased. They found that 15 of the 30 acres of arable land were under cultivation. The property held several outbuildings, a poultry house and brooders for 2,200 chickens, a barn and the original ranch house, which could be repaired and serve for a time as a home until a more permanent structure was

McKim Cottage, seen here in 1975, was part of the original 1946 purchase for Mount St. Francis. True to the original health care vision of the Sisters, it is currently in use as a mental health facility. SSAA P0221

erected. The poultry business was yielding a monthly profit of $200 and the vegetable garden and orchard were expected to produce an income in addition to supplying food for the home. The Sisters' favourable report led to approval by the general council in July 1947, enabling the Sisters to pay $12,000 for the required portion of the property and the house. Bishop Johnson contributed $1,000.

In the interim a committee met to draft sketches, select an architect, address fundraising, and to approach the government for financial assistance. The committee also assuaged the concerns of a largely non-Catholic population who feared discrimination. Assurances were forthcoming. Few of the committee members were Catholic, but they showed great enthusiasm for the concept, reassuring the populace that guests would be admitted on the basis of need as recommended by the BC director of welfare and social assistance.[489] The deputy provincial secretary promised a government contribution of one-third the cost, as long as there was assurance that the home would be open for old-age pensioners and social-assistance cases, that it would be maintained on a non-sectarian basis, and the plans approved by the provincial architect.[490] On September 1, 1947, the general council granted permission for the project to proceed.

Local architect W.F. Williams drew up plans and a fundraising campaign was launched in the *Nelson Daily News*, spearheaded by the owner, F.F. Payne. The list of donors illustrates the broad spectrum of support for Mount St. Francis. Heading the list were district doctors, followed by local businesses such as the T. Eaton Company, Woogmans, Woolworths and Hudson Bay Company; local fraternal and non-profit groups such as the Knights of Columbus, the Catholic Women's League, the Fraternal Order of Eagles, Rotary, Gyro, Soroptomists, Lions and Kiwanis; and many individuals.[491] The response was so good that when the sod was turned for a permanent building on September 13, 1947, the Sisters received $45,217.31 in public donations.[492]

The Sisters did not wait for the completion of a new building to begin their ministry in Nelson and their sixth foray into BC health care. On May 13, 1947, Quebec-born Sister Mary Seraphina, previously superior in Kamloops, and Sister Mary Itha arrived on the Kettle Valley train to stay with the Sisters of St. Joseph, who operated St. Joseph School in Nelson, while "the cottage" on the McKim estate was being prepared. Sister Mary Seraphina came as founder and first superior of this new endeavour.

They moved in on June 3 and the first three boarders at the facility arrived on July 14 from a home in Moyie in the East Kootenay—John Jarvie, John Anderson and Carl Holm. Bishop Johnson continued to be an enthusiastic supporter, regularly visiting the elderly men, sometimes walking two or three miles to the house in winter after abandoning his car in deep snow since there were no finished or plowed roads to this isolated location.

Sister Mary Seraphina invited a group of the original supporters to form the first official advisory board, which met October 17, 1947, electing Judge E.P. Dawson as chair and Walter Hendricks as vice-chair. Progress was slowed by the sudden death of architect Williams in December. His widow, Ilsa, also an architect, stepped in.

In October 1948 the bids from the first tenders were too high to permit proceeding. Further negotiations were needed with both levels of government. Bishop Johnson, Dr. H.H. Beauchamp, a Dr. Shaw and Sister Mary Seraphina met with officials in Victoria. By the time they returned to Nelson, the project was no longer the home for aged men that had originally been discussed, but was to be designated as an infirmary, which called for an enlarged and changed structure. Victoria architect Don Wagg was retained to alter the plans to meet the standards required for a BC infirmary. Ilsa Williams and another architect, Arthur Morton, were to guide the subsequent construction in Nelson.

Mount St. Francis would be one of the biggest undertakings ever in the district. A reinforced steel and concrete fireproof building would contain nine four-bed wards and sixty-two private rooms, with accommodation for the Sisters and a small chapel, at a cost four times the original estimate.

The second round of tenders were opened at the advisory board meeting held at Bishop Johnson's home on February 20, 1949, resulting in the contract being awarded to Marwell Construction of Vancouver. The board took on the responsibility of raising another $50,000 for furnishings. A solicitation letter to R.W. Diamond, manager of Consolidated Mining and Smelting in Trail, and a member of the board, elicited a very generous donation of $15,000, kick-starting the campaign. When the campaign was over, the federal government had contributed $147,000—or $1,500 per bed—and the provincial government one-third of the total, $171,528; the Sisters of St. Ann provided the remainder, $151,000.[493]

Construction began on April 5, 1949, 1½ years after the turning of the sod. Two thousand people participated in the formal opening of Mount St. Francis on Wednesday, July 5, 1950. There were speeches by Bishop Johnson, Health and Welfare Minister A.D. Turnbull,[494] Mayor N.C. Stibbs, R.W. Diamond and Judge E.P. Dawson, board chair. Ilsa Williams handed the ceremonial keys to the building over to Mother Mary Ludovic, the provincial superior. The *Nelson Daily News* wrote that Mount St. Francis was a "fitting monument to those pioneers whose energy and faith in their land built this" and that "it is a beautiful, practical testimony to the selflessness of the new generation and its full acceptance of responsibilities towards senior citizens."[495] The formal ceremonies over, visitors toured the new building under the leadership of members of the Kiwanis Club.

Bishop Johnson blessed the building and celebrated the first Mass in the chapel on July 26, the Feast of Saint Ann, prior to the residents moving in on August 2. The Sisters left the McKim "cottage," which would now house other hospital staff, and moved into the Mount. By the end of the year there were sixty-two male and female patients. Many people had contributed to the cleaning, furnishing and supplying of both locations. Of note was the Uphill Circle, an association of local women formed in

Originally envisioned as a home for elderly men, Mount St. Francis was designated a general infirmary before the completion and official opening of its new structure in 1950. SSAA P0212

1950 who decided to make Mount St. Francis their special project. Their help was invaluable as they busied themselves sewing linens, constructing mattress pads, making beds, cleaning rooms and raising funds through teas and special events. When Sister Mary Patrick arrived as the new superior in 1951, she asked the women to relinquish the Uphill Circle name to become known as the "Ladies' Auxiliary" in order to be eligible for funds from the Community Chest (renamed the United Way in 1963).

There were other projects in the wind in the Nelson Catholic population in the 1950s. In July 1954 a fundraising campaign was initiated to raise $400,000 from the Catholic community for the building of an institution of higher learning near Mount St. Francis, to be called Notre Dame College. The Sisters gave 5.4 acres of the original McKim property for this purpose; the Sisters at the Mount donated $100, and the patients $1,000.[496] Father J. Joyce, SJ, Ph.D., was the first dean and also served as chaplain for the Sisters.

Close connections were maintained with the college. Sisters who studied or lectured there lived at the Mount. Sister Mary Catherine of Sienna was instrumental in gaining approval from the Canadian Association of Medical Record Librarians for a medical records school in 1964. In May 1966 many Sisters attended the graduation of Sister Mary Gonzaga, who was the first to receive a degree in the new medical record science program.

Over the years, despite the isolation of Mount St. Francis, many distinguished visitors would tour the hospital and visit those who called it home, among them BC Premier Byron Johnson, several lieutenant-governors, Archbishop Joseph Charbonneau and young adults in the federal Katimavik program.[497] Premier W.A.C. Bennett arrived in November 1957 and invited patients to join him on his bus as the first people to officially cross the new million-dollar cantilever bridge over Kootenay Lake. The following year the BC Centennial vans brought historical displays—the province celebrated its hundredth anniversary as the Sisters observed the same anniversary of their arrival in British Columbia.

The Sisters at Mount St. Francis were very involved in the broader community. From 1964 to 1976, Sister Mary Ellen McDonald taught in the commerce department at Notre Dame University, was secretary to the faculty association and a member of the convocation committee. To these duties she added membership on the hospital advisory board and activities in the local parish.[498] Sister Mary Catherine of Sienna conducted a retreat for Anglican women in 1965. Sister Mary Luca and Sister Mary Ann Celesta were elected chair and secretary of the West Kootenay Regional Health Council in September 1967.

In the early years they shared their abundance of garden produce with Kootenay Lake Hospital, Willow Haven Private Hospital, Notre Dame College and the Sisters of St. Joseph. Starting in December 1967, they provided hot meals from their kitchen for the Meals-on-Wheels program for shut-ins. Sisters Mary Luca and Mary Patrick presented diplomas and pins to the graduates of the practical nurse class of 1968 at the Nelson Provincial Vocational School. The Soroptomist Club members, who had always been generous in donating equipment and furnishings to the hospital, elected Sister Mary Luca to their board in 1969. After the city declared March 2 to 8, 1980, to be "Mount St. Francis Week," emphasizing the value of the facility to the community, Sister Margaret Doris suggested that the residents might enjoy being "adopted" by individuals or families. More than thirty people responded. When Rick Hansen rolled into Nelson on his worldwide "Man in Motion" tour, the patients presented him with the $1,100 they had raised. The Sisters and

Following in the footsteps of past premiers, Dave Barrett (middle) is welcomed by Sister Mary Barry to Mount St. Francis in the mid-1970s. SSAA P0223

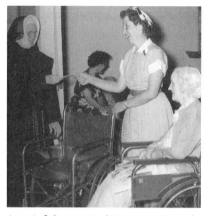

A grateful superior, Sister Mary Patrick accepts a wheelchair on behalf of Mount St. Francis. SSAA P0218

the hospital residents were definitely attuned to the world beyond their doors.

Since the congregation provided opportunities for its members to pursue advanced education, it was natural to celebrate related milestones. The Sisters at the Mount honoured Sister Mary Margaret of Scotland when she received her Ph.D. from Cornell University (1965) and Sister Mary Ellen McDonald on attaining her master's degree in business administration from the University of Notre Dame in Indiana (1968).[499] The Second Vatican Council changed the manner in which women religious pronounced their final vows. Often this ceremony would occur in their home parishes. This enabled the Sisters at Mount St. Francis to celebrate the final profession of Sister Leanne Marie (1966) in her home parish of Kaslo, BC, and to entertain Sister Andrea Marie and her parents after she made her final vows in Kimberley, BC (1966).

As in most new endeavours—and despite the welcoming community—there were a few setbacks.

In May 1958, Municipal Affairs Minister W.D. Black, city engineer E.E. Olson and Mayor T.S. Shorthouse called the Sisters with assurances that the road in to Mount St. Francis would be blacktopped that spring. Two years later, when the work had still not been done, the general council in Lachine granted permission for the Sisters to contract out the work themselves at a cost of $6,320.[500] They had waited a long time to have a decent road. During a December 1952 visit by Edith Pringle, inspector of hospitals, Sister Mary Luca informed her that the "religious policy of our Infirmary is precisely that of the provincial and public hospitals throughout British Columbia." When some voiced questions about the policies of Mount St. Francis again, Sister Mary Dositheus was quoted in the local paper as saying:

Concerning religion, Mount St. Francis welcomes everybody regardless of denomination or religious affiliation. The clergy of every denomination or sect are encouraged to visit their members. In a word, our policy in this regard is identical with the policy of the Nelson, Trail or Rossland hospitals.[501]

An important step in the evolution of care was the designation on December 1, 1965, of Mount St. Francis as one of seven extended-care hospitals in British Columbia under the Hospital Act. Henceforth all patients would be screened by a medical committee and if they were deemed eligible, would be covered by an all-inclusive per diem rate and would personally pay $1 a day, just as patients in acute-care facilities. Mount St. Francis expressed concern for those patients who would not fit the criteria. Fifty-eight of the Mount's residents were eligible and the forty who were not were allowed to remain, but no more in their category would be admitted. Further, Mount St. Francis officially became a bona fide public institution under the *Hospital Act* in May 1966, entitling it to exemption from the federal sales tax.[502] Another significant step was the granting of three-year accreditation on June 17, 1972. Mount St. Francis would continue to earn accreditation every three years until its demise.

Tea time in the activity room for the long-term residents. The woman in the middle might have been a member of the Doukhobors, a Russian religious and pacifist sect active in the Kootenays. SSAA P0217

Despite Nelson's remoteness, the Governor General and his wife, Roland and Norah Michener, stopped by for a visit in 1971. Sister Mary Luca, hospital administrator, is on the right. SSAA P0216

More discussion ensued on the need to expand. Shortly after Sister Mary Barry arrived as the new administrator—replacing Sister Mary Luca—a regional hospital district referendum on December 11, 1971, voted $550,000 toward renovations and extension to Mount St. Francis. With the arrival of approval from British Columbia Hospital Insurance Service (BCHIS), the hospital began planning. In February 1972 the Victoria firm of Wagg & Hambleton was chosen as architects and the actual work began in October. David Hambleton regularly inspected the work in progress and also attended board meetings. The Sisters moved to "the cottage" to make room for displaced patients during the expansion. The official opening of the newly renovated hospital and its additions was celebrated with great fanfare on Saturday, June 8, 1974, followed by tea and tours. The bed complement had been reduced from ninety-eight to eighty-four, due to the incorporation of up-to-date physiotherapy and other treatment areas and centralized dietary services. In 1984 further renovations provided administration and support services areas.

Sister Margaret Doris replaced Sister Mary Barry as administrator in September 1978. Accompanying her was Sister Betty Janelle, who remained

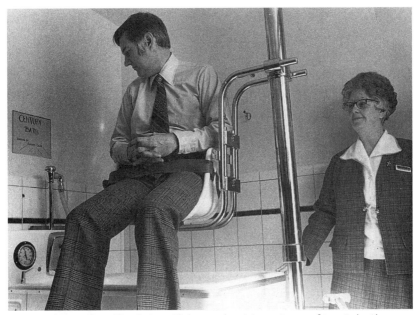

Contemplating the gift, a Rotary Club member tries out one of two tubs they donated to the hospital in 1974, while Sister Mary Barry looks on. SSAA P0222

for seven years, filling several roles. She helped with patients—transporting them to activities and visiting those who had no other visitors—and taught conversational French part-time to St. Joseph's Elementary School students. She tells of the Doukhobor families who would come to visit their elders bringing bags of Russian food or those who would come in traditional dress to sing and entertain the residents. Almost all the kitchen staff were Doukhobors, and they put borscht on the menu frequently.[503]

Sister Margaret Doris focused on enriching and enlarging the patients' lives. In 1981, the United Nations Year of the Disabled, she solicited families and friends to raise about $20,000 with the goal of purchasing a bus that could seat six wheelchairs and carry an attendant. This would open a whole new world. "It would enable them to become integrated into normal community living once again."[504]

Another change of leadership occurred with the arrival of Sister Rita Downey as the new administrator in September 1981. She had spent the past two years at the University of Toronto, where she received a degree in health administration. Not only was she a graduate of St. Joseph's School of Nursing, but her credentials included nine years of teaching in the school. She became an active member of the Nelson community and implemented a quality assurance program at the hospital when it was introduced as an essential element in the standards for accreditation in 1983. She also shepherded friends and volunteers who rallied to feed and care for the patients during a general strike in June 1987 that had been called by BC unions to protest against the Social Credit government's Bill 19, which limited the power of unions to call strike action. (The bill was withdrawn in 1991 by the NDP government.)

But it was clear through the 1980s that it would be impossible to continue staffing Mount St. Francis with Sisters of St. Ann. A change of governance would take place. The Marie Anne Blondin Society was created and incorporated under the Society Act on October 19, 1990, as a separate legal entity for the ownership and operation of the hospital. The McKim residence was registered in the name of the Sisters of St. Ann and the hospital was registered in the name of the Marie Anne Blondin Society.[505] The board of directors of the society delegated the responsibility for the operation of the hospital's affairs and financial management to the board of management, which then had the legal and moral responsibility for the conduct of the facility in all its aspects. In January 1992 Sister Frieda Raab, provincial superior and director of the Marie Anne Blondin Society, informed management and staff that for the first time a lay administrator would be engaged.[506]

Always a joyful time of the year, Christmas was a good excuse for the community to join the hospital in celebration. SSAA P0220

A meeting of the hospital board in the 1970s. At the far right is Sister Virginia Surina, with Sister Margaret Doris at the other end of the table, also on the right.
SSAA P0225

She appointed Sheila Hart on September 15, 1992. Sister Rita Downey had retired on September 1, 1992, after serving eleven years as administrator.

Even with these changes it became impossible to continue as a Catholic denominational facility. In 1997 the Sisters signed an agreement to amalgamate the hospital with the local health authority, after which the Marie Anne Blondin Society dissolved at its last meeting on November 15, 1997. The BC government required the Sisters to transfer title to the facility and its lands to them without compensation. The Sisters retained ownership of the adjacent property, including the McKim cottage, which they sold to the Nelson and Area Health Council in December 1999 for less than their assessed values, keeping faith with the past, placing a covenant on the property restricting its use to health care purposes. In March 2004 the Sisters agreed that part of the property could be developed by a private purchaser in partnership with the Interior Health Authority, to become a new residential care facility.

As this book was being written, the former Mount St. Francis facility was still owned by the Interior Health Authority but used only as a storage facility. The McKim cottage continued to be used by the same authority for mental health purposes.

Epilogue

Wherever there were new frontiers there were congregations of women religious helping to establish a presence for the values of the Catholic Church by founding schools, orphanages and hospitals. They saw themselves as God's instruments, eschewing praise for their works of charity. The Sisters of St. Ann had their frontier in Victoria at the start of the 1858 gold rush and soon pioneered new ventures throughout British Columbia, the Yukon and Alaska.

In branching out from teaching into nursing, they were responding to a profoundly human need that transcends the physical, accompanying patients at the most vulnerable time in their lives, not just listening to but hearing the individual. They carried out this service throughout British Columbia in a truly committed and professional manner. But, like all religious communities, they have continually adjusted their ministries to changing circumstances. As Sister Rita Larivée said when she was elected congregational leader in 2008: "When we wrap our labor in compassion and empathy that moves us beyond ourselves and makes our needs second to the hopes and dreams of a wider community, then we are engaged in ministry."[507]

As the number of Sisters of St. Ann in British Columbia decrease they are ensuring their legacy in a thoughtful and deliberate manner. When a new Mount St. Mary Hospital was built in 2003, the board initiated a fundraising drive to enable the construction of the Blessed Marie Anne Blondin Chapel. The expense for this chapel, which is at the heart of the facility, was not covered by the government. In recognition of the contribution of the Sisters to health care in British Columbia, and to support the continuation of this important ministry, the Congregation, located in Lachine, Quebec, gave a sizeable gift. In 2006 the Mount St. Mary Foundation established an endowment fund honouring the Sisters, called the Sisters of St. Ann Legacy Fund. The Sisters were pleased to contribute a generous start-up amount, knowing it would go toward supporting and enhancing the lives of the residents who make Mount St. Mary their home.

Marking their 150th anniversary in British Columbia in 2008, the Sisters donated two $150,000 endowments to the University of Victoria—one for a graduate nursing scholarship for nurse practitioners, the other an undergraduate education bursary, both with preference given to a student who intends to work in rural communities. These endowments were officially announced at the special celebrations of their anniversary at the Victoria Conference Centre on June 7, 2008, at which Kim Campbell, Canada's first female and nineteenth prime minister, and former student of St. Ann's Academy, was the keynote speaker. On March 1, 2010, the Sisters signed an agreement that would see the sale of their Queenswood property in the Gordon Head area of Victoria to the university. "The agreement is in keeping with the shared history of the Sisters of St. Ann and UVic, and their shared commitment to education and health promotion."[508]

Property in Duncan originally settled by the Sisters in 1864, later home to St. Ann's Convent School, has for the last thirty years been

Happy to be celebrating their 150th anniversary in British Columbia in 2008, Sister Mary Ellen King, congregational leader (left), and Sister Marie Zarowny, province leader (right), announced two $150,000 endowments to the University of Victoria for nursing and education students intending to work in rural communities. The Right Honourable Kim Campbell (centre), 19th prime minister of Canada and former student at St. Ann's Academy, Victoria, was pleased to be the keynote speaker at the event celebrated at the Victoria Conference Centre. PHOTO BY TONY SOUTHWELL

under the stewardship of the Vancouver Island Providence Community Association, a registered society "operating creative and innovative programs for adults in the Valley with mental health issues, brain injuries and developmental challenges." This 400-acre parcel of land and its buildings, known as Providence Farm, were formally transferred in perpetuity to the association by Sister Marie Zarowny, province leader, at a ceremony on September 12, 2009. Sister Marie announced that the Sisters were entrusting to the Providence Community Association their "legacy of serving the needs of the people of the Cowichan Valley."

Other donations include a generous sum given to Little Flower Academy, a school the Sisters operated in Vancouver for many years, for a much-needed new building. Yearly since 2000 they have awarded the Marie Anne Blondin Bursary to offer financial assistance to women wishing to pursue theological or church ministry studies and have donated a bursary to Camosun College in Victoria for licensed practical nurse education.

A continuing priority, of course, is ensuring that the remaining forty-three Sisters (as at June 2011) in St. Joseph's Province (British Columbia) will have a secure retirement. St. Ann's Residence, a care home for the elderly and ill Sisters, is scheduled to close at the end of 2012, and the residents will need to move to public care facilities. Despite the financial requirements of providing for these needs, the Sisters' simple lifestyle and commitment to others allows them to continue to aid many charitable causes.

The greatest of these efforts is in solidarity with their Sisters in Haiti who operate schools and clinics. St. Joseph's Province has given funds to help provide salaries for all staff in the five Haitian schools of the Sisters of St. Ann so that they may continue to educate the children in this devastated country, and they have established a fundraising project to provide others the opportunity to join them in this endeavour. They also have a presence in Chile. Until 2010 they had a region in the Cameroon (since the 1960s); the Sisters are withdrawing from their one mission in the Congo during 2011. Closer to home, they continue involvement in areas concerning social justice. A priority for the Sisters in recent years has been to respond justly and compassionately to the painful experience of generational suffering arising from the Indian Residential Schools. The Sisters of

St. Ann were involved as teachers and caregivers in four of the schools and have provided leadership in partnership with members of First Nations in developing and participating in programs of healing and reconciliation.

There are visible reminders of their presence in Victoria. On Humboldt Street, St. Ann's Academy—both building and grounds—which was designated a BC heritage site in 1984, is still just across the way from the 1908 addition to St. Joseph's Hospital. On July 12, 1997, St. Ann's officially re-opened when the first stage of its restoration was completed. Visitors can now see the parlours and the chapel in all their beauty as they were when the Sisters lived in them. The most noticeable of reminders is a still-active and vibrant Mount St. Mary Hospital on the site of the original St. Joseph's School of Nursing.

The skills, dedication, integrity and professionalism that the Sisters of St. Ann brought to the service of British Columbians were given willingly. They responded to the needs of an emerging society, making an enormous unpaid contribution. They were energized spiritually by "working in God's vineyard." Their legacy will be seen in the values they passed on to the nursing students at St. Joseph's School of Nursing, staff in their hospitals throughout the province, students in their classrooms and, indeed, to the thousands they have influenced in their many ministries. They have had an immeasurable impact on the story of British Columbia.

Acknowledgements

I am most grateful to the Sisters of St. Ann who shared their experiences of ministry in health care with me and to others involved in the Sisters' hospitals who agreed to be interviewed. I thank Dr. Patricia Roy for her insights and suggestions, which enhanced my understanding of BC history. I appreciate those Sisters who with foresight preserved the many records and artifacts of their history. I thank Michaeleen King, Sisters of St. Ann archivist in Victoria, for the many hours spent aiding my search and pointing me in new directions; and Sister Margaret Cantwell and Carey Pallister, also of the Sisters' archives. I appreciate the welcome and friendship of all those in the Begbie Street office where the archives are situated.

Thanks to many along the way who have offered assistance in some manner—Barbara Lathem, Sylvia Van Kirk, Lynne Damant, Joy Olesky and Monsignor Michael Lapierre. I am grateful to Anna Comfort and Harbour Publishing for accepting and publishing this history.

This book would not have been finished without the patience and support of my husband, Tony, and the encouragement of our children and their spouses—John and Alice, Diane and Nick, and Marianne, the nurse in our family.

And I could not forget to thank Sister Sheila Moss for inviting me to take on this project.

Appendixes

Appendix 1:
Administrators/Superiors at St. Joseph's Hospital 1875–1968

Sister Mary Providence	1875–80
Sister Mary Winifred	1880–81
Sister Mary Providence	1881–82
Sister Mary Stephen	1882–83
Sister Mary Winifred	1883–85
Sister Mary Providence	1885–90
Sister Mary Anne of Jesus	1890–94
Sister Mary Placide	1894–95
Sister Mary Bridget	1895–98
Sister Mary St. Sauveur	1898–1900
Sister Mary Providence	1900–03
Sister Mary Bridget	1903–17
Sister Mary Margaret	1917–19
Sister Mary Mark	1919–25
Sister Mary Mildred	1925–31
Sister Mary Ludovic	1931–35
Sister Mary Alfreda	1935–41
Sister Mary Kathleen	1941–47
Sister Rose Mary	1947–53
Sister Mary Angelus	1953–59
Sister Mary Ann Celesta	1959–65
Sister Mary Lucita	1965–68

Appendix 2:
Directors of St. Joseph's School of Nursing 1900–1981

Sister Mary Gertrude of Jesus	1900–13
Sister Mary Anna	1913–24
Sister Mary Alfreda	1924–26
Sister Mary Gregory	1926–33
Sister Mary Gabriella	1933–34
Sister Mary Gregory	1934–36
Sister Mary Beatrice	1936–37
Sister Mary Gregory	1937–49
Sister Mary Claire	1949–50
Sister Mary Gregory	1950–54
Sister Mary Lucita	1954–57
Sister Mary Justinian	1957–59

Sister Mary Ronalda	1959–62
Sister Mary Doris	1962–66
Sister Mary Ronalda	1966–68
Lilian Knighton	1968–73
Anne McKenzie	1974–75
Sylvia Brough	1976–81

Appendix 3:
Sisters Known by Both Religious and Birth Names
This list contains names of Sisters of St. Ann who are included in this history and may be known by both their religious and birth names.

Mother Mary Ann	Marie Esther Blondin***
Sister Andrea Marie	Marie Zarowny
Sister Celine Marie	Marie Baines
Sister Elizabeth Marie	Betty Janelle
Sister Frieda Marie	Frieda Raab
Sister Joan Marie	Molly Conlon
Sister Kathleen Mary	Margaret Cantwell
Sister Leanne Marie	Virginia Surina
Sister Marie des Sept Douleurs	Marie Mainville
Sister Mary Ida of the Eucharist	Ida Brasseur
Sister Mary Angèle	Angèle Gauthier
Sister Mary Angelus	Mary Barry
Sister Mary Ann Celesta	Sheila Griffin
Sister Mary Anna	Margaret Daly
Sister Mary Anne of Jesus	Elizabeth Rowan
Sister Mary Aquina	Kathleen Cyr
Sister Mary Beatrice	Beatrice Wambeke
Sister Mary Benedicta	Theresa Clarkson
Sister Mary Catherine of Sienna	Catherine Moroney
Sister Mary Conception	Mary Lane
Sister Mary Doris	Margaret Doris
Sister Mary Eileen	Eileen Kelly
Sister Mary Ellen	Mary Ellen McDonald
Sister Mary Faustina	Grace Down
Sister Mary Fidelis	Lucy DuMont

***

*** Since her beatification on April 29, 2001, she has been called Blessed Marie Anne Blondin.

Sister Mary Gladys	Kathleen Moroney
Sister Mary Gonzaga	Joan Brophy
Sister Mary Gregory	Mary Dina Hughes
Sister Mary Henrietta of Jesus	Rose Anna Gareau
Sister Mary Janita	Janita Stephenson (now McHugh)
Sister Mary Joan	Joan Bell
Sister Mary Josepha	Mary Ellen King
Sister Mary Justinian	Norah Shine
Sister Mary Laurena	Mary Powell
Sister Mary Luca	Catherine Kirwan
Sister Mary Lucita	Mary McGarrigle
Sister Mary Lumena	Virginie Brasseur
Sister Mary Margaret of Scotland	Edith Down
Sister Mary of the Sacred Heart	Salome Valois
Sister Mary Osithe	Elizabeth Labossière
Sister Mary Patrick	Teresa McLeod
Sister Mary Perpetua	Sheila Hughes
Sister Mary Providence	Mary Ellen McTucker
Sister Mary Ronalda	Ronalda McGauvran
Sister Mary Theodore	Victoria Pineault
Sister Miriam Anne	Anne Deas
Sister Miriam Jude	Theresa Doogan
Sister Miriam Rita	Rita Downey
Sister Miriam Theresa	Irene Wheldon
Sister Rita Marie	Thérèse Brousseau
Sister Rose Mary	Alice Beatrice Daly
Sister Sheila Marie	Sheila Moss

Selected Bibliography

1. Books

Auclair, Rev. Elie J. *History of the Sisters of Saint Ann: The First Fifty Years 1850–1900.* Translated by Sister Mary Mildred Welsh, SSA. Lachine: Saint Ann's Press, 1939.

Barman, Jean. *The West Beyond the West: A History of British Columbia.* Toronto: University of Toronto Press, 1991.

Baskerville, Peter A. *Beyond the Island: An Illustrated History of Victoria.* Burlington, ON: Windsor Publications, 1986.

Bates, Christina, Dianne Dodd and Nicole Rousseau, eds. *On All Frontiers: Four Centuries of Canadian Nursing.* Ottawa: University of Ottawa Press, 2005.

Berton, Pierre. *Klondike: The Last Great Gold Rush 1896–1899.* Toronto: McClelland and Stewart, 1997.

Bicknell, Jacquie, and Vicky White, eds. *Oliver Area: Secrets and Surprises.* Oliver, BC: South Okanagan Writers and Publishers, 1995.

Bourgon, Nan. *Rubber Boots for Dancing and Other Memories of Pioneer Life in the Bulkley Valley.* Edited by Marjorie Rosberg. Smithers: Hetherington 1979.

Bowering, Marilyn. *To All Appearances a Lady.* Toronto: HarperCollins, 1997.

Brown, Debra. *The Challenge of Caring: A History of Women and Health Care in British Columbia.* British Columbia Ministry of Health, 2000.

Cantwell, Margaret, SSA, and Mary George Edmond, SSA. *North to Share, The Sisters of Saint Ann in Alaska and the Yukon Territory.* Victoria: Sisters of Saint Ann, 1992.

Carr, Emily. *The Book of Small.* Vancouver: Clarke, Irwin and Co. Ltd., 1966.

Chaput, Don. *Nellie Cashman and the North American Mining Frontier.* Tucson, AZ: Westernlore Press, 1995.

Chronicle of the 20th Century. Mount Kisco, NY: Chronicle Publications, 1987.

Coccola, Nicolas. *They Call Me Father: Memoirs of Father Nicolas Coccola.* Edited by Margaret Whitehead. Vancouver: University of British Columbia Press, 1988.

De Baets, Maurice. *The Apostle of Alaska.* Translated by Sister Mary Mildred Welsh, SSA. Patterson, NJ: Guild Press, 1943.

De-Pathmos, Marie-Jean, SSA. *A History of the Sisters of Saint Anne.* Vol. 1, *1850–1890.* Translated by Marie Anne Eva, SSA. New York: Vantage Press, 1961.

Down, Edith E., SSA. *A Century of Service.* 2nd edition. Victoria: Sisters of St. Ann, 1999.

Downs, Barry. *Sacred Places: British Columbia's Early Churches.* Vancouver: Douglas and McIntyre, 1980.

Edwards-Rees, Desirée. *The Story of Nursing.* Don Mills: Longmans Canada, 1965.

Fialka, John J. *Sisters, Catholic Nuns and the Making of America.* New York: St. Martin's Press, 2003.

Forbes, Elizabeth. *Wild Roses at Their Feet: Pioneer Women of Vancouver Island.* Vancouver: Evergreen Press, 1971. British Columbia Centennial Project.

Forster, Merna. *100 Canadian Heroines: Famous and Forgotten Faces.* Toronto: Dundurn Press, 2004.

Gibbon, John Murray, and Mary Mathewson. *Three Centuries of Canadian Nursing.* Toronto: Macmillan, 1947.

Glavin, Terry, and Former Students of St. Mary's. *Amongst God's Own: The Enduring Legacy of St. Mary's Mission*. Mission, BC: Longhouse Publishing, 2002.

Gould, Jan. *Women of British Columbia*. Saanichton, BC: Hancock House, 1975.

Green, Valerie. *No Ordinary People: Victoria's Mayors Since 1862*. Victoria: Beach Holme Publishing, 1992.

Greene, John, Marc Lapprand, Gerald Moreau and Gerald Ricard. *French Presence in Victoria B.C. 1843–1991*. Victoria: L'Association Historique Francophone de Victoria, C.B., 1991.

Gregson, Harry. *A History of Victoria 1842–1970*. Victoria: Victoria Observer, 1970.

Helmcken, John. *The Reminiscences of Doctor John Sebastian Helmcken*. Edited by Dorothy Blakey Smith. Vancouver: University of British Columbia Press, 1975.

Hume, Stephen. *Lilies & Fireweed: Frontier Women of British Columbia*. Madeira Park, BC: Harbour Publishing, 2004.

Humphreys, Danda. *Building Victoria: Men, Myths, and Mortar*. Victoria: Heritage House, 2004.

Kluckner, Michael. *Victoria: The Way It Was*. North Vancouver: Whitecap Books, 1986.

Lillard, Charles. *Seven Shillings a Year: The History of Vancouver Island*. Ganges, BC: Horsdal and Schubart, 1993.

Lugrin, Nancy de Bertrand. "When the Sisters Came." In *The Pioneer Women of Vancouver Island 1843–1866*. Edited by John Hosie. Victoria: Women's Canadian Club of Victoria, 1928.

McDonough, John Thomas, OP. *Charbonneau & Le Chef*. Toronto: McClelland and Stewart, 1968.

McNally, Vincent. *The Lord's Distant Vineyard: A History of the Oblates and the Catholic Community in British Columbia*. Edmonton: University of Alberta Press, 2000.

McPherson, Kathryn. *Bedside Matters: The Transformation of Canadian Nursing 1900–1990*. Toronto: Oxford University Press, 1996.

Mansell, Diana RN. *Forging the Future: A History of Nursing in Canada*. Ann Arbor, MI: Thomas Press, 2004.

Mary Theodore, Sister, SSA, a.k.a. Victoria Pineault (attributed to). *A Chaplet of Years 1858–1918*. Victoria: Sisters of St. Ann, 1918.

———. *Heralds of Christ the King*. New York: P.J. Kennedy, 1939.

———. *Pioneer Nuns of British Columbia*. Victoria: Colonist Publishing, 1931.

———. *The Seal of the Cross*. Victoria: Sisters of St. Ann, 1939.

———. (attributed to). "The Sisters of Saint Ann on North Pacific Shores." Unpublished manuscript in the Archives of the Sisters of St. Ann.

Morgan, Roland, and Emily Disher. *Victoria Then and Now*. Vancouver: Bodima Publications, 1977.

Morice, Adrien-Gabriel, OMI. *The History of the Northern Interior of British Columbia 1859–1938*. Smithers, BC: Interior Stationery, 1978.

Nelson, Sioban. *Say Little, Do Much: Nurses, Nuns and Hospitals in the Nineteenth Century*. Philadelphia: University of Pennsylvania Press, 2001.

Ormsby, Margaret. *British Columbia: A History*. Toronto: MacMillan, 1958.

Pearson, Anne. *The Royal Jubilee Hospital School of Nursing 1891–1982*. Published by the Alumnae Association of the Royal Jubilee School of Nursing, 1985.

Pethick, Derek. *Victoria: The Fort.* Vancouver: Mitchell Press, 1968.

Pineault, Victoria. *See* Mary Theodore, Sister, SSA.

Reksten, Terry. *More English than the English: A Very Social History of Victoria.* Victoria: Orca Book Publishers, 1986.

Roy, Louise, SSA. *The Correspondence of Mother Marie Anne.* Translated by Eileen Gallagher, SSA. Lachine: Les Editions Sainte-Anne, 1977.

———. *The Sisters of Saint Anne: A Century of History,* Vol. 2, *1900–1950.* Translated by Eileen Gallagher, SSA. Lachine: Les Editions Sainte-Anne, 1994.

Roy, Patricia E., and John Herd Thompson. *British Columbia: Land of Promises.* Vol. 5, *The Illustrated History of Canada.* Don Mills, ON: Oxford University Press Canada, 2005.

Sage, Walter N. *Sir James Douglas and British Columbia.* Toronto: University of Toronto Press, 1930.

Schoenberg, Wilfred P., SJ. *Jesuit Mission Presses in the Pacific Northwest 1876–1899.* Fairfield, WA: Ye Galleon Press, 1994.

Shalof, Tilda. *A Nurse's Story: Life, Death, and In-between in an Intensive Care Unit.* Toronto: McClelland and Stewart, 2004.

Shervill, R. Lynn. *Smithers from Swamp to Village.* Smithers, BC: Town of Smithers, 1981. Sixtieth anniversary project of the Town of Smithers.

Taylor, Jeanette. *River City: A History of Campbell River and the Discovery Islands.* Madeira Park, BC: Harbour Publishing, 1999.

Trudeau, Pierre Elliott. *Memoirs.* Toronto: McClellland and Stewart, 1993.

Van Kirk, Sylvia. *Many Tender Ties: Women in Fur-Trade Society, 1670–1870.* Winnipeg: Watson and Dwyer, 1999.

Whitehead, Margaret. *The Cariboo Mission, a History of the Oblates.* Victoria: Sono Nis Press, 1981.

Whittaker, Jo Ann. "The Search for Legitimacy: Nurses' Registration in British Columbia 1913–1935," in Barbara K. Latham and Roberta J. Pazdro, eds., *Not Just Pin Money: Selected Essays on the History of Women's Work in British Columbia.* Victoria: Camosun College, 1984.

2. Booklets, Pamphlets, Brochures, Papers

Canonical Legislation Concerning Religious. Authorized English translation. Vatican City: Libreria Editrice Vaticana, 1949.

Caritas Christi Urget Nos. Catholic Health Association of British Columbia Anniversary Booklet. "Living The Mission 1940–1990."

Catholic Directory for British Columbia and the Yukon 2000–2001. Published by the Archdiocese of Vancouver.

Cimichella, OSM. Bishop Andre-M. *Mother Marie Anne, Esther Blondin: Woman of Hope.* Booklet, part of a collection—no. 22—*Our Great Figures;* Archdiocese of Montreal, 1988.

Customary of the Sisters of Saint Ann of Montreal. Lachine: Sisters of St. Ann, 1928.

Fort St. James National Historic Site. Pamphlet published by Parks Canada by authority of the Department of Canadian Heritage, 1981.

In the Service of the Sick at St Joseph's Hospital. Pamphlet produced at the completion of the expansion program, March 19, 1952.

In This Fiftieth Year. St. Joseph's School of Nursing 50th anniversary Yearbook, 1950.

Kerr, J.F., B.Sc.N. *Nursing Education in Canada.* St. Joseph's School of Nursing, March 1968.

McRae, Edward Davidson. *The Story of the British Columbia Health Association.* Published by the British Columbia Health Association to mark its 75th anniversary in 1993. Vancouver, 1992.

Medicine in the Pacific Northwest. American Medical Association Clinical Session. Seattle, Washington, November 27–30, 1956.

Nelson Centennial Book 1897–1997. A publication of the Nelson Centennial Committee.

Reminiscing Commemorative Yearbook 1900–1981. Victoria General Hospital, 1981. Published at the closing of St. Joseph's School of Nursing.

Saint-Pierre, Odette, SSA. *The Charism of Mother Marie Anne.* Translated by Eva Mondor, SSA, and Lucienne Babin, SSA. Lachine: Sisters of St. Anne, 1974.

Scott, Marian. "The Quiet Evolution" in *Canadian Geographic* September/October 2006.

Solemn Blessing and Laying of Corner Stone. St. Joseph's Hospital, March 18, 1928.

St. Ann's Academy: A Building Brought Back To Life. 1997. *St. Ann's Academy: A Life Remembered.* 1997. *St. Ann's Academy: Grounds For Celebration.* 1998. Provincial Capital Commission. Produced for the opening of the restored building, the chapel and the grounds.

St. Joseph's School of Nursing 75th anniversary Yearbook, 1975.

Turnbull, A. Douglas. *Memoir: Early Years of Hospital Insurance in British Columbia.* BC Studies, no. 76, Winter 1987/88. Vancouver: University of British Columbia.

100 Years of Service 1876–1976: The Hospital Story. Centennial Committee.

Notes

Chapter 1

1. Marie-Jean de-Pathmos, SSA, *A History of the Sisters of Saint Anne,* vol. 1, *1850–1900,* trans. Marie Anne Eva, SSA (New York: Vantage Press, 1961), 36.

2. Sister Mary Theodore, SSA, *The Seal of the Cross* (Victoria: Sisters of St. Ann, 1939), 4.

3. Ibid., 6.

4. Elie J. Auclair, *History of the Sisters of Saint Ann: The First Fifty Years 1850–1900* (Lachine: Saint Ann's Press, 1939), 21.

5. Andre-M. Cimichella, OSM, *Mother Marie Anne, Esther Blondin: Woman of Hope* (Archdiocese of Montreal, 1988), 16.

6. Sister Mary Theodore, SSA (attributed to), *A Chaplet of Years 1815–1918* (Victoria: Sisters of St. Ann, 1918), 8.

7. Sister Mary Theodore, SSA, *The Seal of the Cross,* 94.

8. Louise Roy, SSA, *The Sisters of Saint Anne: A Century of History,* vol. 2, *1900–1950,* trans. Eileen Gallagher, SSA (Lachine: Les Editions Sainte-Anne, 1994), 12.

9. Bishop James M. Hill, "The Most Reverend Modeste Demers, D.D., First Bishop of Vancouver Island," Canadian Catholic Historical Association, *Report,* 20 (1953), 29.

10. Auclair, *History of the Sisters of Saint Ann: The First Fifty Years,* 112–22.

11. Chronicles of the Sisters of St. Ann 1858–68. Recorded by Sister Marie des Sept Douleurs, December 1876. SSAA S24-01-01.

12. Sister Mary Theodore, SSA (attributed to), *A Chaplet of Years 1858–1918,* 19.

13. Sister Mary Theodore, SSA, *Pioneer Nuns of British Columbia* (Victoria: Colonist Publishing, 1931), 40.

14. De-Pathmos, *A History of the Sisters of Saint Anne,* vol. 1, 136.

15. Journal of Sister Mary Angèle. SSAA S24. This journal, sent to her parents in Quebec, provides a clear log of the trip and arrival of the first contingent of the Sisters of St. Ann in Victoria.

16. Charles Lillard, *Seven Shillings a Year: The History of Vancouver Island* (Ganges, BC: Horsdal and Schubart, 1993), 107.

17. Lugrin, Nancy de Bertrand. "When the Sisters Came." In *The Pioneer Women of Vancouver Island 1843–1866.* Edited by John Hosie. Victoria: Women's Canadian Club of Victoria, 1928.

18. The attributes of Sir James Douglas, stalwart friend of the Sisters, were such that the *Globe and Mail* in 2005 named him the greatest British Columbian of all time, a claim generally accepted by such modern historians as Jean Barman, Daniel Francis, Lily Chow and Thomas Berger.

19. Margaret A. Ormsby, "Sir James Douglas," in *Dictionary of Canadian Biography Online (Library and Archives Canada)* (accessed March 25, 2011). http://www.biographi.ca/

20. Sylvia Van Kirk, *Many Tender Ties: Women in Fur-Trade Society, 1670–1870* (Winnipeg: Watson and Dwyer, 1999), 138–39.

21. Lillard, *Seven Shillings a Year,* 153.

22. "From Log Cabin to Modern Hospital," *The Torch* (July 1963).

23. Harry Gregson, *A History of Victoria 1842–1970* (Victoria: Victoria Observer, 1970), 12.

24. Jean Barman, *The West Beyond the West: A History of British Columbia* (Toronto: UTP, 1991), 77.

25. Gregson, *A History of Victoria 1842–1970*, 25, 101.

26. Michael Kluckner, *Victoria: The Way It Was* (North Vancouver: Whitecap Books, 1986), 81. All five "birdcages" remained until the 1890s, when four were demolished to be replaced by the current legislative buildings. The fifth burned down in 1957.

27. "Jewish Roots Unveiled," review of Cyril Leonoff's *Pioneer Jews of British Columbia* in *BC Bookworld* vol. 20, no. 1 (Spring 2006): 32.

28. A plaque in the Inner Harbour of Victoria commemorates this arrival.

29. Unattributed article in historical data file. SSAA S24-03-05.

30. Walter N. Sage, *Sir James Douglas and British Columbia* (Toronto: UTP, 1930), 191.

31. The pioneer convent, one of the oldest buildings in British Columbia, was moved to the grounds of the Royal BC Museum, adjacent to Helmcken House, in the 1970s.

32. John Adams, "First Pioneer Square Burial 150 Years Ago," *Victoria Times-Colonist*, February 20, 2005.

33. Barman, *The West Beyond the West*, 76.

34. Sister Mary Theodore, SSA, *Pioneer Nuns of British Columbia*, 6–8.

35. Sister Mary Theodore, SSA, *Heralds of Christ the King* (New York: P.J. Kennedy, 1939), 175.

36. John Greene, Marc Lapprand, Gerald Moreau and Gerald Ricard, *French Presence in Victoria B.C. 1843–1991* (Victoria: L'Association Historique Francophone de Victoria, C.B., 1991), 57.

37. Ibid.

38. Chronicles of the Sisters of St. Ann. SSAA S24-01-02a.

39. Hill, "The Most Reverend Modeste Demers," 31.

40. This hundred-year-old iron hand press, weighing a few hundred pounds, was given to Bishop Demers by the Society of the Propagation of the Faith in Paris and arrived in Victoria from California in 1856.

41. First Prospectus for St. Ann's Academy, SSAA S35-01-05.

42. Wilfred P. Schoenberg, SJ, *Jesuit Mission Presses in the Pacific Northwest 1876–1899* (Fairfield, WA: Ye Galleon Press, 1994), 81–84. The Sisters gave this press to the Royal BC Museum when St. Ann's Academy closed in 1973.

43. Chronicles. SSAA S24-01-02a.

44. Sister Mary Conception to Sister Mary of the Purification (March 22, 1859). SSAA S17-09-10.

45. Mother Mary Providence to Lachine (April 23, 1860). SSAA S17-09.

46. De-Pathmos, *A History of the Sisters of Saint Anne,* vol. 1, 125.

47. Lugrin, "When the Sisters Came," 141.

48. Auclair, *History of the Sisters of Saint Ann: The First Fifty Years, 123.*

49. Sister Mary of the Sacred Heart, Victoria, to mother superior in Saint-Jacques, Quebec (November 9, 1859). SSAA S17-09-06.

50. Auclair, *History of the Sisters of Saint Ann: The First Fifty Years,* 130.

51. De-Pathmos, *A History of the Sisters of Saint Anne,* vol. 1, 140.

52. Account by Sister Mary Theodore, SSA, of the life of Mother Mary Providence. SSAA S24-3-10.

53. Maurice De Baets, *The Apostle of Alaska,* trans. Sister Mary Mildred Welsh, SSA (Patterson, NJ: Guild Press, 1943), 282–83.

54. Bishop Seghers' extensive library, including Latin folios and the works of the Fathers of the Church, is deposited in trust in the Special Collections of the University of Victoria Library.

55. Sister Mary Theodore, SSA, *Pioneer Nuns of British Columbia,* 6.

56. Ibid., 9–11.

57. Sister Mary Theodore, SSA, *Heralds of Christ the King,* 236; De Baets, *The Apostle of Alaska,* 113.

Chapter 2

58. John Murray Gibbon and Mary Mathewson, *Three Centuries of Canadian Nursing* (Toronto: Macmillan, 1947), 111.

59. Derek Pethick, *Victoria: The Fort* (Vancouver: Mitchell Press, 1968), 223–24. Quoting from the minutes of the House of Assembly for August 17, 1858.

60. Gibbon and Mathewson, *Three Centuries of Canadian Nursing,* 122.

61. John Greene, Marc Lapprand, Gerald Moreau, and Gerald Ricard. *French Presence in Victoria B.C. 1843–1991* (Victoria: L'Association Historique Francophone de Victoria, C.B., 1991) 120–23. "La Societe Francaise de Bienfaisance et Secours Mutuels de Victoria—1860."

62. Sister Mary Lumena's Journal, 139. This would have been the cemetery in Pioneer Square. Father Joseph Marie Mandart made the coffin, which was transported to the "burying ground" in a horse-drawn carriage.

63. Marie-Jean de-Pathmos, SSA, *A History of the Sisters of Saint Anne,* vol. 1, *1850–1890,* trans. Marie Anne Eva, SSA (New York: Vantage Press, 1961), 156.

64. Beatrice Wambeke, SSA, *History of St. Joseph's School of Nursing.* Published by the Sisters of St. Ann to celebrate the 75th anniversary of the school in 1975.

65. Sister Mary Theodore, SSA (attributed to), *A Chaplet of Years 1858–1918* (Victoria: Sisters of St. Ann, 1918), 90.

66. "Graveyard of the Pacific: Shipwrecks on the Washington Coast," essay 7936, The Online Encyclopedia of Washington State History (accessed September 27, 2006). http://www.historylink.org/essays/output.cfm?file_id7936

67. Necrology of the Sisters of St. Ann 1930–1938, 17, SSAA.

68. *Daily British Colonist,* August 23, 1875. The original copy of Bishop Seghers' speech was given to the Sisters of St. Ann by Dr. J.S. Helmcken's daughter, Dolly, in a letter dated December 27, 1923, after her father's death. SSAA S37-02-01.

69. Buildings and demolitions, articles and reviews, SSAA S37-01-10.

70. *100 Years of Service, 1876–1976: The Hospital Story* (Centennial Committee), 9.

71. John Helmcken, *The Reminiscences of Doctor John Sebastian Helmcken,* ed. Dorothy Blakey Smith (Vancouver: UBC Press, 1975), xxv.

72. Ibid., xxvii.

73. *Medicine in the Pacific Northwest,* brochure. American Medical Association Clinical Session in Seattle, Washington, Nov. 27–30, 1956. Dr. James D. Helmcken, son of Dr. John Sebastian Helmcken, appointed secretary of the association. SSAA S37-02-02b.

74. Chronicles of the Sisters of St. Ann 1876. SSAA S25-02-01.

75. *Catholic Sentinel,* June 26, 1876, SSAA S37-01-13. This is the oldest Catholic paper on the North American west coast.

76. Centenary address given by an anonymous Sister in 1976. SSAA S37-01-16a.

77. Chronicles 1875–1888, SSAA S25-02-01. Consolation and support also came in the form of a letter from Mother Mary Ann to Sister Mary Providence and her Sisters assuring them of her great interest in and promise of her prayers for the foundation in Victoria. Louise Roy, SSA, *The Correspondence of Mother Marie Anne,* trans. Eileen Gallagher, SSA (Lachine: Les Editions Sainte-Anne, 1977), 205.

78. Chronicles 1875–1888, SSAA S25-02-01.

79. Peter A. Baskerville, *Beyond the Island: An Illustrated History of Victoria* (Burlington: Windsor Publications, 1986), 44.

80. Elizabeth Forbes, *Wild Roses at Their Feet: Pioneer Women of Vancouver Island* (Vancouver: Evergreen Press, 1971), 25–26. British Columbia Centennial Project.

81. St. Joseph's Hospital Society Rules, SSAA S37-10-01.

82. SSAA S37-10-01.

83. Ledger for St. Joseph's Hospital 1895–1903, SSAA S37-02-15.

84. Patient Register 1904–07, SSAA S37-10-06.

85. Michael Kluckner, *Victoria: The Way It Was* (North Vancouver: Whitecap Books, 1986), 102.

86. Barry Downs, *Sacred Places: British Columbia's Early Churches* (Vancouver: Douglas and McIntyre, 1980), 63.

87. Sister Mary Theodore's notes on St. Joseph's Hospital, SSAA S27-23-07.

88. Valerie Green, *No Ordinary People: Victoria's Mayors Since 1862* (Victoria: Beach Holme Publishers, 1992), 117–22.

89. Chronicles 1888, SSAA S24-02-01.

90. Harry Gregson, *A History of Victoria 1842–1970* (Victoria: Victoria Observer, 1970), 140.

91. Sister Mary Theodore, SSA, "The Sisters of St. Ann on North Pacific Shores," unpublished manuscript, 284. SSAA.

92. Gibbon and Mathewson, *Three Centuries of Canadian Nursing,* 228.

93. The Sister leader was called "provincial directress" from 1863 to 1866, when she was called "vicar directress." The title changed again in 1874 to "vicar superior" and finally in 1891 to "provincial superior" when four distinct provinces or jurisdictions of the Sisters of St. Ann were canonically erected for the fifty houses of the institute.

94. Sister Mary Theodore's notes on early Victoria, SSAA S27-23-10.

95. Sister Mary Theodore, SSA, *Pioneer Nuns of British Columbia* (Victoria: Colonist Publishing, 1931), 83.

96. Ibid., 121.

97. Necrology 1850–1930, 293. SSAA.

98. By 1958, the hundredth anniversary of the Sisters' arrival, 202 girls from BC, other parts of Canada, England, Belgium, Ireland, Germany, France, the United States and Alaska had pronounced their religious vows in Victoria. Edith E. Down, SSA, *A Century of Service,* 2nd ed. (Victoria: Sisters of St. Ann, 1999), 111.

99. De-Pathmos, *A History of the Sisters of Saint Anne,* vol. 1, 300.

100. Patricia E. Roy and John Herd Thompson, *British Columbia: Land of Promises* (Don Mills, ON: Oxford U Press Canada, 2005), 65.

101. Baskerville, *Beyond the Island,* 122.

102. Bill Dale, "John Blair and George Fraser's Beacon Hill Park's Scottish Heritage," Victoria Historical Society newsletter, Spring 2002.

103. Gibbon and Mathewson, *Three Centuries of Canadian Nursing.*

104. Roland Morgan and Emily Disher, *Victoria Then and Now* (Vancouver: Bodima Publications, 1977), 71–72.

105. Danda Humphreys, "A Birthday Fit for a Queen," *Focus* magazine, May 2006, 68.

106. Pierre Berton, *Klondike: The Last Great Gold Rush 1896–1899* (Toronto: McClelland & Stewart, 1997), 113.

107. Sister Mary Theodore, SSA, *Heralds of Christ the King* (New York: P.J. Kennedy, 1939), 255.

Chapter 3

108. Sister Mary Theodore, SSA (attributed to), "The Sisters of St. Ann on North Pacific Shores" (unpublished manuscript), SSAA S27-22.

109. Louise Roy, SSA, *The Sisters of Saint Anne: A Century of History,* vol. 2, *1900–1950,* trans. Eileen Gallagher, SSA (Lachine: Les Editions Sainte-Anne, 1994), 14–19.

110. SSAA S27-23-10, S24-03-06.

111. Mother Mary Providence also served as superior at St. Joseph's Hospital 1881–82, 1885–90.

112. In 1982, the University of Victoria named one of its $2,000 regional entrance scholarships the Sister Mary Providence Memorial Scholarship. It is given each year to "students with high academic standing and broad interests." In seeking the Sisters' permission to honour Sister Mary Providence, UVic president Howard Petch, explained to Sister Kathleen Cyr, provincial leader, on July 13, 1982, that "to honor a person of regional significance, the scholarships are named after men and women who contributed to the advancement and development of the region and its people and who were highly respected members of their community." SSAA S24-03-14.

113. Home Visits 1923–24, SSAA S37-10-08.

114. Register of postings for the hospital Sisters, 1897, SSAA S6-02-04.

115. *Customary of the Sisters of Saint Ann of Montreal* (Lachine: Sisters of St. Ann, 1928), 6.

116. The first one was set in 1848 and revised four times, before the 1916 Customary was written and adhered to until the Second Vatican Council in the 1960s. (Roy, *The Sisters of Saint Anne*, vol. 2, 93.)

117. *Customary of the Sisters of Saint Ann of Montreal*, 140.

118. A year after the Customary was renewed, Rome promulgated the 1917 Code of Canon Law to regulate the life of the whole Church. Women had not participated in drawing up codes, so it was not surprising that the restrictions applied to them seemed an attempt to place sisterhoods under more direct control of the diocese and the bishop. The new expectations that dictated set times for prayers, meditation and Eucharist and disallowed travel and going out alone posed an onerous burden. Sioban Nelson, *Say Little, Do Much: Nurses, Nuns and Hospitals in the Nineteenth Century* (Philadelphia: University of Pennsylvania Press, 2001), 157–59. But the Sisters worked with the rules and the bishops as best they could, letting their common sense prevail when the need arose.

119. Acts of Provincial Council 1904–24, SSAA S12-01-02a.

120. The *Daily Colonist*, March 1908.

121. Acts of Provincial Council 1904–24, SSAA S12-01-02a.

122. *Daily Colonist*, October 4, 1908; the *BC Orphan Friend*, October 1908.

123. Ibid. Richard McBride was the first premier to serve after party politics were introduced in BC. He held office as a Conservative, 1903–15.

124. Elizabeth Forbes, *Wild Roses at Their Feet: Pioneer Women of Vancouver Island* (Vancouver: Evergreen Press, 1971), 52.

125. John Murray Gibbon and Mary Mathewson, *Three Centuries of Canadian Nursing* (Toronto: Macmillan, 1947), 229.

126. Terry Glavin and Former Students of St. Mary's, *Amongst God's Own: The Enduring Legacy of St. Mary's Mission* (Mission, BC: Longhouse Publishing, 2002), 85.

127. Emily Carr, *The Book of Small* (Vancouver: Clarke, Irwin and Co. Ltd., 1966), 105.

128. In conversation with the author, Sister Catherine Moroney spoke concerning Chinese and other ethnic groups in relation to St. Joseph's Hospital, August 1996.

129. Data collected by Sister Mary Anne of Jesus and Sister Mary Theodore, SSAA S27-23-01.

130. Correspondence from Father Auguste Brabant to mother provincial, April 22, 1909, SSAA S17-09-17. The earliest burials were near the original log convent. In 1869–85, burials were behind St. Ann's Academy. Those remains were removed to the front of St. Ann's in 1885 and this cemetery was used until 1908. From 1909 on, Ross Bay Cemetery was used, two bodies per plot. R. Hayward (July 19, 1952), managing director of B.C. Funeral Co. Ltd., who had appraised the situation, stated that the Sisters' section should last another ten years. On March 3, 1964, the Sisters paid $14,000 for two hundred double plots in Hatley Memorial Gardens in Colwood, BC.

131. Data collected, SSAA S24-03-01.

132. Ibid.

133. Acts of Local Council 1909, SSAA S85-03.

134. Gibbon and Mathewson, *Three Centuries of Canadian Nursing*, 373.

135. Bishop Alexander MacDonald, "To Whom It May Concern," 1912, SSAA S17-09-22a.

136. In addition, three members of the Christian Brothers of Ireland took on the educational duties at St. Louis College (1915), and the first Conference of the St. Vincent de Paul Society was formed in 1915.

137. *Chronicle of the 20th Century* (Mount Kisco, NY: Chronicle Publications, 1987), 241.

138. Patricia E. Roy and John Herd Thompson, *British Columbia: Land of Promises,* vol. 5, *The Illustrated History of Canada* (Don Mills, ON: OUP Canada, 2005), 103–4; Terry Reksten, *More English than the English: A Very Social History of Victoria* (Victoria: Orca Book Publishers, 1986), 151–52.

139. Chronicles 1921–22, SSAA S25-02-03.

140. Ibid.

141. Genevieve Allard, "Caregiving on the Front: The experience of Canadian Military Nurses during World War I," in *On All Frontiers, Four Centuries of Canadian Nursing,* ed. Christina Bates, Dianne Dodd and Nicole Rousseau (Ottawa: University of Ottawa Press, 2005), 153. Gibbon and Mathewson: *Three Centuries of Canadian Nursing,* 294.

142. "In This Fiftieth Year 1900–1950," St. Joseph's School of Nursing Golden Jubilee Souvenir Book.

143. Acts of Local Council 1915, SSAA S85-03-02.

144. Patient Register for St. Joseph's Hospital 1891–1904, SSAA S37-10-04.

145. Acts of Provincial Council, SSAA S12-01-02a. It was not uncommon for various "houses" in St. Joseph's province to borrow from the provincial council.

146. "Influenza," research by Johanna Boffa and Richard Johnson, source the World Health Organization, United Nations and The Centre for Infectious Disease Research (*Globe and Mail,* October 6, 2005).

147. Janice Dickin McGinnis, "The Impact of Epidemic Influenza: Canada, 1918–1919," Canadian Historical Association, *Historical Papers 1977.*

148. Barry Gewen, review of John M. Barry's *The Great Influenza* in the *New York Times Book Review* (March 14, 2004).

149. Acts of Provincial Council, October 21, 1921, SSAA S12-01-02a.

150. Nelson, *Say Little, Do Much,* 160–61.

151. Chronicles 1920, SSAA S25-02-03. "By 1929 over half of all Catholic hospitals had met minimum standards as compared to only a quarter of non-Catholic hospitals." Nelson, *Say Little, Do Much,* 161.

152. Edward Davidson McRae, *The Story of the British Columbia Health Association* (Vancouver: BC Health Association, 1992), 10.

153. Acts of Local Council 1921, S85-03-02.

154. McRae, *The Story of the British Columbia Health Association,* 19.

155. Chronicles 1922, SSAA S25-02-02.

156. Ibid; Acts of Local Council 1922, S85-03-01.

157. Chronicles 1926, S25-02-03.

158. McRae, *The Story of the British Columbia Health Association,* 18–19.

Chapter 4

159. Charles Lillard, *Seven Shillings a Year: The History of Vancouver Island* (Ganges, BC: Horsdal and Schubart, 1993), 181.

160. Acts of Local Council 1923, S85-03-02.

161. Mother Mary Leopoldine to Pius XI; copy of indult giving permission, SSAA S37-02-6a.

162. Chronicles 1927, SSAA S25-02-03.

163. Chronicles 1928, SSAA S25-01-02

164. Necrology of the Sisters of St. Ann 1930–38.

165. Brochure issued during first appeal, SSAA S37-01-09.

166. It was the same trowel used by Dr. J.S. Helmcken to lay the cornerstone of St. Joseph's Hospital in 1875. His daughter, Dolly Higgins, gave the trowel to Sister Mary Bridget as a Christmas present in 1922.

167. A.M.D.G. = *"ad majorem Dei gloriam"* (for the greater glory of God); *"Pro Deo et Humanitate"* = for God and humanity.

168. Program for the "Solemn Blessing and Laying of Corner Stone" (March 18, 1928), Diocese of Victoria Archives.

169. *Daily Colonist,* May 24, 1929.

170. Chronicles 1924–26, SSAA S25-02-03; Acts of Local Council 1924–26, SSAA S85-03-01; *Daily Colonist,* March 17, 1928.

171. Board of Management minutes 1924, SSAA S34-04-17.

172. Ibid.

173. Ibid. The Income Tax Act had been declared in 1917 as a temporary measure to finance the First World War, but was never repealed.

174. Board of Management minutes 1928, 1929, 1932, 1937, SSAA S34-04-17.

175. Sister Mary Theodore, SSA. "The Sisters of Saint Ann on North Pacific Shores" (unpublished manuscript) SSAA, 417–420.

176. Don Chaput, *Nellie Cashman and the North American Mining Frontier* (Tucson, AZ: Westernlore Press, 1995); *Daily Colonist,* January 11, 1925; Chronicles 1925, SSAA S25-02-03.

177. Diana Mansell, *Forging The Future: A History of Nursing in Canada* (Ann Arbor, MI: Thomas Press, 2003).

178. www.can-aiic.ca/CAN/about/history (accessed January 15, 2008).

179. Jo Ann Whittaker, "The Search for Legitimacy: Nurses' Registration in British Columbia 1913–1935," in Barbara K. Latham and Roberta J. Pazdro, eds., *Not Just Pin Money* (Victoria: Camosun College, 1984), 317.

180. Acts of Provincial Council 1927, SSAA S12-01-04.

181. Chronicles 1931, SSAA S25-02-04.

182. Board of Management minutes 1931, SSAA S34-04-17. Acts of Local Council 1925, 1930, SSAA S85-03-03.

183. Chronicles 1930, SSAA S25-02-04.

184. Correspondence, SSAA S17-09-23.

185. Board of Management minutes 1934, SSAA S34-04-17.

186. Acts of Local Council 1933, 1938, SSAA S85-03-03.

187. *Victoria Daily Times,* March 18, 1933.

188. Chronicles 1935, SSAA S25-02-04. Women gained the vote and the right to run for office for the first time in BC provincial elections in 1917. In 1929 the Privy Council in England ruled that the term "person" in the *British North America Act* included women, hence women could serve in the Canadian Senate.

189. St. Ann's Academy Journal, April 1934, SSAA S26-04-08; Chronicles 1934, S25-02-04.

190. Chronicles 1935, SSAA S25-02-04.

191. Board of Management minutes 1938, SSAA S34-04-17. In January 1938 they had five patients who had been in hospital more than 300 days.

192. Chronicles 1936, SSAA S25-02-04.

193. Chronicles 1936–1941, SSAA S25-02-04; Board of Management minutes 1936–40, SSAA S34-04-17; Acts of Local Council 1936–41, SSAA S85-03-03; Acts of St. Joseph's Province 1936–40, SSAA S12-01-06.

194. Mansell, *Forging the Future*, 148.

195. St. Joseph's School of Nursing booklet, *In This Fiftieth Year 1900–1950*.

196. Jean Barman, *The West Beyond the West* (Toronto: UTP, 1991), 262.

197. Ibid., 264.

198. Acts of Local Council 1942, SSAA S85-03-03.

199. Chronicles 1939, SSAA S25-02-04.

200. Board of Management minutes 1942, SSAA S34-04-17.

201. Acts of Local Council 1945, SSAA S85-03-03.

202. Chronicles 1943, SSAA S25-02-06; Acts of St. Joseph's Province 1943, SSAA S12-01-06.

203. *CHABC Anniversary Booklet 1940–1990*, 11.

204. Chronicles 1947, SSAA S25-02-06.

205. Interview May 19, 2005, with Sister Margaret Doris, who received her diploma in pharmaceutical chemistry in 1945. At this time there was no bachelor of science in pharmacy program at UBC, so apprenticeship was the way to earn a diploma. Penicillin at this early date was only available in liquid form, with pills coming later.

206. Chronicles 1944, SSAA S25-02-06.

207. Roy, *The Sisters of Saint Anne*, 476–89.

208. *History of the CHAC* (online). The organization had three name changes, with the last in 1976 being Catholic Health Association of Canada, its mission "to strengthen and support the ministry of Catholic health care organizations and providers." www.chac.ca/about/history.htm (accessed June 28, 2007).

209. *CHABC Anniversary Booklet*, 6. For thirty years the executive of the conference only included Sisters from religious congregations.

Chapter 5

210. Acts of Local Council 1943, SSAA S85-03-03.

211. Board of Management minutes 1944, SSAA S37-05-01. In October 1945 the caveat was put on that the government would pay the one-third expense if it did not exceed $1,250,000.

212. Mansell, *Forging the Future*, 170.

213. Acts of St. Joseph's Province 1945–46, SSAA S12-02-01.

214. Bishop John Cody to Mother Mary Mildred, July 30, 1945, SSAA S17-09-23.

215. Historical reviews and articles, SSAA S37-01-05a.

216. Chronicles 1946, SSAA S25-02-06.

217. Ibid.

218. Board of Management minutes 1947, SSAA S37-05-01. Sister Catherine Moroney mentioned that St. Joseph's Hospital benefited by receiving Jewish interns who were being turned away from the Royal Jubilee Hospital.

219. Board of Management minutes 1947, SSAA S37-05-01.

220. Board of Management minutes 1949, SSAA S37-05-01.

221. Ledger 1928–68, SSAA S37-02-07c.

222. Mrs. Marguerite Spratt, who died in July 1946, owned Victoria Machinery Depot. She left part of her estate for the maintenance of her dog. When "Rip" died in June 1949, the Sisters of St. Ann at St. Joseph's Hospital received another $24,000 from the residue of the Spratt estate.

223. Chronicles 1948, SSAA S25-02-06.

224. Acts of Local Council 1949, SSAA S85-03-03.

225. Acts of Provincial Council 1949, SSAA S12-02-01.

226. No. 17 of the *Hospital Insurance Act* stated: "Where a person entitled to the benefits provided by this Act requests and receives care in addition to the public ward care, the Hospital shall be paid from the Hospital Insurance Fund on the basis of public ward care as provided in this Act and the Hospital may collect from the patient the difference in rates and retain the difference."

227. Edward Davidson McRae, *The Story of the British Columbia Health Association* (Vancouver: BC Health Association, 1992), 24.

228. A. Douglas Turnbull, *Memoir: Early Years of Hospital Insurance in British Columbia* (BC Studies no. 76, Winter 1987/88), 67.

229. Minutes of Local Council, September 3, 1960, SSAA S85-03-04.

230. Turnbull, *Memoir,* 81.

231. Louise Roy, SSA, *The Sisters of Saint Anne: A Century of History,* vol. 2, *1900-1950,* trans. Eileen Gallagher, SSA (Lachine: Les Editions Sainte-Anne, 1994), 19, 514.

232. Fr. Joseph Birch, OMI, to provincial superior April 11, 1950, SSAA S17-09-23.

233. Roy, *The Sisters of Saint Anne,* vol. 2, 50.

234. David MacDonald, "When Asbestos Caught Fire," *Reader's Digest,* December 1989, 108; Vincent McNally, *The Lord's Distant Vineyard* (Edmonton: U of A Press, 2000), 326.

235. Pierre Elliott Trudeau, *Memoirs* (Toronto: McClelland and Stewart, 1993), 63.

236. Chronicles 1950, SSAA S25-02-06.

237. In later years a square at Place Ville Marie was named Place Joseph Charbonneau in recognition of his part in history. On September 20, 2005, a bronze and marble representational sculpture meant to symbolize the man and his spirit was unveiled there. *Times Colonist,* August 26, 2005.

238. *Victoria Daily Times,* March 20, 1952.

239. Chronicles 1952, SSAA S25-03-01.

240. Chronicles 1950, SSAA S25-03-01.

241. *In the Service of the Sick at St. Joseph's Hospital,* pamphlet produced for the official opening of the Collinson Street wing, March 19, 1952, SSAA S37-01-14.

242. Ibid.

243. Acts of Local Council 1953, SSAA S85-03-03.

244. *CHABC Anniversary Booklet 1940–1990,* minutes from November 29, 1944, meeting, 6.

245. Board of Management minutes 1953, SSAA S37-05-01.

246. Board of Management minutes 1955, 1957, SSAA S37-05-01.

247. The board also stressed their opinion that more acute beds would not be needed in Victoria if the government implemented the suggested program to build chronic care beds.

248. Patricia E. Roy and John Herd Thompson, *British Columbia: Land of Promises,* vol. 5, *The Illustrated History of Canada* (Don Mills, ON: OUP Canada, 2005), 151.

249. Board of Management minutes 1946, SSAA S37-05-01.

250. Edward Davidson McRae, *The Story of the British Columbia Health Association* (Vancouver: BC Health Association, 1992), 45.

251. Board of Management minutes 1957, SSAA S37-05-01.

Chapter 6

252. Chronicles 1956, SSAA S25-03-01.

253. Chronicles 1955, SSAA S25-03-01.

254. Chronicles 1957, SSAA S25-03-01.

255. Sister Marguerite Lalonde, interviewed by the author on December 15, 2005.

256. Chronicles 1954–60, SSAA S25-03-01.

257. Minutes of Local Council, October 1957, SSAA S85-03-03.

258. Acts of Provincial Council 1935–69, SSAA S12-01-06, S12-02-01, S12-04-01.

259. Hospital news release, July 22, 1959, SSAA S37-02-05.

260. G. Fitzpatrick Dunn, interviewed by the author on June 8, 2005.

261. Acts of St. Joseph's Province, April 1959, SSAA S12-02-02.

262. Hospital news release, July 22, 1959, SSAA S37-02-05.

263. Chronicles 1959, 1960, SSAA S25-03-01.

264. Acts of Local Council 1959–64, SSAA S85-03-04.

265. Treasurer's Office 1960, SSAA S20-02-03.

266. *Columbia* vol. 85 no. 12, December 2005, 11.

267. Erin Dwyer, *Whose Leaves Never Fade* (Saint John, NB: Sisters of Charity of the Immaculate Conception) 2003, 3.

268. Acts of Local Council, September 10, 1951, SSAA S85-03-03.

269. *Bulletin,* no. 194, August 16, 1963, published for the staff of the hospital.

270. Chronicles 1969, SSAA S25-03-02.

271. Sister Kathleen Cyr, interviewed by the author on March 3, 2006.

272. Chronicles 1967, SSAA S25-02-06.

273. Chronicles 1961, SSAA S25-03-02.

274. Dr. Embert Van Tilburg, interviewed by the author on October 17, 2005.

275. Chronicles 1966, SSAA S25-03-02.

276. Acts of Local Council 1967, SSAA S85-03-04

277. Acts of Local Council 1968, SSAA S85-03-04.

278. Board of Management minutes 1967, SSAA S37-05-02a.

279. Chronicles 1967, SSAA S25-03-02.

280. Treasurer's Office, January 1959, SSAA S20-02-03

281. Acts of Local Council 1968, SSAA S85-03-04.

282. *Victoria Times*, November 14, 1969.

283. Minutes of South Vancouver Island Hospital Society 1969, SSAA S37-05-02b.

284. Minutes of the SVIHS, April 1971, SSAA S37-05-02b.

285. *Daily Colonist*, February 22, 1976, SSAA S37.01-19-07.

286. *Victoria Times*, April 25, 1972.

Chapter 7

287. *Daily British Colonist*, August 23, 1875.

288. Two of her sisters followed her to Victoria—Sisters Mary Armella and Mary Hilda.

289. Biography of Sister Gertrude of Jesus, SSAA S37.01-02-09.

290. *In this Fiftieth Year 1900–1950*, St. Joseph's School of Nursing 50th anniversary Yearbook, 1950.

291. Sister Mary Gertrude's notes, SSAA S37.01-01-01.

292. Beatrice Wambeke, SSA. Unpublished manuscript, SSAA S37.01-01-01; *Daily Colonist*, June 1, 1975.

293. Roy Harding and Jack Nazaroff graduated together in 1965, the first male students since Anthony Williams at the beginning of the twentieth century.

294. Chronicles 1930–1940, SSAA 25-02-04. The hospital continued two intakes per year, one in the fall and one in January, until 1961.

295. Beatrice Wambeke, SSA, in St. Joseph's School of Nursing 75th anniversary book.

296. Ibid.

297. Wambeke, unpublished manuscript. SSAA S37.01-01-01.

298. *Reminiscing: Commemorative Yearbook 1900–1981*, 72. When the school closed in 1981 it had graduated 2,321 nurses.

299. *In This Fiftieth Year*. Chronicles 1944, SSAA S25-02-06.

300. Wambeke, 75th anniversary book.

301. Alumnae information, SSAA S37.01-26-03.

302. *Reminiscing*, 114.

303. Chronicles 1929, SSAA S25-02-03.

304. *Daily Colonist*, May 11, 1947; *In This Fiftieth Year* states the colours a bit differently: "Red for the zeal which ideals inspire, White for each thought and each heart's desire"; Memories of the Class of 1933 uses another phrase for the meaning of the school colours: "to bind the true white of your devotedness with the red of nobility," SSAA S37.01-19-15.

305. Christina Bates, Dianne Dodd and Nicole Rousseau, eds., *On All Frontiers: Four Centuries of Canadian Nursing* (Ottawa: U of Ottawa Press, 2005), 188.

306. Chronicles 1930, SSAA 25-02-03.

307. John Murray Gibbon and Mary Mathewson, *Three Centuries of Canadian Nursing* (Toronto: Macmillan, 1947), 374–79; Anne Pearson, *The Royal Jubilee Hospital School of Nursing 1891–1982* (The Alumnae Association of the Royal Jubilee School of Nursing, 1984), 62–64; Mrs. J.F. Kerr, instructor at St. Joseph's School

of Nursing, *Nursing Education in Canada,* report to the provincial superior, 1968, SSAA S37.01-05-15a.

308. Gibbon co-authored this book with Mary Mathewson. It became virtually the bible of Canadian nursing history until the end of the twentieth century.

309. Acts of Local Council 1943, SSAA S85-03-03.

310. *Daily Colonist,* July 28, 1942.

311. Acts of Local Council 1946–48, SSAA S85-03-03.

312. Chronicles 1951–54, SSAA S25-03-01.

313. Interview with author, February 13, 2007.

314. Interview with author, March 3, 2006. Sister taught community mental health. The other two women who inaugurated the program were Dr. Isabel MacRae and Kathleen Maxwell.

315. Chronicles 1961, SSAA S25-03-02.

316. *Victoria Daily Times,* December 21, 1968.

317. *Reminiscing,* 94.

318. A Catholic organization for females that practised a special devotion to Mary.

319. Diocese of Victoria Archives, Bishops' Correspondence, correspondence of November 30, 1965, from Rev. Edward Bader, CSP, to Bishop De Roo; correspondence of December 4, 1965, from Bishop De Roo to Monsignor O'Connell; correspondence of January 7, 1966, from Rev. Bader to Monsignor O'Connell.

320. Diocese of Victoria Archives, Bishops' Correspondence, Archbishop William Duke, archbishop of Vancouver, to Bishop James Hill, bishop of Victoria, March 6, 1947.

321. *Nursing Education in Canada,* report by Mrs. J.F. Kerr, instructor, St. Joseph's School of Nursing, to Mother Mary Gladys, provincial superior, May 1, 1968, SSAA S37.01-05-15a.

322. *Victoria Daily Times,* November 30, 1973.

323. Ephemera, SSAA S37.01-02-10; Chronicles 1920, SSAA S25-02-02.

324. *Reminiscing.* This bursary and another named in honour of Sister Mary Anna and started in 1964 were turned over to the RNABC to administer when the school closed in 1981.

325. In 2008 the administration of the bursary was turned over to the Registered Nurses Foundation of BC. In 2008 two students received $1,000 each from this bursary.

326. *Reminiscing,* 117.

327. Ibid, 151.

Chapter 8

328. The legal name of the society through which the Sisters of St. Ann established Mount St. Mary as an extended-care hospital in British Columbia. Named for Blessed Marie Anne Blondin, founder of the Sisters of St. Ann, and incorporated under the *Societies Act* in October 1990.

329. Diocese of Victoria Archives, Bishop's Correspondence, letter from Bishop John Cody to the Sisters of St. Ann, April 23, 1939. Chronicles 1939, SSAA S43-07-01.

330. Chronicles 1939, SSAA S43-07-01.

331. Chronicles 1939, SSAA S43-07-01.

332. Register of private patients, SSAA S43-03-05. Died November 30, 1944.

333. These same doors now form the entry to the modern 2003 Mount St. Mary Chapel in its new location.

334. The provincial infirmary was established in 1937 for the care of any person who, being a chronic patient affected with some bodily disease, did not require, nor was not likely to benefit from care or treatment in a general hospital, but required institutional care.

335. Chronicles 1941, SSAA S43-07-01.

336. Chronicles 1943, SSAA S43-07-01.

337. Chronicles 1952, SSAA S43-07-01.

338. Chronicles 1951, SSAA S43-11-01.

339. SSAA S43-03-12b.

340. SSAA S43-03-13.

341. Reports and financial statements 1959, 1969, SSAA S43-07-03 and S43-02-08.

342. Report and financial statement, December 31, 1963, SSAA S47-04-03.

343. A history of Mount St. Mary 1941–91, SSAA S43-04-03d; Correspondence, letter from K.G. Wiper, senior administrative officer of BCHIS, to Sister Mary Justinian, September 23, 1971, SSAA S43-04-12.

344. Paper by planning group designing a 150-bed extended-care hospital for BCHIS, SSAA S43-02-07.

345. SSAA S43-04-03.

346. Chronicles 1966, SSAA S43-07-02.

347. Board of Management minutes, May 23, 1968, SSAA S43-05-01.

348. Local and Vicarial Councils minutes 1967, SSAA S12-03-01.

349. SSAA S43-02-07.

350. SSAA S43-02-08.

351. Necrology written around the time of her death in 1988 by Sisters Catherine Moroney and Beatrice Wambeke, SSAA.

352. Chronicles 1991, SSAA S43-07-02.

353. Little Flower Academy in Vancouver also adopted this new governance model under the name of the Jane Rowan Society.

354. SSAA S43-05-07, S43-04-08a.

355. A history of Mount St. Mary 1941–91, SSAA S43-04-03d.

356. *Catholic Health Association of BC Annual Report,* May 1996, by J.B. McMahon.

357. Interview with author, March 24, 2009.

358. SSAA S43-04-08b, S43-04-26a.

359. Parcel 1 was sold and developed as condominiums.

360. *Times Colonist,* February 18, 2000, C1.

361. Mount St. Mary staff newsletter March and June 1999. The number of "houses" increased to 16 after the government committed to funding 200 beds instead of the 150 first promised.

362. Board of Management minutes, May 2000, SSAA S43-11-02.

363. *BC Catholic,* April 7, 2003.

364. From Bernard McHugh, "The New Mount St. Mary," in the *Diocesan Messenger* of July 2003.

365. Newsletter to St. Joseph's Province, 2004, SSAA S43-04-26b.

366. Chronicles 1995, SSAA S25-03-08.

367. Sandra McCulloch, "A Nun on the Move" *Times Colonist,* October 7, 2006; Chris Coleman, "Sister Lucy and the Royal Victoria Marathon, "*Diocesan Messenger,* December 2008.

368. Letter to author from Janet Lowe, March 3, 2009.

369. Quoted in Brennan Clark, "New Era for Mount St. Mary," *Victoria News,* March 26, 2003, 3.

Chapter 9

370. Traditionally known as Lourdes hospital.

371. Jeanette Taylor, *River City: A History of Campbell River and the Discovery Islands* (Madeira Park, BC: Harbour Publishing, 1999), 91, 95.

372. Chronicles 1926, SSAA S25-05-08.

373. Chronicles 1926, 1927, SSAA S25-05-08.

374. Superiors' Correspondence, Bishop Thomas O'Donnell to Sister Mary Mark, March 13, 1926, SSAA S17-01-11.

375. *Daily Colonist,* December 14, 1929.

376. Board of Management minutes, January 30, 1930, SSAA S42-02-01.

377. Chronicles 1926–39, SSAA S25-05-08, S25-05-09.

378. Taylor, *River City,* 125.

379. Chronicles 1944, SSAA S25-05-09.

380. SSAA S42-02-09, article from *Campbell River Courier-Islander,* March 21, 1997, and an oral history interview with the handyman Willie Grandlund in 1991. These two statues went to Mount St. Francis Hospital in Nelson when Lourdes hospital closed.

381. Ibid.

382. Taylor, *River City,* 132-37.

383. At one point a navy ship was anchored off Campbell River, ready to evacuate the town should it become necessary.

384. Chronicles 1942, SSAA S25-05-10.

385. SSAA S37.01-19-03, clipping from *Vancouver Province.*

386. Chronicles 1928, SSAA S25-05-08.

387. Chronicles 1935, SSAA S25-05-09.

388. Interview with the author, February 10, 2005.

389. Taylor, *River City,* 154.

390. Acts of St. Joseph Province Council, SSAA S12-03-02.

391. Chronicles 1948, SSAA S25-05-10.

392. Superior's Correspondence, SSAA S17-01-11.

Chapter 10

393. R. Lynn Shervill, *Smithers from Swamp to Village* (Smithers, BC: Town of Smithers, 1981), 9.

394. The Grand Trunk Pacific Railway (online) http://collections.ic.gc.ca/cnphoto/english/gtp3_ang.html (accessed December 1, 2004).

395. Shervill, *Smithers from Swamp to Village,* 91.

396. *British Columbia Medical Association Archives* (online), "Dr. Cecil Hazen Hankinson," http://aabc.ca.ca/aabc/bcma/bio_CHHankinson.html, (accessed January 5, 2005).

397. Shervill, *Smithers from Swamp to Village*, 91.

398. Monograph, SSAA S67-01-05.

399. Correspondence March 22, 1933, SSAA S17-06.

400. On October 20, 1940, the village suffered the tragic loss of S. Mayer and another well-known resident when a CNR locomotive plunged off the track, which had been swept away as Lorne Creek flooded.

401. Correspondence March 22, 1933, SSAA S17-06.

402. Biography of Sister Mary Osithe, SSAA #646.

403. J.M.J.A. stood for Jesus, Mary, Joseph and Ann, a short prayer that the Sisters of St. Ann put on many of their documents.

404. Monograph, SSAA S67-01-05.

405. Correspondence, SSAA S17-06-01.

406. Chronicles October 15, 1935, SSAA S25-08-07; P. McGrath, VB, to Sister Superior, October 11, 1935.

407. Correspondence, SSAA S17-06-01.

408. Nicolas Coccola, *They Call Me Father: Memoirs of Father Nicolas Coccola* (Vancouver: UBC Press, 1988) 89, 91, 175.

409. Monograph, SSAA S67-01-05. In these years the Sisters did not usually speak at public events.

410. Monograph, SSAA S67-01-05.

411. Board of Management minutes, February 8, 1939, SSAA S67-02-01.

412. Chronicles, SSAA S25-08-17.

413. Nan Bourgon, *Rubber Boots for Dancing and Other Memories of Pioneer Life in the Bulkley Valley*, ed. Marjorie Rosberg (Smithers, BC: Hetherington, 1979), 105.

414. Board of Management minutes, November 13, 1954, SSAA 67-02-02.

415. Chronicles December 6, 1937, SSAA S25-08-17.

416. Chronicles January 21, 1938, SSAA S25-08-17.

417. Chronicles April 15, 1941, SSAA S25-08-17.

418. Correspondence August 4, 1939, SSAA S17-06-01.

419. Board of Management minutes, March 8 and September 13, 1944, SSAA S67-2-1.

420. Board of Management minutes, October 31, 1951, SSAA S67-2-2.

421. Chronicles June 4, 1937, SSAA S25-08-17.

422. Chronicles December 26, 1935, SSAA S25-08-17.

423. When Sister Mary Patrick died in 1991 at the age of one hundred, Sister Beatrice Wambeke said of her, "It was her insight into who she was in relationship to her God Whom she knew from experience loved her and all other human beings that made her into a compassionate and loving person, filled with empathy for the sufferings of others." This compassion exhibited itself profoundly in her support of the widow on the sudden death of Mr. Moroney, father of two Sisters of St. Ann, Sisters Mary Catherine of Sienna and Mary Gladys. How grateful they all were for the solace and strength she showered on them. Sisters' Biographical Notes, SSAA.

424. Father Doherty, OMI, an Irish priest on his way to Fort St. James, escaped while sailing on one of a convoy of boats sunk by submarines in 1942, with the loss of thirteen lives.

425. Louise Roy, SSA, *The Sisters of Saint Anne: A Century of History,* vol. 2, *1900-1950,* trans. Eileen Gallagher, SSA (Lachine: Les Editions Sainte-Anne, 1994), 473.

426. Board of Management minutes, July/August 1943, SSAA S67-02-01.

427. Chronicles July 18, 1947, SSAA S25-08-18.

428. The first triplets to be born in the northern district—Peter, Paul and John—were born at Sacred Heart hospital, the sons of Mr. and Mrs. John Murray. Chronicles March 16, 1954, SSAA S25-08-18.

429. Chronicles October 7, 1942, SSAA S25-08-18.

430. Chronicles May 7, 1945, SSAA S25-08-18.

431. Correspondence October 1, 1946, SSAA S17-06-01.

432. Chronicles February 23, 1945, SSAA S25-08-18.

433. Correspondence October 1, 1946, SSAA S17-06-01.

434. Board of Management minutes, April 13, 1938, SSAA S67-02-01.

435. Chronicles April 10, 1947, SSAA S25-08-18.

436. Board of Management minutes, September 14, 1955, SSAA S67-02-02.

437. Chronicles February 19, 1949, SSAA S25-08-18.

438. Chronicles July 20, 1948, SSAA S25-08-18.

439. Chronicles June 13, 1948, SSAA S25-08-18.

440. Chronicles April 17 and June 6, 1949, SSAA S25-08-18. "DP" was used for "displaced persons" after the Second World War, but later became a derogatory term.

441. Chronicles March 5, 1948, SSAA S25-08-18.

442. Notes by Sister Mary Barbara, August 21, 1949, SSAA.

443. Notes by Sister Mary Thomasina, March 8, 1953, SSAA.

444. Board of Management minutes, October 31, 1951, SSAA S67-02-02. Trout was in Smithers October 9–11 speaking on drugs and their uses, obstetrics and care of the newborn.

445. Board of Management minutes, October 1952, with notes from the BC Hospitals' Association bulletin, SSAA S67-02-02.

446. Board of Management minutes, December 1, 1952, SSAA S67-02-02.

447. June 7, 1954, A. Pitkethley to H. Whittaker, SSAA.

448. Chronicles November 1954, SSAA S25-08-19.

449. Chronicles August 21, 1955, SSAA S25-08-19.

450. Chronicles February 11, 1955, SSAA S25-08-19.

451. Board of Management minutes, March 31, 1955, SSAA S67-02-02. From an article in *Interior News.*

452. Chronicles March 30, 1955, SSAA S25-08-19. Quotation from a speech by Mother Mary Luca.

453. Chronicles September 11, 1955, SSAA S25-08-19.

454. Correspondence July 12, 1955, SSAA S17-06-01.

455. Chronicles August 5, 1951, SSAA S25-08-19.

456. Diocese of Prince George (online), http://www.pgdioceses.bc.ca/History (accessed February 24, 2005).

457. Board of Management minutes, February 29, March 28, and April 25, 1956, SSAA S67-02-02.
458. Correspondence August 6, 1956, SSAA S17-06-02, Sister Mary Velma to Mother Mary Luca, provincial superior.
459. Correspondence December 4, 1957, SSAA S17-06-02, Sister Mary Lucita to Mr. A. Pitkethley.
460. SSAA 1967 speech by Sister Mary Colombe-de-Jesus to the Smithers Rotary Club when invited by Mr. Capewell to speak on "What the Sisters of St. Ann Have Done for This Town."
461. Acts of the Provincial Council, March 23, 1962, SSAA S12-02-03.
462. Correspondence February 13, 1967, SSAA S17-06-02, J.F. MacDonald, Mayor of Smithers, D. Moore, MD, Hospital Planning Commission, and C.M. Spicer, alderman, all members of the Bulkley Valley District Hospital Board to W. Black, minister of health services and hospital insurance.
463. In 1963 the Sisters received permission from the general council in Lachine to purchase 16.4 acres on Lake Kathlyn for $4,500 from Kenneth B. Warner; in November 1964 they received permission to spend $8,000 to build a cottage.
464. Janita McHugh, interviewed by the author, May 18, 2005.
465. Smithers Chamber of Commerce to Health Minister Eric Martin, February 6, 1964.
466. Acts of the Provincial Council, November 23, 1968, SSAA S12-04-01.
467. Board of Management minutes, February 6, 1969, SSAA S67-02-03.
468. Donald Cox, deputy minister of hospital insurance, wrote to the board on January 28, 1969, that no grant would be forthcoming to purchase the hospital as a grant had been made when it was built in the 1930s.
469. Archbishop Douglas Hambidge, interviewed by Mark Forsythe on *CBC Almanac,* April 11, 2005; and interviewed on the phone by the author on July 6, 2005. Archbishop Hambidge was pastor at the first St. James Anglican Church in Smithers in 1958–64.

Chapter 11

470. Church of Christ the King 50th anniversary booklet, SSAA S60-01-12.
471. www.oliver.ca (accessed September 2, 2008).
472. Jacquie Bicknell and Vicky White, eds., *Oliver Area, Secrets and Surprises* (Oliver, BC: South Okanagan Writers and Publishers, 1995), 81–82.
473. Chronicles 1941, SSAA S60-05-07.
474. March 16, 1940, Mother Mary Mark to the Oliver–Osoyoos Hospital Society, Chronicles 1940, SSAA S60-05-07.
475. Chronicles 1942, SSAA S25-07-11. In time three auxiliaries were formed—one in Oliver, which met in the afternoon; a junior auxiliary (1952), which met in the evening; and another auxiliary in Osoyoos.
476. Chronicles 1942, SSAA S25-07-11
477. History of the Sisters in the Nelson Diocese by Sister Mary Barry (date unknown), SSAA S60-01-03.
478. Chronicles 1944, SSAA S25-07-11.
479. *Osoyoos Times,* December 4, 1991.

480. John Murray Gibbon and Mary Mathewson, *Three Centuries of Canadian Nursing* (Toronto: Macmillan 1947), 249.
481. Chronicles 1948, SSAA S25-07-11.
482. Chronicles 1966–1972, SSAA S25-07-13, S25-07-14.
483. Chronicles 1972, SSAA S25-07-13.
484. Chronicles 1971, SSAA S25-07-14.
485. Chronicles 1973, SSAA S25-07-14.
486. *Oliver Chronicle,* December 4, 1975. The east wing was dedicated at the same time to Dr. Norbert Ball, friend of the Sisters and supporter of the hospital.

Chapter 12

487. http://www.city.nelson.bc.ca/html/founding.html (accessed July 21, 2009).
488. Patricia E. Roy and John Herd Thompson, *British Columbia: Land of Promises* (Don Mills, ON: OUP Canada, 2005), 75; Jean Barman, *The West Beyond the West* (Toronto: UTP, 1991), 124.
489. March 12, 1947, Bishop Johnson to Mother Mary Mildred, SSAA S17-04-03.
490. July 24, 1947, N. Baker to Mother Mary Mildred, SSAA S17-04-01.
491. SSAA S61-01-13.
492. Chronicles 1947, SSAA S25-11-17.
493. Chronicles 1949–51, SSAA 25-11-17, Monograph by Sister Margaret Cantwell, October, 1995, SSAA S61-01-26.
494. Turnbull was also the MLA for Rossland–Trail and, when not in politics, an engineer with Cominco.
495. *Nelson Daily News* editorial, June 5, 1950.
496. Chronicles 1954, SSAA S25-11-17, Correspondence November 2, 1970, Sister Mary Luca, administrator, to Sister Kathleen Moroney, provincial superior, S17-04-05.
497. Katimavik is a national volunteer service organization that aims to empower youth to make a significant contribution to local communities and participate in nation-building.
498. Article by Sister Patricia Dickinson, *Diocesan Messenger,* September 2009, 24.
499. Chronicles 1965 and 1968, SSAA S25-11-18.
500. Chronicles 1958 and 1960, SSAA S25-11-17.
501. *Nelson Daily News,* March 6, 1961.
502. Chronicles 1965 and 1966, SSAA S25-11-18.
503. Sister Betty Janelle interview with author, February 1, 2005.
504. SSAA S61-01-10.
505. Patrick Delsey to Sister Patricia Donovan, April 5, 1991. SSAA SS61-05-10.
506. January 24, 1992, Sister Frieda Raab to management and staff at Mount St. Francis, SSAA S17-19-17.

Epilogue

507. *National Catholic Reporter,* September 19, 2008.
508. *The Ring,* March 2010.

Index

Photographs marked in **bold**.